COOKIE

COOKIE

By

BARBARA QUINN

BARTHOLOMEW
HOUSE
LTD

BARTHOLOMEW HOUSE LTD.
First Printing June 1971

Library of Congress Catalog Card Number: LC 70-155025
International Standard Book Number: ISBN 87794-026-6

Published by Bartholomew House Ltd.,
a subsidiary of Bartell Media Corporation.

Manufactured in the U.S.A.

This book
is dedicated to
Leslie
and to all the others
who were just passing through

And to my son Mitchell:

Some day you will understand
why I couldn't be there until now

All of the incidents
reported in this book
are completely true,
but many of the names
have been changed

Part One: BUM'S ROCK

Part Two: GRASSLANDS

Part Three: THE PLAZA

Part Four: SYNANON

Part Five: THE BEGINNING

☼ CHAPTER ONE ☼

It was Leslie who introduced me to drugs.

That was really odd in a way because Leslie was quite a bit younger than me, and I'd always prided myself on being well ahead of my own age group.

I was eighteen going on nineteen when I started on heroin and Leslie was barely sixteen, but there'd been two and a half years of my life away from home—being married to Eddie, giving birth to little Mitchell, then getting my separation from Eddie—so that I hadn't been able to follow Leslie through adolescence.

I used to play with Leslie when she was ten or eleven—I was about thirteen then—and once she was asleep her brother Bruce and I used to fuck. Now she was grown-up, amazingly grown-up, a young woman who knew where life was at, a student hairdresser by day, a frequenter of the "in" spots in Greenwich Village at night.

Compared to her I was just a hick.

I was really happy when I ran into her in August of 1960. For the past eight months I'd been living at home again in Yonkers, cooped up in my mother's apartment with my son, Mitchell, getting more and more depressed, feeling more and more out of things. I was unwilling to mix with the young suburban mothers who sat with their baby carriages on the sterile patio of the apartment complex while they discussed formulas and bowel movements and their husbands' careers, and I was too tied down by domestic obligations to live it up with the younger set with whom I'd lost all contact when I got married. Dr. Tollman, our family physician, had put me on pep pills, tranquilizers, and sleeping pills but that hadn't been able to get me out of my depression, and the psychiatrist I used to see twice a week in Manhattan had also been unable to help me. Nothing exciting had happened to me in the eight months since I'd left Eddie, aside from a brief affair I'd had with a man called Boris whom I'd picked up in a bar on South Broadway one dreary afternoon—and that had ended with a traumatic abortion, which was probably the direct cause of my depression and withdrawal.

I was pushing my eighteen-month-old baby when I met Leslie again. She was with a friend, Sally, who lived in the new apartment building facing my bedroom window, right on the site of my old haunted house that had burned down five years earlier. Leslie invited me to the candy store and we sat over a Coke and we talked about old times and everything that had happened in between. Then Leslie told me about all the exciting new things that were happening in her life and I knew suddenly that if I could only get in with Leslie and her crowd I'd come to life again, I'd really be able to enjoy myself once more.

My mother didn't need much persuasion. She was happy to send me to hairdressing school where I could learn a useful trade, and she was glad to see me perk up and go out more and meet people. She didn't know that Leslie and Sally and I were hanging out in lesbian dives in Greenwich Village and she didn't know that we were turning on with opiated cough syrup and she didn't know that Leslie was carrying on with Max who was twenty-four and a dope addict. My mother, as always, was too busy working at the jewelry factory in the city, and when she came home, cleaned the house, cooked my father's dinner, and stretched out in front of the TV, she was really too exhausted to cope with anything more than surface problems.

I guess deep down she did know, but she just couldn't bring herself to believe the evidence and accept what was happening to her younger daughter. She knew, for instance, that I brought a young butch home to sleep with me one night because my mother made breakfast for her next morning and had quite a friendly chat with her, but she didn't let it register as meaning something serious, not even later when I cut my hair short and took to wearing men's pants. It was only when she found a man-styled tee shirt in my dresser drawer that she started asking questions, and when I told her I didn't know where it had come from and threw it in the garbage, she was mollified.

Leslie and Sally and I had been drinking cough syrup for perhaps two months—two or three bottles each, bought daily at the friendly drug stores in the neighborhood—and we were stoned from morning to night, playing hooky from hairdressing school more days than we attended, spending our time just sitting around in my mother's apartment, drinking cough syrup, listening to some way-out African drum music. Mitchell was away all day with the baby-sitter, so there was nothing to do but enjoy ourselves during the days when we weren't at hairdressing school, and in the evening, when Mitchell was asleep and my mother and father were watching television, we'd be downtown mixing with the lesbian set, hanging around the edges of the drug scene, really having a ball.

But cough syrup was a drag; it had a horrible taste. I had to hold my nose while I was swallowing it so that I wouldn't smell the stuff and throw up, and I had to have a handful of candy ready to suck to take away the taste, and then I had to smoke cigarette after cigarette to take away the cloying cherry flavor that went with it. And I was getting terrible stomach cramps from the syrup.

I tried doing without the syrup but that gave me cramps, too, and it left me jittery from the amphetamines I was getting from Leslie in exchange for the doctor's Miltowns that I didn't need. I knew there was an easier way of getting the same effect—with heroin.

Many of the dykes and the fems who hung out at Barbo's on Thompson Street in Greenwich Village were into heroin and they used to warn me against it. I knew all about dope addicts and what happened to them but I wasn't scared. I knew that I was too strong a person to let myself get addicted. I knew that when I was ready I could take dope, take it when I wanted to and stop when I wanted to. The only thing that really scared me was the thought of having to shoot it with a needle. I was scared of needles, so scared in fact that at one time I hadn't wanted to go through with my marriage to Eddie because of the blood test we had to take. But I knew I didn't want to stay with cough syrup and the awful taste and the stomach cramps. There was an easier way: It came in a little glassine envelope and gave people the same lift and the same feeling, nodding and enjoying just like we did on cough syrup—but without the hassle.

I had a suspicion that Leslie was on to the real stuff. After all, she was Max's girl friend and Max was an addict and knew where to get it, and Sally and I both had a shrewd idea that Leslie, who was much more interested in the lesbian scene than in boys, wouldn't be hanging around with Max unless she had a really good reason.

We were coming home one sunny Friday afternoon from hairdressing school, Leslie and Sally and I, sitting in the back of the bus and giggling. It was late September or early October. We were talking about dope and syrup and then suddenly Leslie spilled the beans.

"I've been getting high on dope," she said, whispering to us so that the other passengers wouldn't hear. "Heroin's where it's at. Cough syrup isn't what's happening, man. You've got to try heroin. It's easier. You don't have to drink it and the high is dynamite."

I was excited. The thought that Leslie, my close friend, was already on dope. Wow! And then I realized that if I asked her to, she'd help me turn on with heroin—and that scared me.

"I'm afraid of needles," I told her.

"That's nothing, Cookie," she told me. "You don't even feel it. You just shoot it and you don't even feel the needle."

I started thinking: No cough syrup, no holding nose, no gagging, no candy, no cigarettes, just a couple of seconds with a needle and you get it over with.

Sally was watching the two of us for clues. I thought about it for a while longer, and then I jumped up from my seat and clapped my hands to my face with excitement and said "Wow!" and then I said "Wow!" again. I could feel the tingle of excitement right through my body. We were going to do something, we were really going to do it. We didn't have to discuss it any further; it was quite clear we were going to get some dope and turn on. I stretched out on the empty back seat of the bus and covered my eyes with my hands and said "Oh wow!" There just wasn't anything to say and I couldn't have said it if I'd wanted to. It was just too exciting for words.

As we got off the bus I asked Leslie what time we were meeting that night. I didn't have to go into any more detail.

✡ CHAPTER TWO ✡

My parents had moved to Yonkers in 1955, when I was thirteen. We were one of the last Jewish families to move out of the part of Manhattan's Lower East Side where I'd grown up.

Until then, the Lower East Side had seemed to me to be the only place to live. Eldridge Street was home to me: the street outside as much as our three-room, third-floor apartment at number 43. I remember it as a bustling street with crowded tenements and a forest of fire escapes on which people slept on hot nights. Many of the little stores still had lettering in Hebrew, although some of the owners were more likely to speak Spanish than Yiddish, and instead of Yiddish books and Hebrew prayer books they sold votive candles and plaster saints. There was a noisy and lively world just beyond Eldridge Street. Hester Street, at one end, had grocery stores with smoked whitefish and lox and pickle barrels on the sidewalk. Grand Street, a block beyond, had fabric shops and dress shops crowded to the rafters with dresses and coats and stiff petticoats and shoes. Everything you could want hung in front of the shop from lengths of rope. The next block over, toward Little Italy, was Forsyth Street and a small park; in the other direction there was Orchard Street, packed every Sunday from curb to curb with pushcarts and shoppers. Essex Street with its huge covered market was another couple of blocks farther; Delancey Street to the north, where the buses went over the Williamsburg Bridge to Brooklyn, had all the big stores. East

Broadway had the Yiddish newspapers and the Educational Alliance; Canal Street and the Manhattan Bridge were a couple of blocks south of us; and on the other side of Canal Street was Chinatown.

That part of the Lower East Side was still predominantly Jewish when I was born there on January 27, 1942. Over the years, the Jews had moved out to Queens and Westchester and New Jersey, to be replaced by a further influx of Italians plus Chinese, Irish, and Puerto Rican newcomers. I wasn't aware of the change but my parents were very conscious of it; to me the streets seemed as alive and as friendly as ever. I was as happy eating a pizza as eating a knish. The Lower East Side was where I grew up and where I went to school. It was home to me.

My memories go back to infancy. I can see it clearly. I'm standing in my crib, next to it is a closet and then a bed. I'm clutching an empty bottle and sobbing out, "Where's Mommy? Where's Mommy?" My grandmother—has she just come in?—I see her sitting on the bed, a tiny woman, thin and frail with a mass of dark hair pinned to the back of her head. She picks me up and rocks me and I keep on sobbing, "Where's Mommy? Where's Mommy?" She takes me to the window. Diagonally across the street on the other side of Eldridge Street in a building just like ours at a window on a level with ours, I can see a head of flaming red hair bent over some work. The red hair stands out: It's my mother's. She'll be home later, she'll hold me and hug me and put me to bed. Seeing her, I feel better. My grandmother sings an old Jewish tune to me. I look up into her eyes and I feel warm and safe.

My mother was always out at work. My grandmother baby-sat for me when I was little and then, when I was three, my sister Sandra who was five years older walked me to nursery school at the Educational Alliance on East Broadway every morning, and picked me up again on her way home from school and then baby-sat with me until my mother came home from her job at the jewelry factory across the street. While Sandra was bent over her school books, I'd sit at the window playing with my dolls and watching that red hair bob up and down, up and down. Sometimes, however, I'd break out in a cold sweat and then the terror would overtake me: My mother had disappeared, the red head was no longer at the window opposite. There were many times when I climbed out on the fire escape and bawled hysterically, convinced that my mother had disappeared, that I would never see her again, that she would never come home.

But there was always my grandmother. I'd see her on my way to school and on my way home. A thin figure hunched over her work at the kosher poultry store, plucking away at the feathers, clouds of white down settling in her hair and growing into a heap around her ankles. She'd been an actress in the Yiddish theatre—Lena Lesch was her stage name—but now she was separated from my grandfather and her health had gone and she spent her days plucking kosher chickens. Each time I walked in she gave me a kiss and a hug—and a feather to take to school, where I would sit and let the soft fuzz tickle my face. Even when I was little I felt sorry for her, but proud of her, too, and I often brought my school friends in to meet her and to get a feather for themselves.

I was a star pupil in nursery school. My parents were proud of me. I acted in little playlets and served as a child model for the adults' dress-making classes. And in the Educational Alliance's nursery school I had my first experience with sex: petting and kissing with a very dark and handsome boy, Geraldo, a Puerto Rican.

I don't know where I got those ideas from. They didn't come from the other children in nursery school, I'm sure, but I may have gotten them from watching grown-ups on television. We had the first television set on Eldridge Street—in fact my father used to boast that he was one of the first fifty Americans to have TV—a huge wooden cabinet with doors that enclosed a tiny screen, a set that had cost him over five hundred dollars.

To my mind my parents were wealthy, outstandingly wealthy. Our apartment was furnished with what probably passed for opulence in that neighborhood, and we had a huge car, blue and white with lots of chrome. Friends and neighbors crowded into our living room to watch the television and when I was angry at a girl in school I'd threaten that my father wouldn't let her come up any more to watch and that we wouldn't take her for a ride in our car.

My father, Danny Goodman, actually worked very hard and long for our luxuries. Except on Friday evenings he never came home until we'd already finished having dinner, but on Friday we ate together; it felt festive to me, the whole family together at home. He worked uptown for a printer—he was a paper cutter—and in my eyes he was glamorous. He'd been an amateur prizefighter in his youth and he'd hung out at pool halls with racketeers, all of which made me think of him as a big shot and something of a rebel. He reminded me of Gary Cooper—and I was secretly in love with him. He was Jewish in little more than name, but his father, a tailor, was Orthodox, in fact he served also as a cantor at his *shul* in Brooklyn. I visited my father's family quite often but they were seldom over at our place.

My grandmother wasn't around much as I grew older. She had cancer. She was in and out of the hospital and we would drive over to Welfare Island on a Sunday afternoon to see her; my mother and father went upstairs and Sandra and I waited outside for her to come to the window high up and wave to us. Then she would come home for a few months, back to her apartment above the chicken place, back to her job with the chickens, only to be off again to the hospital. Soon she stopped waving to us from the window and a little while later my mother woke me up in the middle of the night to tell me that Grandma was dead. I was five and a half at the time.

Grandpa, her husband, loved me and I loved him back. He was so handsome, so manly, so strong. His name was Murray. He was a gay blade, a man about town, a restaurateur and a wheeler-dealer. He seemed like Superman to me, bigger and more powerful than my father, and I used to wish he would come to live with us. When he came visiting he used to bring us gifts and he'd put me on his knee and give me an extra special gift. I knew I was his favorite, his special pet. Sometimes he took Sandra and me to the restaurant where he'd been chef, to watch the cooks at work and to peek into the pots, and then he'd give us a little tidbit: a slice of pastrami, a knish, some sweet and delicious pastry. He went to live in Miami about the time my grandmother died, but he visited us frequently and then he'd cook spicy dishes for us—my mother seldom had the time or patience to do any fancy cooking.

Cooking at the Goodmans varied considerably with the weekly calendar. Saturday we ate out at a restaurant—Chinatown or the Automat were the favorites. Sunday we ate out with family in Brooklyn. Monday through Thursday, Sandra or I would cook for Dad. But Friday was really the big day: Mom came home early and did the cooking for all of us.

My mother, Minnie, seemed a huge and powerful woman to me, a giant in my child's eye, a five-foot-three giant, the biggest woman in the world. She sensed my rebelliousness early and kept comparing me with my sister, Sandra, the studious one who never gave any trouble and always did what she was told. When my mother was angry she beat me with her hands or with a stick, she pummeled me and knocked me against a wall. My father seldom intervened. He was always quiet and tried to stay out of conflicts.

There was only one time that I felt that my mother was taking my side. That was shortly after I'd started first grade in PS 42 on Hester Street. The teacher wanted me to eat a peanut butter sandwich for lunch and I wouldn't. I cried, "I don't want it! I don't want it!" and the teacher tried to force me and finally I threw the plate at her and she slapped me. I ran around the corner to the chicken place, but my grandmother was no longer there, and the next day my mother came to school and got into a big fight with the teacher.

I wasn't happy at school. The other children were always picking on me. They mocked me because I was Jewish—there were very few Jewish children at the school then. I didn't really know what Jewish meant, and for a long time I used to think we were the only Jews in the world. There was nothing really Jewish about us though, except our name, Goodman. We never celebrated any Jewish festivals and we never went to *shul.* The one *Jewish* thing we adhered to was not having a Christmas tree and so every year my mother spread out our presents under an Italian neighbor's tree. And every year on the Yom Kippur fast, my mother would warn me not to eat on the street in case the neighbors saw.

The first poem I ever knew was:

Matzo, matzo, two for five,
That's what keeps the Jews alive.

I heard those taunting lines at school and on the way home, day after day. The children made fun of the *mockies* who were supposed to be cheap, and so I stole nickels and dimes from my mother to treat the girls in school to soda and candies, jelly apples and ices, to prove I wasn't what they thought I was.

There was one Italian boy, John DeFanto, with whom I was madly in love when I was in first grade; he was two or three years older. I used to stand at our window waiting to catch sight of him and I used to run after him and tell him I wanted to be with him. He was easily the prettiest boy on the block and everyone was in love with him, and I thought the only reason why he didn't care for me in return—I was a very pretty child myself and I knew it—was because I was Jewish: John never called me anything except kike.

But names were always quite confusing for me. I was convinced my given name was Cookie. When I got into second grade a teacher once called out Barbara and I didn't answer. I didn't know it was my name. Everyone had always called me Cookie.

My archenemy was Doris Gasparin, a short but tough girl in my class who really terrified me. She bullied me unceasingly and got her friends to beat me up too—just because I was Jewish. It got so bad that eventually I stole a little rhinestone cross on a chain from Woolworth's and wore it to school to make the girls think I was a good Christian, too. I'd keep it on until I got home, then hide it under the stairs from my mother and put it on again the next day to go back to school.

Despite that, I did have quite a few friends in school. I was especially close to two Italian girls, Francine Valisi and Sharon Graddo. We promised to marry each other when we were grown-up and in the meantime we necked and kissed and rehearsed our marriage lines daily, taking the role of priest, bride, and groom in turn. Francine and Sharon and I were very close. The only Jewish children I was close to—in fact the only Jews I knew apart from my family—were Philip and Sam Stomberg who lived in the apartment directly above ours. They had an aunt, Anne, a young ballerina, a beautiful and glamorous woman on whom I tried to model myself. They called me up to meet her whenever she came by for a visit and I watched her with fascination as she applied her makeup; I tried to copy her every step and gesture. She took a liking to me and when I was about five, she talked my parents into sending me to dancing school.

At that age, too, I started becoming serious about Philip. Somewhere or other I must have heard people talk about fucking and I wanted to see what it was like. I told Philip directly that I wanted to fuck him—I was never shy about speaking my mind. I got him to lie down on the floor of his apartment and I lay down on top of him. With my skirt up and my panties down, I tried to get him to put his little penis into my belly button. He tried very hard and we giggled a lot and I got very hot in the face while he was doing it, but finally we gave up: Obviously I hadn't got my information down correctly. But we kept up our petting and necking game for years, always in their apartment (I didn't want my sister Sandra to spy on me at home), watching their new television set with one eye and looking by mirror reflection into the kitchen with the other eye so that we could quickly rearrange our clothes the moment Mrs. Stomberg left her pots to come into the living room.

I really wanted to be grown-up. I made myself a bra out of scraps of cloth and showed it to Philip and also to John DeFanto, the big boy with whom I was in love, but John wasn't impressed. Philip was, however, and for him I used to sneak out from home wearing my mother's see-through blouse with my bra straps showing prominently underneath. Being a grown woman was very important for me.

Geraldo, the boy with whom I'd started petting when I was in nursery school, refused to have anything to do with me later in public school. He claimed I wasn't old enough for him—I was seven—and, for support, he pointed out that I had no hairs on my pussy; he went only with older women, he said. I felt slighted.

Every day I examined myself to see if the hair had sprouted yet and I tried putting some black salve on my vagina to make it grow faster. I wanted to help my friends grow up, too, and I put salve on their vaginas when they came up to play. Sharon's mother found out and came storming up to my mother one evening. "Your daughter is putting all sorts of ingredients on my daughter's privates," she said. "Tell her to stop it."

My mother didn't just tell me—she beat it into me. She caught me by the head and started beating me against the wall. *Smash, smash, smash!* Luckily my father walked in just then for his dinner and told her to stop, but she was so furious that my dad had to actually pull her off me.

Seven was a turning point in my life: At seven I became a rebel. I really felt I ought to be older. I looked older and I was taller than anyone else my age. I felt in a way that I was different from the whole world, something special, something of a freak. I was so different from my sister—good, plump, obedient Sandra, always with her books, always doing what my mother told her. I had a warm spot for my father (after all, he'd been a rebel in his youth, he'd been a fighter and he knew all the racketeers) and a warm spot for my grandfather whom no one could tame. I went shoplifting with impunity, mainly for the thrill of something forbidden, partly to acquire cosmetics and trinkets for myself and to give away to my friends. The girls admired me for my generosity. They had no idea that I'd stolen the things.

I needed to be popular. I wanted to be grown-up. I wanted to wear nylon stockings and tight skirts, but Doris Gasparin wouldn't let me. For years she bullied me. She waited for me as I walked to school to beat and punch and pummel me. She forced me to give her money which I stole from my mother. If I wore stockings and a tight skirt, she'd force me to go home and change into bobby socks and a pleated skirt. If I combed my hair pretty, she'd make me comb it in an ugly way. If I wore makeup, she'd make me wash it off. If she found me carrying a record, she'd smash it. I tried to dodge her and avoid her but it just didn't help. Finally, I took to wearing sneakers to school with bobby socks over my nylons. I carried my ballerina flats in a bag, and wore a loose pleated skirt over my tight one. Once I was in school

I could change into my "glamorous" clothes, but then Doris would beat me up again during the lunch break. She was tough and aggressive, rather short and heavy like a bulldog, with a Buster Brown hairdo. I was terrified of her for years—until I was about eleven—and I assumed the reason why she hated me was not simply because I was Jewish but because I was both pretty and sexy.

Sex had always been a major interest for me, from around the time, I guess, when I discovered that playing with my pussy gave me a good feeling. By the time I was seven, sex had become a preoccupation. One of my sex games was with a Chinaman who lived across the street right next to where my mother worked. I never saw him on the street, only at the window. He was quite old. My game was to undress for him at the window when I knew he was watching, taking my clothes off slowly like a stripper, wiggling my ass, spreading my legs, shaking my hips suggestively, turning around slowly like a dancer so that he could see every part of me, pretending I didn't know he was there. I wanted to tease him, and it excited me.

I did other things besides teasing. I eventually became John DeFanto's sweetheart. We necked together every lunch period and when movies were shown in school, he'd arrange to sit next to me so that he could run his hands up inside my skirt and play with me. There were many others—girls as well as boys—with whom I used to play sex games. Having other people stroke my pussy was even better than doing it myself. I held boys' penises when they asked me, but there was something about them that made me scared; I'd hold them and even stroke them, but always with a sort of feeling that they'd bite me any moment. "Your privates" was how my mother used to refer to my pussy when she sent me to the bathroom to wash. That word always made me want to giggle. Private indeed! It was public as far as I was concerned. It was mine to play with, to enjoy, and to share and she had no business telling me what to do with it.

My mother was becoming more and more aware of my rebel nature. Sometimes she'd beat me and sometimes she'd threaten to have me put away. She would make believe she was calling the police, dialing the number on the phone but keeping her finger on the bar, and she'd say, "Hello? Police? I want you to come and take my daughter to reform school." I was terrified. I'd scream and sob hysterically, "I'll be good. I'll really be good now. I'll do what you want me to. Please don't let them take me away." And then she'd go through the motions again and say, "It's all right now. She's promised to be good. You don't have to come after all."

In school, however, I continued to be a good student. There were few complaints from teachers: My English was good and so was my spelling. I had good grades and was a little above average. I enjoyed acting and I was always in plays: I acted many roles, from the planet Saturn to a pirate in *The Pirates of Penzance.* I was also good at art. And at dancing school I was an outstanding student. My parents used to come and watch all my performances and I knew they were proud of me. I was always sure of acceptance by my father, but the only time I was sure of my mother's approval was when she came to watch and admire as I performed in public.

I was the choreographer of Eldridge Street. I arranged dances on the sidewalk, devising new steps and organizing all my girl friends into a little troupe that performed among the legs of startled shoppers. Except for Doris Gasparin, who was still making my life miserable, I was popular. I was still rehearsing my wedding with Francine and Sharon who continued to be my best friends. On Sundays I even used to accompany them to church without my parents' knowledge, and I used to watch with envy and fascination as they walked up to the altar rail to take communion. I wanted to join them there, but they told me I'd have to go to confession first. So one Saturday I went with Francine to confession. She'd coached me to start off by saying, "Forgive me, father, for I have sinned," but I forgot what I had to say after that. I gathered my wits quickly, though, and told the confessor that I'd been in the hospital for two years with polio and that I'd forgotten my prayers. Would he please prompt me and I'd repeat after him. It worked. He asked me what my sins were and I told him that I'd cursed my mother and that I'd lied. He ordered me to say the Act of Contrition and told me to go and sin no more.

Next day I took communion. The priest placed a wafer on my

tongue. It melted very fast and left no taste. I was quite disappointed; I'd expected some magic revelation to come over me and I said to myself, "Is that all?" Anyway, it had satisfied my curiosity and I never felt the need to go to church again.

What I assumed to be my parents' wealth embarrassed me. Weren't Jews supposed to be mean and tightfisted? I knew *we* weren't and I was determined to prove it. The kids on our block were mostly poor, some had no toys; they needed a club, a place to go and play after school and on weekends. I was going to play Lady Bountiful. *I* was going to provide the club.

One Sunday morning I took forty dollars from my mother's purse while she was asleep. I'd been taking nickels and dimes for years and had recently graduated to quarters and dollar bills, but I'd never tried taking any sum like this! I hid the money and waited for my mother to say something. Nothing happened—perhaps my mother was afraid to tell my father of her loss. On Monday, with no alarm out, I went to Haber's on Essex Street and bought toys, a whole forty dollars' worth. Forty dollars! It got me a real treasure trove. I brought them upstairs to my room in boxes with some story of minding them for a friend and later I arranged the clubhouse in an adjoining building: The upstairs was being used for workshops, but the downstairs part was vacant and there was easy access from the back. The downstairs became our clubhouse. When I came home from school in the afternoon, my close friends were allowed to help me down with the toys, and then I'd arrange the toys and games and let the club members play with them. The club was *my* thing. *I* made the rules. *I* told the kids what they could play with and how and when. It really made me important. It made me the most important girl in the neighborhood. I was one up on Doris Gasparin.

I played my role as benefactress and administrator to the hilt, but it only lasted for two or three days. Sharon Graddo wanted a bigger say in the running of the club. I wouldn't let her. We had a fight and I kicked her out. Sharon went straight to my mother and complained.

I see it now as if it had happened yesterday. My mother leans out of the window of the third floor, her face framed by her fiery red hair. She calls to me, "Cookie!" She often calls to me from that window but this time there is an ominous threat in her voice. *"Cookie!"* My heart drops into my shoes. I don't want to go up, I'm afraid, I want to hide, but the voice is insistent and I go on and up, trembling and expectant.

As soon as I open the door she grabs me by the blouse and pulls me into the apartment. She slaps me across the face. Slap, sting, slap! She lashes out at me, on my head, on my arms, on my legs. My mother is absolutely wild. She screams wordlessly and lays into me with all the strength of her powerful body; I cry, beg, scream, promise. Nothing helps; my mother is determined to get her revenge. Eventually my father and Sandra have to intervene to pull her off my bruised body. My mother collapses hysterically.

They took the toys back the next day to Haber's for a refund—all except Howdy Doody, my favorite toy, a huge cuddly puppet that I had kept all to myself and wouldn't let any of the others play with. Howdy was damaged, not much but just enough to make Haber's refuse him, so he stayed home, on the top shelf of my father's closet, so near and yet so far. Every morning when my father got dressed I stood right behind him and watched as he opened the closet to take out his clothes. My eyes were on Howdy Doody, but I was never allowed to play with him again.

There was one more beating that I got from my mother which sticks in my mind because I still have the scars. I was nine and I wanted, as always, to be grown-up, more grown-up. I especially wanted John DeFanto to notice me more. I took some of my mother's hair dye and bleached a neat reddish streak into a hank of my hair at the front. My hair was long and it was, with all due modesty, a really professional job. But my mother wasn't impressed with my skills. She started beating me. She banged my head against the walls, then she got a silver-headed baton that I'd brought home from the circus and beat me with it till the baton snapped into little pieces. My mother dyed my hair back to its natural dark brown shade, but within a week I was back at it again, bleaching a few hairs at a time so that she would hardly notice a gradually widening and deepening streak of red in my dark hair to mark me as a grown woman.

☼ CHAPTER THREE ☼

When I was ten, I met Stella. Stella was a grown-up woman of sixteen. She was tall, she was popular, she had long black hair, she wore all the latest clothes, and she looked terribly sexy. Popularly she was known as the Whore of Mott Street. She became my idol; I wanted to be just like her. I wanted to be really grown-up and learn how to fuck properly with grown men. Since there was no other way to find out how to do it properly, I became friendly with Stella and got her to coach me.

In school I had been head and shoulders above my classmates, doing everything years before they thought of doing it, but with Stella I felt inferior and inadequate. Stella readily took me on as her protégée. I followed her around like a kitten and got her to introduce me to all her grown-up friends. She started schooling me, showing me how to wear makeup properly—she used to wear so much makeup it looked almost like a mask—and how to wear my skirts even tighter and how to wiggle my ass as I walked. I told Stella I was a virgin—I felt really ashamed to admit it—and asked her to help me lose my cherry.

Stella thought she could set it up. Not just a fuck but a rape, not just an ordinary rape but a gang-bang. I already knew one of the boys she had in mind, George, a blond Irish boy of about fifteen, five feet five inches, with freckles, a pug nose, and blue eyes. I'd first met George when I was going to the St. James Street Settlement House to have my teeth fixed, and he really turned me on. George had a close friend, Ralph, an Italian boy with sandy hair and a funny protruding jaw that gave him the look of a frog. I didn't care much for Ralph, but Stella made it clear that they always operated as a pair and that George wouldn't do anything without Ralph.

So that's how it was set up. It was supposed to be a surprise and I pretended that I didn't know what was happening—in fact we hadn't said it would *definitely* happen—but I put on some really tight dungarees and my highest heels and met Stella at her home after dinner one day. Stella made some last minute adjustments to my makeup and my hair, and we were ready. We walked to an apartment on Mulberry Street, a walk-up in a tenement building that a salesman friend of hers used as storage for toys. It was a dismal, dingy, dirty apartment, no furniture in the whole place except for a wrought iron bed with noisy springs and a thin mattress, no sheets and no blankets.

But it had toys. Every closet, every shelf, was crowded with boxes of toys, and what especially stuck in my mind was the array of dolls, hundreds of them, all alike: stuffed clowns with a body of plaid fabric and a painted plastic face, no hands, no feet. I took one for myself off a shelf in the little kitchen and hugged it while I waited with nervous anticipation.

George and Ralph arrived a few minutes later on a prearranged schedule. We walked into the bedroom—the bed was the only place to sit on in the apartment—and we talked for perhaps two minutes. "Hi!" "How are you?" "Isn't it cold for November?" and so on, and then George started kissing me.

I was sitting with George on one side and Ralph on the other with Stella behind us. As soon as George and I were kissing, Ralph grabbed my pants and pulled them off and George forced me down on my back and got on top of me. He had his pants off before I even knew it and his penis was hard and big—the first grown-up penis I'd ever seen, so big, so straight and so red, it both thrilled me and frightened me.

I'd had some romantic ideas about rape. I also had some rosy notions about fucking. What I hadn't expected was the violence that went with it. Violence wasn't in the cards. Violence went with Doris Gasparin slapping me, or my mother beating me, but it had no place in my romantic ideal of grown-up sex. I started struggling. Stella, who'd been prepared for some token resistance on my part, pinned my arms. Ralph grabbed my legs and held them wide. George positioned himself between my thighs and tried to force his cock into me. I struggled. I tried to pull my arms away from Stella; I tried to kick with my legs; I started crying. George tried again to force his way inside me. I really wanted to be fucked but I was too scared by all the violence. Stella whispered to me, trying to reassure me, telling me not to be scared, to just relax and enjoy. But I couldn't enjoy and I was so clammed up from fear that George couldn't get anywhere with me—quite apart from the difficulty he might have had with my virginity.

George gave up after a while and changed places with Ralph, holding my arms while Ralph tried to rape me with his cock. But if George had frightened me, Ralph enraged me. I didn't want him. He turned me off. I couldn't bring myself to look at him. I screamed and cried and begged them to stop. I told Stella that I'd changed my mind, I didn't want to, I really didn't.

Stella may have thought in the beginning that my protests were all part of my act, but by now she was convinced I meant it. She signaled to George and Ralph; they got dressed and we were left alone.

"The trouble with those two is they're only boys," Stella said, apologizing for having bungled my rape. "They're too rough. What you need for the first time is an experienced man. I'll find one for you. Someone who really knows how to take a girl's cherry. Then when you know how to do it properly, you can try it with George again."

Everyone in our neighborhood was too busy at that time preparing for Christmas, working overtime, buying gifts, visiting and partying. It wasn't until January, 1953, a week or so before my eleventh birthday, that Stella was able to make the arrangements. She introduced me to Leo, a twenty-two-year-old truck driver. I liked him: He was strong, Italian, and mature, and I realized I'd found a *real* man at last. Stella told him I was thirteen and that I wanted him to take my cherry and he said sure, he'd had lots of experience with virgins and he'd be pleased to help.

To my mother I said simply that I was spending the weekend

with my friend Stella—she had no idea that Stella was a whore, in fact she thought she was rather a nice girl. My part of the preparation was to wear a bra with falsies—I had a chest like a boy—and then I went over to Stella's and she applied a half-dozen layers of makeup so that I could hardly smile without fear of cracking my face. Then Leo arrived with another man for Stella and we all got into Leo's car to drive up to his father's cabin in the Catskills.

Stella and her man sat in the back, necking. I sat in the front with Leo, but I kept over to my side of the seat by the door, too excited to move or to talk. The lights of the city danced by, glamorous and exciting. We started getting into more open country and Leo was saying, "Come here, come here." I inched over toward him and he put his right arm around my shoulders. Occasionally, when the road was clear, he let me steer. It was very cold outside and snowing lightly. We drove for two or three hours, then we went off the road and bounced along a dirt track and parked among the trees. It was a bitterly cold night, well below zero with an icy wind.

The cabin was a rough place, not quite finished. There were boards and planks all over. Leo tried the lights; they weren't working. He groped around with matches, lighting one after the other, looking for light bulbs. Finally he found some candles and lit those. Stella and her man went off into one room, Leo and I took the other. There was just a mattress in the room, propped up against the wall among the boards and the wood shavings. I took off my clothes but immediately wrapped myself in my coat; I had goose pimples and I was shivering.

Leo was gentle. "I wish you didn't have to wear that coat. I'd like to see you. Here, open it a little way and let me see."

I opened my coat and did one quick pirouette, imagining myself to be a dancer on the stage or a slave girl in a harem. Leo came close, stroked my breasts with chilly hands, then wrapped my coat around me again and hugged me. He was still dressed. We started kissing and then Leo gently lifted me up in his arms and laid me down on the mattress.

It was too cold for any loveplay—and I didn't need any to get me ready. I may have been shivering on the outside, but inside I was hot and expectant and eager. Leo unfastened his belt, unzipped his fly, and came down on top of me. He was a big man, but his weight on me was light. "You have a lovely body," he told me, "a lovely body." He had one hand on my crotch, the fingers in my vagina. His other hand was stroking my face. "I'll be gentle," he said, "don't worry. I know what to do."

He moved his hands to my buttocks, pinching them and raising me slightly. I could feel his penis pushing against my thigh, then against my vagina. I was thrilled. It was really going to happen! Really going to happen!

The tip of it was at my cunt. I was numbed. It was a dull feeling, a blunt point pressing against me. It went in deeper. I couldn't feel it much because of the numbness I was feeling everywhere, everywhere except for my heart and that was pounding against my ribs. I was in love with Leo—really in love! Then Leo started moving up and down, very gently, and I tried to move with him. I had my legs wrapped around his legs—his pants felt rough and cold. I tried to stop my teeth from chattering. His hands were under my ass, with one thumb pressing at the back of my vagina.

"Gently now!" he said. He sounded anxious. "Don't worry, it won't hurt much." It didn't. There was just one sharp stab and then a duller pain, but it all dissolved in a pleasant feeling. I was enjoying it, a lot. My first fuck!

"You're a good fuck," he told me, "real good. We're gonna be together from now on, you and me. We'll do it often. You're a good fuck." A good fuck! It was like a diploma. I'd graduated.

His movements were faster now but still gentle. Then he got very fast, his breath came in short gasps, he moaned and it was over. He lay on me gently for a while longer, then he rolled off, zipped up his fly, and stood up. Stella and her man were also finished and they came in from the other room. "How was it?" Stella asked. "Great!" I said. I felt like dancing with the joy. "She's a great fuck," Leo said.

"There," said Stella, "I knew you'd enjoy it. Leo's good."

I found my clothes and put them on. The others were all wrapped in their overcoats. We'd planned to spend the whole weekend there, just enjoying and having fun, but it was too cold to stay one minute longer than absolutely necessary. Leo helped me on with my coat, kissed me, blew out the candles, and locked the door behind us.

So that was that! I could go home now, back to Eldridge Street. I was a virgin no longer! I dozed on Leo's shoulder, trying to get some warmth back into my body. Then the lights grew closer together. We were back in the city. I had a feeling of strength and power. I was a woman. I'd been fucked. I wondered if anyone could guess it. I wondered whether it would show on my face. I knew I'd be different from now on, a woman at last, no need now to prove it by pretense. I'd lost my cherry and I'd fucked with Leo and I was a woman.

We got back to Stella's flat around dawn. I was tired but too excited to sleep. We were planning who I'd fuck next, how to do it, where to do it. First of all, there'd be George of course—without Ralph if possible. I'd prove to George that I was a woman now, not afraid to fuck. Then there were other friends of Stella. She gave me full descriptions of each one, praising his good points, glossing over the bad ones—and of course I'd get to fuck a lot with Leo, a genuine grown-up, the man with whom I'd fallen in love.

I came home from Stella's on Sunday evening. My mother asked me if I'd had a good weekend.

"Yeah, I guess so," I told her. "It was all right, I guess."

I went with Leo a few more times. Then he found out I was only eleven, not thirteen as I'd told him. That must have been a blow to his masculinity. I kept seeing him driving his truck in the neighborhood, but from then on he kept making excuses when I asked to meet him evenings. It hurt me; I'd felt so important when people had seen me driving around with a twenty-two year old. I started calling him at work but he kept putting me off. Then one day I had a real urge to get together with him. I called him again on the phone and he told me he couldn't, he had diarrhea. I never called him again.

Life became easier for me once I knew I was a woman. I had a reputation among the kids at school and in the neighborhood; I didn't have to prove myself anymore. I got as much attention from boys and men as I wanted; I no longer had to act up. I gained a lot of self-confidence, enough to let me stand up at last to Doris Gasparin and her bullying. I just started fighting back—and that scared Doris so much she soon left me alone. I felt so powerful at having stood up to her that I turned around and played her role myself with a girl called Laura at dancing school: I made her give me money, I made her wear bobby socks, I made her comb her hair straight, I made her wear pleated skirts. I guess I didn't have too much originality.

I'd been going to dancing school almost every afternoon since I was five. It had been rewarding for a long time: It was something my sister couldn't do because she was too heavy; it was something I could demonstrate for hours to the other kids; it made my parents proud of me; it made me more like Philip and Sam's Aunt Anne, for whom I always demonstrated whenever she came to visit. My father used to come with me Saturdays to pick out leotards and dancing shoes—I easily went through half a dozen of those shoes in a year because I'd wear them everywhere so that I'd look shorter and wouldn't stand out so much like a freak—and it was a good feeling to have my father pick out my costumes for me. I learned toe dancing, tap dancing, modern dance—everything. I did so much dancing my parents kept on having to find new schools for me every couple of years because I'd outgrown what the current one could teach.

It was a Mr. Karp, manager of the last dancing school I attended on Lexington Avenue, who finally turned me off. He was married, in his forties, very bald—and I was convinced he was a pervert because of the way he used to leer at us in our leotards. I took to phoning him evenings at the studio while my mother was washing the dinner dishes.

"Mr. Karp," I said the first time in my Mata Hari voice, "this is Marlene. I've fallen in love with you. I'd like you to take me to bed, Mr. Karp, and fuck me. I want you to stick your gorgeous cock into my pussy."

I'd thought Karp might hang up but he went right along with me. "I don't know who you are but you sound exciting. I think I might fall in love with you." He asked me about my breasts and my pussy and told me what he'd like to do to me and asked me what I liked.

The second time I called, he asked to meet me and I arranged a date, giving him a voluptuous description of myself so that he could recognize me. The day after our planned date I called him to apologize that I hadn't been able to keep it because I was with another man but that I still wanted to meet him. This went on for a few weeks. Every time I saw him in dance school I'd giggle and tell my friends what a pervert he was but without going into the details. Finally I got sick of Karp, his school, and dancing altogether and I told my mother I didn't want to go anymore.

If she had any regrets over the years of effort I'd put into dancing and the money she'd spent, she didn't show it. "Whatever you want, dear," she said. "We can't force you if you don't want it."

I gave up calling Karp but started another round of mischievous phone calls. I'd call a name chosen randomly from the directory. If a man answered I'd hang up; if a woman answered I'd ask for the man.

"I want to speak to Bill."

"Who's this?" she'd ask and I'd reply by asking, "Who are *you?*"

"I'm Mrs. Williams."

"Oh!" I'd say, feigning shock and surprise. "Bill didn't tell me he was *married.*" Then I'd hang up and call back a few minutes later and just breathe deeply into the phone. No sex talk, just mischief for the hell of it.

I was a tease. I used to sit at the window by the fire escape, my sweater puffed out with falsies, making eyes at the workers in a factory across the road—*not* my mother's place. In school I used to put a pocket mirror on the floor and stand over it with my panties drawn up tight so that almost nothing was obscured. The boys got a big thrill just from looking into the reflection at my feet—and it was great promotion for my reputation.

In summer camp I flirted with the counselors. Camp Star was a farm camp with cows and horses, but what interested me more than the animals were the counselors and kitchen help, big grown-ups as I thought at the time. I seemed to get crushes on one after another and did all I could to seduce them. They were all willing prey but only one sticks in my mind: Bob, who looked like an Italian, short, with curly black hair. We used to make out in the hayloft.

The next vacation we went to visit my grandfather and his girl friend in Miami. We stayed at a hotel; I made out with bellboys and lifeguards.

I was tough and I had a reputation. People knew who I was and admired me. We had a sort of gang in our neighborhood—it wasn't a very strong gang and it didn't last too long so that I don't even remember the name, but it was a gang: twenty or twenty-five kids, all Italians, from our school and from Forsyth Street. We met in the park on Forsyth Street. There wasn't much purpose to the gang except to challenge other gangs to fights in order to prove that ours was the toughest block. I set out to prove that I was the toughest girl in our gang.

Our first real fight was with the gang from the Henry Street Settlement House, really tough kids and the girls were even tougher. We marched over to Henry Street, proud in our swagger. The Henry Street gang was waiting for us. Boy! Were they tough! There was one girl that I especially admired. Her name was Mary, a little-bitty thing of a girl—I towered way above her. She swaggered over to me and started pushing, trying to get me to fight. "Come on!" she said, "you're bigger than the rest of them. Let's see you fight. You're bigger than me. Let's see how you fight." All the time she kept shoving me I knew I ought to push her back to keep up my reputation, but I shoved only hard enough to keep my balance, not hard enough to give her a pretext to start swinging. I suddenly felt very humble. I was scared. Some boys from my gang had to wade in to rescue me and then a fight developed with garrison belts flailing on both sides. Our gang got the shit beaten out of it before the police arrived with screaming sirens and scattered us all. That marked the end of our gang.

I started hanging out at the Henry Street Settlement House instead.

☼ CHAPTER FOUR ☼

We moved to Yonkers in March of 1955, two months after my thirteenth birthday.

My mother had been wanting to move for a long time. The firm she worked for had moved from Eldridge Street to midtown Manhattan and many of her close friends had moved away, too. She didn't like the changes that were taking place on the Lower East Side and—though she never said this to me—she didn't like the kids I was mixing with. My father, on the other hand, wasn't in a hurry to move. He still felt comfortable in the neighborhood: We had a neat apartment, the rent was low, and shopping was inexpensive.

For a long time I wasn't aware of the tensions. My parents seldom raised their voices at each other, they seemed like such an ideal couple. My mother used to speak her mind; my father either agreed or held his peace. No unseemly arguments.

Now, suddenly, they were having loud and frequent fights. It scared me. I had no idea what they were fighting about. Since I was little I'd had a fear that one day my mother would just get up and go, taking Sandra with her and leaving mc behind. "I should never have brought you home from the hospital when you were born," she often said when she was angry with me, "they must have given me the wrong child." Sandra was her good girl, I was the rebel. Now that my daddy was rebelling too, she'd lump us both together and go.

But she didn't leave, not right away. First she stopped getting beer for my father. I looked in the refrigerator every day: no Rheingold. Then my father stopped coming home for dinner Friday evenings. Friday had always been the big day for me. I couldn't wait to get to the table Friday evening, and when I pulled in my chair I always got a happy rush of good feeling: *Wow! The whole family is here.* It wasn't that we were Jewish; what mattered was that my father was home to eat with us and we were all together. (After dinner my father always went out on Friday evenings, perhaps to meet a girl friend I would think to myself, jealousy gnawing at my insides.)

When my father stopped having dinner with us Friday evenings, I was terribly upset. I knew they were fighting. I spoke to my mother: "Mommy, why don't you buy Daddy his beer? You know that's why he's upset. Buy him his beer again and he'll stop fighting and then he'll stay home and have dinner with us and everything will be fine again." And I told my father that I'd talk to Mommy about the beer so that he wouldn't be upset anymore.

But my mother didn't get the beer and my father didn't come home Friday evenings, and then suddenly my mother left and went to stay with her father in Miami. Just my mother. Sandra and Daddy and I stayed home.

I felt terribly sorry for my father. Sandra shopped and cooked for us. I cleaned the house and dusted the furniture and mopped the floors. I wanted to take care of our home, I wanted to take care of my father, I wanted to play mother to everyone. I was important, the house was mine, I felt free. Mommy had gone and I was independent. But I was mad at my mother for having left Daddy—not for leaving us, only for leaving Daddy—and I felt he must be so lonely without her. I spent a lot of time crying, for him, I told myself, not for me.

Mommy called us frequently from Miami. I was really too angry to want to speak to her but I did. "You didn't have to fight with Daddy," I told her, "you could have got him his beer. He's so lonely without you. Why don't you come back?"

She came back three weeks later. There was Rheingold in the refrigerator again, Daddy had dinner with us Friday evenings. I was very proud: I'd brought them together.

We moved to Yonkers on March 17, 1955, into a two-bedroom apartment on the ground floor of a huge cooperative development on Riverdale Avenue, just a few hundred yards over the line from New York City.

It was a revelation to me, a new world, an all-American dream come true. Between Riverdale Avenue and South Broadway was a maze of curving streets lined with trees and sumptuous homes of ten or twenty rooms, each set in a picture book garden with well-kept lawns. Boys and girls, looking for all the world like my idols from the *Archie* comics, rode their bicycles on the sidewalks. Facing our apartment was a huge lot with an old ramshackle house that was reputed to be haunted. Beyond that, across the city line, was a Catholic college and a pond with real ducks.

We moved in the middle of my first year at JHS 65 and I was transferred to Nathaniel Hawthorne JHS, five minutes away on Riverdale Avenue. Sandra was in her last year in Seward Park High School; my parents left her there and she had to commute an hour and a half to school every day by bus and three subway trains. My mother and father left early in the morning to go to their jobs in midtown Manhattan. I had to prepare my own breakfast before I went off to school and when I came home in the afternoon, I sat by myself, watching television, looking out at the haunted house, or decorating the room I shared with Sandra. I fixed it up with pictures on the wall: Elvis Presley and my heroine, Liz Taylor. I kept scrapbooks about Liz Taylor and saw her in *National Velvet,* and then I discovered the riding stables in Van Cortland Park and I went there as often as I could, talking to the grooms, helping with the horses, getting free rides, imagining I was Liz herself. I let my dungarees get heavy and stiff with the smell of horses, and at night I curled them in a ball and put them on my pillow so that I could fall asleep with the smell in my nostrils and pretend I was sleeping with the horses.

The Nathaniel Hawthorne school thrilled me at first. It was just what I'd wanted. All that space and all those trees and girls coming to school in bobby socks and bucks and black and white saddle shoes, just like Archie's friends, Betty and Veronica. I would have liked to dress like that on the Lower East Side but there it wasn't "in" and in fact I'd had my fights with Doris Gasparin just *because* I wouldn't wear bobby socks. Nylon stockings and ballerina shoes were "out" in Yonkers, but I didn't mind. I went and bought the thickest bobby socks I could find and saw myself in a new image, athletic, collegiate, really neat.

But school was all wrong. On the Lower East Side I'd been a good student. Here I was floundering. The students were more advanced than I was. I couldn't understand the math they were doing; as for social studies, I'd never even *heard* of that. The girls all seemed to be Jewish. I saw them as a bunch of goody-goodies who thought they were better than anyone else—just as I'd heard Jews described by my old Italian friends. They were much like my sister, always carrying around a load of books and spending a lot of time over their homework and raising their hands to every question the teachers asked. I thought they'd be impressed by my toughness, I hoped that would get me a reputation soon, but they weren't impressed. The tables were turned: I was going to school with a bunch of kikes and I was the only *goy* in class.

They had a football team and the girls were cheerleaders. Cheerleaders! Like in all the movies. I knew I could wow them with that. Six years of dance school hadn't been for nothing. I'd get on that cheering section and show them some neat footwork and get them to pay attention to me and my skills. But they weren't interested in dancing, they didn't know a thing about good dancers. "To be admitted to participate in the activities of our cheering squad, students must prove their attitude and dedication to the ideals of the school by achieving consistently good grades."

Shit on that! Take it and stuff it! They're nothing but a bunch of faggot guys and chicken-shit girls. I'll show them I'm tough. I'll get me a reputation and get them all to look up to me.

I was lonely in Yonkers, terribly lonely. I didn't have a single friend. I used to lie in bed in the morning after the rest of the family had gone off to work or school, and I would masturbate. I'd have a quick breakfast and go to school. I walked home from school by myself.

Once home, I would go to the living room window and look out at the ramshackle house. People said Nathaniel Hawthorne had lived there once and that his ghost still haunted the place.

One day after school I made my way through the dense foliage and underbrush to the house. An old frame house, a mansion sagging at the corners, it had been boarded up, but vandals had ripped off many of the boards. I climbed up to an opening, then dropped down on the other side. Piles of dust rose all around me. Light came through the gaps in the siding. The house creaked. There were rotten stairs with missing steps and shaky banisters. Upstairs, where you could see the sky through the shattered roof, was too spooky for me. I was too scared to go upstairs. I was happy enough walking through the downstairs rooms feeling the spirits. It was silent except for the creaks. I cried. I cried every day, every afternoon that I came here direct from school. I cried to the spirit of Nathaniel Hawthorne: "It's your school. It's named after you. Why do you let them do this to me?" I cried for my grandmother sitting in the dark, hunched over her pile of dead chickens. "A feather, Grandma. Please give me a feather to take to the kids in school so that they'll like me. I want to tickle my face with a white feather." I cried for Major, the first dog I'd owned when I was about eleven. "Hello Major," I'd say to the spirits, "how's Major?" Major was a little mutt, black and white with two white patches for his eyes, hardly more than a puppy. Major had died, died terribly, in an accident. I loved him so much. Now he was dead like Buttons, the other dog I had, and Joe Gandolfo, a friend of my mother who'd given me Buttons when Major had died and who'd taken me to spend a couple of weeks with his family at his home in the country. I'd loved Joe Gandolfo, he'd been so good to me and I wanted him to love me in return, love me in a real way, the grown-up way. He was like my father, even more than my father. Joe Gandolfo would have understood what I felt now, the loneliness and the sorrow and being different from anyone else and not having anyone to understand me. But Joe Gandolfo was dead, he'd died a few weeks before we moved to Yonkers. He couldn't help me anymore but I could speak to his spirit, to all the spirits that floated around the haunted house. I felt comfortable with those spirits. They'd take care of me. All I had to do was visit the spirits for five or ten minutes every afternoon when I came home from school, just visit them and talk to them. They'd take care of me.

I never stayed in the haunted house after dark. At dusk I went home and I did whatever homework I felt like doing until Mommy and Daddy and Sandra arrived, late, tired, and grumpy. We had dinner. Then I went out. Hungry. Hungry for friendship.

Friendship was easy to find. There was an orphanage for boys down by the Hudson, a big place with trees and lawns. I only had to walk past, smile, and wiggle my ass and a boy would smile back at me and get into conversation and then we could go off somewhere and fuck. It was so easy and so satisfying. After a while I had a reputation there and the boys would wait for me. Some boys I fucked a second time at some later date; with most of them it was enough for me to fuck them just once. On the grass, under the trees, someone to talk to, someone to care for me. I had to like the way a boy looked and he had to have something manly about him, but otherwise I didn't care much. I never remembered their names. I often forgot their faces.

There were boys, too, at the stables in Van Cortland Park and they had the advantage of smelling of the sweet horsey smell that reminded me of Liz Taylor. From them I could get favors on other occasions, like being allowed to groom the horses or ride them, but that wasn't so important. Some evenings I'd just walk down South Broadway and let a boy or a man in a car pick me up. Sometimes when I'd finished fucking one and it was still too early to go home, I waited around to be picked up again. I had lots of steadies, and if I felt like a particular guy one evening, I almost always knew where to find him—but I wouldn't let any of them come to my house.

I had a crush on Mike, an attendant at the gas station that my father patronized. I walked past the station one evening and got Mike to pick me up. We drove off in his car, way out of Yonkers, far away, and we made love in some park under the open skies. I was lying underneath him, my dungarees folded under my ass for comfort, my legs spread, looking up at him and past him to the stars, and then I saw a shooting star, my first shooting star. I thought that fucking had something to do with it, that the shooting star had come as a sign, blessing me. A reward. I felt good and at ease. It was an omen. Things would go my way.

I was out fucking almost every night. It was an addiction. I had a yearning that needed to be filled. I masturbated morning and afternoon, usually fantasizing that I was talking to Mr. Karp on the phone. It gave me satisfaction and I had an orgasm—something I never associated with men and didn't experience with a lover for another dozen years, marriage and prostitution and all. Masturbation was good, it filled me, but the feeling wore off soon.

My mother thought I was spending my evenings at the Jewish Community Center. I went there just once because it had a pool, but I couldn't make it there. It was full of Jews and the Jews wanted nothing to do with me. I went out and screwed to have someone notice me, to get a reputation, to know I was *somebody.* No one else paid much attention to me. My parents were too tired. My mother did the housework, my father sat in front of the TV, my sister was in our room doing her homework. It was miserable being at home, but once I stepped out of the door I entered a world of excitement. I never knew who might slow down in a car, who would wink at me at a red light, where we'd go and how we'd fuck. It was an adventure. And it made me important: I knew there weren't many girls in Yonkers who'd put out for guys the way *I* did.

In school I was more and more an outsider. I couldn't do anything that would gain me acceptance. I hated the teachers, real old schoolmarm types who spent all their time trying to teach and seemed to have forgotten how to live. I hated the girls with all their prissy Virgin Mary airs. I hated them all for not giving me a chance. It wasn't my fault that they hadn't taught things the same way in Manhattan. It wasn't my fault they couldn't help me catch up now. Toward the end of the school year I was called in to the principal.

"Your grades are unsatisfactory, Barbara. We realize, of course, that with your background and lack of advantages you have problems keeping up with your class, and your parents were probably wrong to take you out of school in the middle of the school year. Your teachers and I concur that in order to get a proper start at Nathaniel Hawthorne Junior High you must avail yourself of every advantage and you should really complete a whole year in seventh grade. Unless, therefore, your teachers report a substantial improvement in what's left of the school year, it would seem to be in your best interest to repeat the seventh grade here with us and become a genuine contributing participant in the educational process on which we pride ourselves at Nathaniel Hawthorne Junior High . . ." and on, and on, and on, with his prissy lecture. ". . . and we feel that parents are an integral part of their children's educational process so that we'd really like to have your parents stop by one morning so that we may discuss the whole problem with them."

I didn't cry in school, I wouldn't give them the satisfaction. The other kids in school may have guessed what was happening, and they probably thought it served me right and that I had no business in their class. I hated them all! It wasn't *my* fault.

I went home from school all alone and threw down my books and rushed over to the haunted house. I burst into tears. I was miserable, miserable and angry. I let old Nathaniel know what I thought of him. "You can't let them do this to me. I'm grown-up. I'm more grown-up than all those namby-pamby goody-goodies in my class. They *can't* keep me back. They *can't* make me repeat a year with twelve-year-old kids. I hate you, Nathaniel Hawthorne! How can you let them do this to me?"

My parents didn't seem to be worried about it. "I guess if that's the way the teachers feel, Cookie. After all, they know what's best for you."

After that I became rebellious. I was going to show everyone how tough I could be. I wasn't going to try and live by their standards; I'd make my own rules. A new girl came to our school, Bobbi Villa, a rebel like me. She and I became fast friends. She looked up to me and followed me around and did everything I suggested. I took her to the haunted house without telling her what it meant to me. She didn't seem terribly impressed; she just thought it was a spooky place and a fun thing for adventures. I decided I wasn't going to share my secrets with her.

We didn't go away that summer. My parents said there'd been a lot of expenses in moving and that we needed time to settle down. Sandra had a big graduation at Seward Park High and she spent most of the summer visiting with girl friends in Manhattan; she was scheduled to start at Westchester Community College in White Plains in the fall. My parents were away working all day. They'd wake me in the morning just before they left and tell me to be good until they came home. I stayed in bed late, masturbating. Then I got dressed and went down to the stables in Van Cortland Park or met with Bobbi and the other girls at Lane's candy store across the road on Riverdale Avenue.

It was there that I met Eddie. I saw him standing outside the candy store in old dungarees and a dungaree jacket, cowboy boots, garrison belt, lolling at ease, a slender, handsome lad of sixteen standing with his hips thrust forward like a cowboy—an Italian-looking cowboy with long sideburns like Elvis Presley and long, light-colored curly hair that fell almost to the collar of his jacket. He was about my height—five feet six inches. He was very fair and had beautiful dark eyes and a chipped tooth. It was the chipped tooth that really got me; I couldn't resist boys who had chipped teeth or a gap in their teeth when they smiled. I fell for him immediately.

I asked one of the kids there, someone I knew, who the new guy was. "That's Eddie Quinones. He's real tough. He's tops. He's a big shot around here. He has his own gang. He's at the Saunders Road Trade School but he lives near Caryl Avenue." He rattled off Eddie's qualifications with admiration.

"Introduce me to him, will you?" I asked.

Eddie overwhelmed me from the first minute; he had such gracious manners. He invited me into the candy store, showed me to a seat, and ordered a milk shake for me. *Archie* comics again! Nobody had ever bought a milk shake for me before. There hadn't even been a place like this on the Lower East Side; the nearest you could get was the newspaper and tobacco stores where you had to buy your soda in a bottle. Here we sat down in pure suburban style, our feet touching the rail, our elbows propped on the counter top, sipping our sodas through a straw while we looked at each other over the top of the glass and passed little messages with our eyes.

I could see that Eddie cared for me as a person whom he wanted to get to know, not just as a girl to make out with. He really cared, he really liked me. We walked around together most of that day, a gentle day of little discoveries. He asked me why I wore so much makeup and such tight skirts. "You don't need them, you're pretty enough just the way you really are, Cookie." It made me feel warm. We walked over to Broadway, through the park to the stables. Everybody seemed to know him and respect him, especially at the stables. We sat on the corral rails for a while, watching the horses, then he showed me through Van Cortland Park, along his private paths to a secret rock hidden from passersby. We had a snack at Little Caesar's, the hangout of Eddie's gang, right on the city line at the edge of the park, directly across from the City Line Diner run by Eddie's stepfather, a German whom he called Poppi.

We walked up to Riverdale Avenue and I invited Eddie to view my own private world, the haunted house. He went through it with a rather superior air. It didn't seem anything special to him, just a tumbledown house in a hell of a mess. I didn't tell him what it had meant to me; it wasn't really as meaningful to me as I'd thought. With Eddie to care for me I wouldn't need those spirits. Then I let Eddie bring me home, just in time for dinner. He was the first boy I'd allowed to see me home, the first one I wasn't afraid to have my mother see.

He called for me after dinner and we walked around together some more. He didn't try to fuck me, he didn't even try to kiss me. He treated me like a princess, like a delicate and valuable treasure. He took me to his home on Saratoga Avenue—a huge frame house set on a rock above the street with flowers in front and a big yard in back—and introduced me to his mother, Alice, and his sister, Nancy, big and plump like my sister, jovial, not too bright. His family was from Puerto Rico, his father had been in the Merchant Marine, but they were really Americanized and Eddie had been born in the United States. They owned their own house. Eddie showed me around, including his room up in the attic where he kept a picture of his brother, George, twenty-one, a ranger and paratrooper whom he idolized. Then we walked up the hill again to Riverdale Avenue, in and out of the shadows cast by the trees, under the widely-spaced street lights with their halos of night bugs. We walked arm in arm. I was his precious possession, he was my prince. We ended up in Valentine

Lane opposite the co-op apartments. There was so much we had to tell each other. We stopped in the dark under the trees, turned, sat on a stoop. Then Eddie reached out and cupped my face in his hands, strong hands, warm hands. He drew my face to his gently, ever so gently, gently and slowly. And then he kissed me. Our first kiss.

Eddie courted me like a gentleman and treated me like a lady. He opened doors for me. He let me walk on the inside. We spent all our time together and he didn't even fuck me. He was respected wherever he went. When he walked with his gang he walked in front and his followers walked a little way behind. No one was allowed to get fresh with me or he'd feel Eddie's anger. I was Eddie's woman.

Eddie had a summer job delivering laundry for a dry cleaner on South Broadway. I always waited for him outside the store and accompanied him on his deliveries. We strolled like lovers through Van Cortland Park, making love under the pine trees behind Caesar's Place, by the bridle paths, on his bed in his room, in the attic of his mother's house, in his jalopy that he was forever fixing. In our spare time we drove over to Rye to get giddy on the rides at Playland Amusement Park or we'd ride the horses in Van Cortland Park. I was Miss Suburban America, loyal, trusting, and kind. I stopped screwing around. I had eyes only for Eddie.

The haunted house burned down soon after I started in seventh grade for the second time. I came home from school one afternoon, and from the entrance hall of our apartment I could see the burning house. I dropped everything and ran to the window. My house was going up in flames. I was paralyzed. I heard the crackling of the timbers crackling in my own bones. I couldn't move. My haunted house was in flames. It was my fault. The spirits were punishing me. I stood rooted to the spot and screamed hysterically. It was all gone. Hawthorne and Grandma and Joe Gandolfo and Major: They were punishing me for neglecting them, for not thinking about them since I'd started going with Eddie. They'd offered me everything I'd wanted, promised me all, and I'd failed them—failed them as I'd failed everyone.

I couldn't move and I couldn't stop screaming. It was Major

again, all over. I'd killed the spirits just as I'd killed Major. I was a witch. Yes, it was true, I'd killed Major, too. I'd been so happy with Major, I'd been so proud of him, I'd had so much fun with him. I was tossing him up in the air in our apartment on Eldridge Street one afternoon when he was only a little puppy, hardly three months old. I'd been throwing him up in the air and catching him and laughing when I caught him, laughing when I heard his doggie laugh. And then I'd thrown him up once too often and he'd slipped from my hands and fallen on the kitchen floor and I stood there and screamed. Stood there paralyzed and screamed as I was standing and screaming now. Poor Major! He gave out such an eerie wail and he tried to drag himself around on the floor, running around in circles, dragging himself with his front paws in tiny little wild circles because his back was broken and he couldn't move his hind legs. My mother found us like that when she came home and she went with me to take Major to the ASPCA, but the vet told us there was nothing he could do; they had to put Major to sleep. I'd loved Major so much. I'd loved him too much and that was how I killed him. I could never do anything right; however hard I tried, things would always go wrong for me.

I was still standing by the window when my mother came home. The fire had long ago burned itself out. The firemen were walking around, rolling up their hoses. I hadn't moved. There were tears in my eyes and streams of tears down my face but I was crying without a sound. My mother couldn't understand it. "Are you crazy?" she asked. "Crying over an old burned house!"

She didn't understand that I'd lost my hopes. Joe Gandolfo had bought me another dog, Buttons, after Major died. I'd really cared for Buttons but he was a wild dog. He chewed up everything in sight. I was scared that my parents would complain and get me to have Buttons put away, so whenever I found one chewed up shoe I'd hunt up its mate and throw them both away and when my parents looked for their shoes I'd say, "What shoes?" When Buttons chewed a hole in the wall, I'd shift the furniture around to hide the broken plaster. But eventually Buttons got too bad. My parents made me get rid of him. My mother had always been threatening to have me put away; now they did it to my dog. I hadn't been able to protect Buttons after all. Chalk up another failure.

And chalk up more failures for Nathaniel Hawthorne, Major, Grandma, and Joe Gandolfo. I'd lost the spirits. They'd burned down their house and left me.

We hadn't taken a vacation that summer, but over the Jewish holy days in the fall we went to a family resort in the Catskills. Two things stick in my mind.

One was that my sister—unhip, bookish Sandra—finally found herself a boy friend. She came in very late one night and when she was getting dressed the next morning, I saw a big red hickey on her neck. I couldn't believe it. Not Sandra! What guy was she with? What was he like? What did he do to her? She couldn't do that! What if he fucked her? What if she wasn't a virgin anymore? I was really disturbed by it. I felt she shouldn't do that, not Sandra, it was wrong, she deserved better. Not Sandra! Not fucking!

I know I wasn't jealous of her; I felt protective about her. She shouldn't be doing such things. It was all right for me, I *had* to, it was my thing, I was the rebel. But Sandra should be pure.

That same day I got into a terrible fight with my mother. She didn't want me running around in dungarees. "It's a Jewish festival. The New Year. What are people going to think of you if you can't even dress right for the holy days?"

I started arguing with her: "Why do you always want to do things to impress other people? Why can't we do things because that's what *we* want?" But then it got into something deeper. I started crying. "Why can't we be Jewish, Mommy? Why do we have to be phony? Why do we have to lie? I *want* to be Jewish. I want to know about being Jewish like Daddy's folks in Brooklyn. I don't just want to dress up and look pretty; I want to go to the temple and be with real Jews and celebrate. I want to know what being Jewish is all about."

My mother looked at me as if I'd dropped from another planet. "Cookie! What's got into you? What do you want with this all of a sudden?"

It made me realize just how much I wanted to belong to something that had meaning, how much I was being cheated out of a sense of belonging. I tried to get my mother to understand but the only thing she seemed able to say was, "When you're Jewish you have to get dressed nice for the holy days."

I couldn't take it anymore. I couldn't get through to her. I couldn't get her to understand. I picked up brushes, scents, clothes, a mirror from the dresser and started throwing them wildly. I screamed and cried and banged my head against the wall in frustration, begging for something to hold on to.

My mother couldn't understand and we didn't go to the Jewish services.

☼ CHAPTER FIVE ☼

Eddie's gang was called the Red Rebels; they had their names stenciled in red on the back of their dungaree jackets.

When I went back to Nathaniel Hawthorne Junior High after the Jewish holidays, I formed my own gang to complement his. Bobbi Villa, my close friend who also stayed back in seventh grade, was one of the members; another was a German girl, new to the school, named Hildy. The other girls in the gang were all older and had stopped going to school. We called ourselves the Black Rebels to show our connection with Eddie's gang, and we tried to live up to the name. There weren't any other gangs in Yonkers—not in that part of Yonkers, anyway—so there were no other gangs to fight with.

But I did plenty of fighting in school. I showed I could be a troublemaker. I showed I wasn't like the other girls—and didn't want to be. My first act was rather a silly one—but symbolic. I rejected the bobby socks values to which I'd tried to cling so hard during the spring, and got Bobbi and Hildy to join me in wearing brightly colored argyle socks to school. To make sure we were noticed, we each wore two obviously dissimilar socks which we decorated with little poodle brooches. The fashion spread to other girls in school and it made the teachers really wild. They tried to tell me I couldn't do that sort of thing and I told them in so many words to go fuck themselves, no one could force me to wear matching socks if I didn't want to. I got the name of troublemaker and I enjoyed the limelight.

We used to ridicule the other girls on the way home from school and pick fights with everyone. I was in my element; I was as powerful and as mean as Doris Gasparin. We called the Jewish girls names and that used to make them angry because they knew I was really Jewish, too. I wanted to have a reputation as the toughest girl: the toughest girl in Nathaniel Hawthorne JHS and the toughest girl in Yonkers. I was Eddie's girl and he used to meet me every afternoon after school. Eddie was a gang leader and I had to show myself worthy of him.

The toughest girl at Nathaniel Hawthorne was called Rosie. I challenged her. I told her she was full of shit, that she didn't know what a real fight was, that she didn't know what a girls' gang was. She took up my challenge—she had no choice really if she wanted to keep her reputation—and we arranged to meet for an all-out fight after school.

We staged the fight just behind my house, at a new primary school that had a large grassy playground. Eddie and his gang and the boys from his school turned out in force to back me. Rosie brought all her supporters. It was to be the fight of the year. We sparred around a bit, mocking each other, feinting, threatening, goading. The circle closed in and Eddie bellowed out, "Give 'em room! Give 'em room!" I didn't really think I could beat her. I wasn't sure I was as tough as I pretended to be, but I'd watched Eddie practicing for fights and he'd taught me how to land a punch. I was ready to fight like a man; Rosie wanted to fight like a woman, pulling hair and scratching. Finally I closed in and landed a punch. Right in her mouth. She went down. I hadn't expected it. Then I went wild. I started kicking her on the ground. I punched her, kicked her, scratched her, pulled her hair. I kicked her on the legs and on the ribs and in the face. I really went wild and lost control. I was going to show them all! I hadn't hated her in particular, but once she was down all my rage came to the surface. I couldn't stop. They had to pull me off in the end and Rosie went limping home. She was in a terrible mess. I broke some of her ribs and gave her a huge black eye, she was scratched and bruised and bleeding all over.

Someone came around to tell my mother that I'd put a girl in the hospital and my mother asked me why I'd done it. "She picked on me," I told her. "I had to stick up for myself." It seemed to satisfy my mother—she was scared of me by now because I was bigger than she was, and she knew that if she tried to hit me as she'd done when I was little, I'd fight right back. But the principal called my mother to school to hear his complaints and she was angry with me for that because it meant her losing a day of work.

I felt sorry for Rosie when she came back to school, sorry enough to run up to her and apologize and ask her to join my gang. She was too scared of me to be angry, too scared to join the gang, and too scared to stay out. She just said yes to everything I said. I'd never seen anyone so humble. Then she faded out of the picture. I was undisputedly the toughest girl around.

I didn't give a damn for the school. It was just one big drag. I did all kinds of crazy things to show them what I thought of the school and the teachers and everything, like the time I went into the room where the kids left their lunches and I went through them, systematically taking one bite out of each sandwich and then putting them back. Of course they guessed it was me because no one else would have done a crazy thing like that but they couldn't prove it. I got sent to the principal I don't know how often. Each time I heard a lecture and the next day my mother had to take another day off from work to talk to the teacher. I shot paper clips and spitballs at the teachers. I stole change from the girls' pocketbooks. Once, Mr. Burne, the science teacher, a dumpy little man whom I couldn't stand, kept me back in school for something or other that I'd done or hadn't done. I knew Eddie was waiting for me outside, and I was furious. While Mr. Burne was out of the room I got a bottle of black ink and emptied it in the tank of the rare tropical fish he was always raving about. The water turned blue, the fish gasped and died. When Burne came back and saw them he got into a furious rage. He called me a dirty tramp and slapped me in the face. I walked right out and the next day my mother had to come in to complain to the principal about Burne's assault.

Eddie was my man. I wanted to marry him but I was still too

young. We fucked almost every night—except when I had my period, because then I was too miserable with pains and cramps to want anything. We never used contraceptives. I wanted to get pregnant because then we'd be allowed to marry by the courts—if you weren't pregnant, the lowest age was sixteen. Month after month I'd hold my breath and keep my fingers crossed that this time it would happen but it never did. My period came on unfailingly.

My parents got to know Eddie and to like him. They thought he was a swell guy, polite, well mannered, with a regular part-time job. They'd have preferred me to go out with a Jewish boy, but Eddie seemed to come from a nice family: His mother owned her own house, his stepfather owned a restaurant. "They may not be Jewish," my mother said to me once, "but they live *like* Jews." That satisfied her. There was never a word of complaint about my staying out late and they never questioned me about my sex life. Eddie often came over to eat at our house and just as often I was over at his house. Eddie was good for me, my parents thought, perhaps he'd help straighten me out and help me get rid of all my foolishness.

During the fall we screwed a lot in the park. We sat around in the park until late at night with the members of Eddie's gang and my gang, drinking quart bottles of Schlitz beer. When it got colder we spent more time at Little Caesar's and then we screwed in Eddie's room up in the attic. Bobbi and I also spent a lot of time together stealing clothes, cosmetics, and odds and ends from the stores on Getty Square; I didn't believe in wasting good money buying things when with a bit of care and hardly any risk at all you could simply take them. My parents didn't ask me where I got the things from; they assumed I'd been saving my allowance or that Eddie had bought them for me.

Another girl I spent a lot of time with was Leslie who lived in our development. She was only eleven—almost a baby to me—and I treated her like a younger sister. I often met her in Lane's candy store and then I'd see her home through the Riverdale Avenue traffic to her apartment. When she got involved with kids I thought weren't right for her, I warned her against them. I was often over at her apartment playing games with her, acting the older sister. I liked caring for little Leslie, but I was really much more interested in her brother Bruce who was about Eddie's age. I wanted to become closer friends with Bruce and I wanted Bruce to understand me. I knew only one way to achieve this: I seduced Bruce. He was reluctant at first because he considered Eddie a close friend, but I had my way and we made love a number of times while Leslie was asleep or off in another room playing with her dolls. Bruce and I became very close. He was the only boy with whom I had sex while Eddie was still in Yonkers and Bruce was scared that Eddie would find out and beat him up.

In the spring my gang went back to Van Cortland Park. Our hangout was at a place we called Bum's Rock, hidden away among some trees. There was a crevice under the rocks where we could hide an old blanket for screwing on. We had a rope in the trees to swing from like Tarzan. The gang met there almost every night to drink beer or Chianti and to yarn and fool around. Some of the girls from my gang were there sometimes, but mostly they'd be busy with other things. I'd introduced Bobbi to Bruce after we stopped screwing together and they were going steady now, though Bruce wasn't in the gang. Many of the girls' mothers were stricter than mine and wouldn't let them stay out late, so often I was the only girl there. Eddie had his gang well under control and they obeyed his orders. When we wanted to make love, for instance, he just had to tell them, "Cookie and me want to be left alone," and they'd all get up and leave.

It was said there was a crazy wild man who was running around Van Cortland Park, scaring and terrorizing people. He was seven feet tall, wore no clothes, and was covered with hair. They called him Nature Boy. Everyone claimed to have seen him somewhere. We'd come to Bum's Rock and find some evidence that he'd been there: The blanket wasn't exactly where it had been the night before or someone had moved the Chianti bottles. Eddie decided we'd have to do something about Nature Boy; if the cops couldn't stop him from terrorizing people, our gang would do the job for them. We had a purpose at last.

Eddie got hold of a hand gun and some bullets (for self-defense only!) and we organized a systematic hunt for Nature Boy. We flushed out some lovers, even pederasts, and we thought we caught glimpses of Nature Boy now and again, but he always eluded us. And then one moonless night while we were hunting him in the dark, I got detached from the rest of the gang. Suddenly I heard footsteps behind me and deep breathing and I could feel a cold shadow fall on me. I started running and screaming with the terror, afraid to look back.

Then I blacked out.

I came to later with Eddie bending over me and kissing me. "He had you," Eddie told me, "Nature Boy had hold of you. He had you in both his hands and then he threw you down."

I was thrilled. We let everyone know that we'd met Nature Boy and that he'd actually carried me and thrown me on the rocks. I was lucky to be alive. I really was.

Now that we had a gun, we had to find some use for it. One of the new members of the gang, a little guy called Shorty, worked at the stables and he said he knew where they kept the daily take. We planned our robbery very carefully and kept revising the details and the date for a couple of weeks. Finally the day came. Four or five guys did the breaking in; I kept chickie, staying on a rock where I could watch Broadway and the bridle paths and let the guys inside know if anyone was coming. Breaking in was easy. They knew the right place to get in and they found the money easily but it was a big disappointment, less than ten dollars. We planned a lot more robberies after that, but each of them fizzled out for one reason or another. The most we ever did in that line was to steal tires from filling stations and sell them.

There used to be a cop—Patrolman Andro—who had a beat near Little Caesar's and he had a special something for Eddie because he was the leader of the gang and had a reputation. One day, out of the blue, Andro stopped Eddie and frisked him. Eddie was carrying the gun and got arrested on the spot. We were all scared they might send Eddie off to Sing Sing and someone even suggested organizing a jailbreak. But Eddie had a clean record and he'd been planning to join the army like his big brother, George. His eighteenth birthday, when the army would have him, was only a few weeks off so they dropped the charges and Eddie was free to spend his last few weeks with us.

Little Caesar had a farewell party for Eddie at his place. He laid on the sodas and the potato chips and the ice cream, and he set the switch on the juke box so that we could play all the records we wanted without having to pay. After Caesar's we all went to Bum's Rock and had our own party with beer. Everyone knew that Eddie and I would be married as soon as I was old enough and we held a ceremony on the rock. We'd exchanged identity bracelets for Eddie's birthday a few days earlier, and now we exchanged rings. We cut our wrists and exchanged vows and drops of blood with the whole gang there as witnesses to hear us swear, "I'll love you forever and I'll die loving you." Then we signaled them to leave and Eddie and I made love on Bum's Rock for the last time, and when we'd finished we went up to his room and lay on his bed until the early hours of the morning, just clinging to each other and crying, both of us crying.

I went home just in time to change my clothes. I took the day off from school—I was playing hooky quite frequently now that I was in the eighth grade—and Eddie and his whole family drove by to pick me up. I said a last and tearful good-bye to Eddie at the Port Authority Bus Terminal before his bus left for the Fort Dix induction center.

I wrote letters every day, three or four pages long, all covered with lipstick from my kisses, and stained with tears. I had some pictures made and sent him one inscribed, "From your future wife, Cookie," and when he replied he often signed himself "Your future husband, Eddie." My mother thought I was rather silly, tying myself down like that at only fourteen and a half. She'd accepted Eddie as one of the family, but she thought that with him gone I'd soon meet someone else and put the idea of marriage at sixteen out of my head. She knew Eddie was good for me, and both my parents had kissed him good-bye before he left, but they felt that with time and his absence I'd find someone else just as good.

The gang just sort of petered out after Eddie left. We were back in school and it was getting colder and we kept hanging around at Little Caesar's. Caesar more or less took over as leader. He gave us lectures and suggested we might do some good things together. It wasn't the same anymore without Eddie. For a while

I kept going back to Bum's Rock, just sitting by myself, crying and looking at the ID bracelet I'd got from Eddie. But I couldn't do without a man for long. Two weeks after Eddie left, I started working on the members of his gang. They were all scared of what he'd do when he came home if he ever found out.

I really wanted to make out with them—I knew that once I was married I'd have to give up screwing around—but since they wouldn't touch me I decided I ought to take care of them some other way. There was a new girl hanging around Caesar's—her name was Gloria—and I knew she liked to fuck, so I arranged a gang-bang for her to introduce her properly to the gang. Shorty, the little five-footer who'd arranged the robbery at the stables, was the first to go with her on Bum's Rock while we stayed behind the trees. I was the only one that stayed close to watch. It was exciting. When Shorty had finished with her he blew a whistle and retired to the edge and that was the signal for Ryan to have his turn. Ryan was a blond Irish kid with freckles and blue eyes and he was Eddie's closest friend. I liked the way he fucked Gloria. He had real style and skill; he really turned me on. Shorty blew his whistle when Ryan was finished so that the next guy could have his turn and he kept signaling until everyone had fucked Gloria. She enjoyed it.

It took me another couple of days to work my way around Ryan and then we sneaked off together and fucked on Bum's Rock. I was still in love with Eddie, madly in love, but for a short while, for just a few nights, I convinced myself I was in love with Ryan, too. He was really scared. All the time while we were fucking he kept telling me that Eddie would kill him if he found out and I kept having to reassure him that Eddie would never find out.

The gang-bang had made me curious about Ryan and Shorty and I wondered if they fucked better than Eddie. When the novelty with Ryan had worn off after one or two fucks, I worked on Shorty. He wasn't any better than Eddie either. I fucked with most of the gang and then I got tired of them and that, more or less, was the end.

I started hanging around a bowling alley. The first night there I picked up a man and he took me to a motel on Broadway just across the city line, and I waited in the car until he got the key. I told him I was a virgin; I pretended to be scared and shy and cried with the pain when he first entered me and he was very proud of having himself a virgin. I liked the idea of screwing in a bed in a swanky motel; I'd become used to the idea of screwing in bed with Eddie—it was so much better than when I'd been fucking on the grass or in the bushes or in the back of a car the way I'd done when I first came to Yonkers nearly two years earlier. The bowling alley became a regular place for me to meet men and I told each one that I was a virgin.

I also hung out in Getty Square with Bobbi, my best friend. Bobbi didn't screw around, but it was fun to have her company while I waited. I looked sexy and provocative, much older than I was. Just to be on the safe side I had stolen my sister's birth certificate and I carried it with me always in case anyone ever asked me for proof of age in a bar. I let men pick me up in coffee shops and in bars, at the lunch counter of Woolworth's, and on the street corner. It was easy. They could tell from my looks that I was willing: My hair was teased, my face was made up with layers of makeup, my clothes were tight and revealing. If a man came on strong and confident, I'd go with him; if he acted weak and unsure of himself, I'd drop him like a hot potato. Most of them took me to a motel and I'd play my virgin game. I liked the sense of mastery I got when a man wanted me and I could satisfy his needs. I liked it when I could get him to hug me and care for me. I didn't climax—but then I didn't even know it was possible for a girl to climax with a man.

Once the man had climaxed, though, and rolled off me, I felt disgust. His sticky juice was inside me. I hated him. He'd had his fun. I'd rush off into the bathroom and wash myself out and then I'd make him take me home and at home I'd have a long soak in the tub to scrub him away.

Sometimes I'd have another friend, Lois, with me while I waited to be picked up. Lois who'd become a member of the gang at Little Caesar's, was with me when I met Waldo. Waldo himself didn't turn me on too much; he was tall and dark and Italian but what I liked about him was his Harley Davidson. Waldo and a friend, both in their twenties, drove by on their bikes while we were standing at Getty Square. They saw us, circled, and came back. Then Waldo said, "Hop on," and we each hopped on the back of a bike. I liked driving around Yonkers on Waldo's bike and having everybody see me. We fucked for about two weeks, every night, first racing up and down Yonkers on his bike, then going to the house of one of his friends to screw.

When I really liked a guy I'd arrange to spend the better part of the night with him. I'd stay with him until eleven and then get him to drive me home. My parents would be watching the late news on television. I'd kiss them good night and go to bed in my street clothes with a pajama jacket over the top. Around one, when my parents were fast asleep, I'd get up and climb out the living room window. He'd be waiting for me with his car parked where the haunted house had once stood, and we'd go off to a motel or down to the Hudson River in his car and fuck and sleep a bit until five; then he'd take me home. I played hooky more often than I went to school, but my mother didn't want me to get into trouble when the truant officer called her so she always lied and told him I'd been sick and had to stay home.

The guy I most often spent the night with was Guido, an auto mechanic in his mid-twenties, an Italian who spoke very little English. I went with him for about a month, then I started getting sores in my vagina. I couldn't screw any more. It got so sore that I had to wear a sanitary napkin to stop the chafing when I walked. I had a discharge like pus from my vagina. I had to stop going to school. My mother found out a short while later when I broke out with a rash on both arms. She took me to a doctor—not our family doctor, Doctor Tollman who had his office nearby, but another doctor who didn't know us. No one questioned me about where I'd got it. I knew it was syphilis. My mother probably knew. The doctor must have known. He gave me a series of injections and no one said another word about it.

One day in late November I didn't go to school. The night before I'd taken the keys to my dad's car from his pocket while he was asleep. As soon as they'd gone off to work I called Lois and then we got into the car. My hair was still in curlers and I wore a scarf over it. I found driving was easy. I maneuvered the turns out of the parking lot, into Riverdale Avenue. It was great! I felt powerful. I hoped no one would recognize me and at the same time I hoped they would. I drove off through city traffic, along highways. I was a great driver.

On Central Avenue a gust of wind tugged at my scarf. I had to straighten it, and to make things easier I let go of the wheel with both hands, steering through the light traffic with my elbows. Suddenly Lois yelled, "Look out!" Too late. I smashed into a double-parked ice-cream truck, bounced off, and hit two more double-parked cars. The impact wrenched off the door so that it was hanging by one hinge. Lois grabbed at the handle to hold it in and I sped off, round one corner, then another, then a third. We left the car in a parking lot and walked off.

We had to get far away, that was clear. Out of the state. We'd find something, do something, but we had to run. We got as far as the old ferry down by the Hudson and crossed over to New Jersey. Where now? Something kept us back. We could hole up here while we planned; it wasn't a bad idea to remain close to home while we prepared for the future, especially as we had almost no money on us. We spent that night in some bushes at the back of a police station only a few hundred yards from the ferry, clinging to each other for warmth. In the morning I called my mother. They'd been waiting for a call. The police had told them of finding my father's battered Chevy and they were out looking for the hit and run driver who'd ruined his car and three other vehicles. My mother said to come right on home. They'd been worried; they knew I'd been involved. If I came home, she said, everything would be all right and they'd work things out with the police.

So we took the ferry back and came home. Lois came from a strict Italian family; when she got home her father beat the shit out of her. When I came home all was forgiven. I couldn't believe it. I said to my father, "Well hit me, say something, do something to me," but he just looked at me sadly and forgiving. "What can I say? You're all right. That's all that matters. It could have been worse." The police didn't press charges. My father had to settle with the owners of the other cars, and on top of that it cost him a few hundred dollars to have our car fixed. But he wouldn't punish me and he wouldn't even show he was angry at me. He did nothing to allay my guilt. I felt cheated.

☼ CHAPTER SIX ☼

Vicky Gordo was a girl in my class. She was a little girl, not quite five feet, fragile, withdrawn, and a real goody-goody. For some reason she irritated me. She didn't smile, she didn't talk to me, she didn't notice me. Possibly she didn't notice anyone else either, but I wanted her to notice *me.* I used to tease her and shove her and trip her just to get some reaction, but she wouldn't react. I challenged her to a fight and she refused my challenge. I couldn't take it. I became convinced she spent her life trying to annoy me and that she was secretly talking about me. I despised her and I hated her guts.

One afternoon shortly before Christmas of 1956 I got my gang together: There was Carol, there was Bobbi, and there was Hildy. I stopped Vicky Gordo and told her we were having a party, would she like to come. Her face lit up. Yes, she said, she'd love to. Poor foolish idiot, I thought, she thinks I've changed my mind about her, she thinks I've suddenly come to like her.

I had no real plans in mind. I was going to take Vicky over to Carol's house and I was going to teach her a lesson; I was going to get her to respect me. We got into Carol's house—her mother was out working—and I shut the door. Vicky looked a bit puzzled. It didn't look like a party. Perhaps she imagined we were going to pull her into our gang; she certainly hadn't lost any of her look of eagerness. It made me mad to think she might even dream we'd want her in our gang.

I slapped her in the face. I called her a slut and lots of other names. Then I slapped her again. "What makes you think you can join our gang, you slut?" I was furious.

Vicky tried to put on a brave front. She was scared and her face was white, but she wouldn't cry. "I don't have to stand for your insults," she said prissily. "I'm getting out."

"Oh no, you're not." I slapped her again and got Hildy to stand in front of the door to make sure Vicky didn't get out. I hated that Vicky. I hated her for her priggish, prissy, holier than thou airs. "Take your clothes off!" I ordered.

"I'll do no such thing."

"You will so!" I said. I started punching her and tearing at her clothes. Vicky saw that I'd get my way whatever she did. "You're forcing me into this," she said. "You'll be sorry." She took off her clothes very deliberately and folded them over a chair. She kept on her bra and panties and her socks. For such a little girl she was surprisingly well stacked, like my sister Sandra at her age, only the rest of her was much slimmer.

"I said take *everything* off!" It excited me. I had a sense of power. I was God, no less.

She didn't say anything. Very calmly she unhooked her bra and folded it away. Her breasts hung incongruously from her little girl body. They were an insult to me. She had no right to such breasts, a foolish little child like her. I was a woman, a grown woman who knew about life, and even I didn't have a bosom like that. Without falsies my chest looked almost like a boy's.

"And your panties!"

She took them off like a martyr facing the heathens. Her hips were small, the triangle of dark hair was well defined. I felt aroused to do something evil to her, something that would leave a mark on her memory. I'd had feelings of sexual arousal around girls before without quite knowing what they meant or what to do about them, but with Vicky I wasn't aroused to do anything directly sexual; I just wanted to punish her.

"Take her into the bedroom," I ordered. I found some lipsticks on the dresser and handed them around. Vicky stood there, her little legs held tightly together, her hands crossed in front of her cunt. She was shivering. We pushed her down on the floor and I went first. I wrote "Cookie" across her belly in lipstick, a big red accusation, a sign of power and possession. I drew a heart around her belly-button and directly below I wrote "Eddie." The girls followed suit and wrote their names on her. It was a great joke; we were laughing and giggling wildly.

Vicky didn't cry. She lay there, stiff and unyielding, and repeated over and over again: "You're going to be sorry. You're going to be sorry."

The more she said it, the more I wrote. All over her body. "Cookie and Eddie." On her belly and on her thighs and on her breasts. Nobody was going to make *me* feel sorry. I didn't give a shit for anyone else; nobody could touch me now. I was powerful. I owned Vicky's body. There was murder in my heart. I knew that if I had to I could finish her off. I got the girls to turn her over and we wrote our names on her back, too. We covered every available square inch. I hated her. I hated everything she stood for, every prissy goody-goody, every virgin bitch, everyone who supported the rules and the teachers and the people who felt I was no good. I wanted to be bad, bad all the way, as bad and as tough as I could be, to break every damn rule there was. I pressed down on Vicky's body, digging my name in red into her white flesh.

When there wasn't any room left to write on, I told the girls to take her into the bathroom. "We'll wash her off." I felt we'd done enough, that Vicky had learned her lesson.

I had every intention of cleaning her up and letting her go and then suddenly I saw a look on her, a sneering look, a look of triumph. She was actually enjoying being the victim! I felt a murderous rage. I let out the hot water that Carol had started to run and let in cold water, icy cold water. I made her stand in the tub and let the icy water rise over her ankles. The other girls stood around and laughed. I opened the shower and let the water pour down over Vicky. She tried to move away and I ordered her back. She stood there shivering, her teeth chattering, her body turning blue under the red lipstick. She'd be a lot more colors before I'd finished with her.

I sent for an egg and broke it over her head. The yolk dripped down her face while we joked, holding our sides with laughter. I sent for ketchup and emptied the bottle over her head. She was crying hysterically. Then she started screaming. I slapped her and ordered her to stop making so much noise. I told her I'd kill her if she screamed again. She had sense enough to realize that I was liable to carry out my threat. She stopped screaming and we turned off the water.

We dragged her into the front room and I propped her up by the window. I opened the window, letting the December air blow in, and shouted, "Look world! Look at her! This is Vicky Gordo, look at her!" Carol got scared. It was her mother's house, after all, and we could get her into trouble. We shut the window and drew the drapes.

"Hold her," I said. "I'll fix her. For good!"

I went in the kitchen looking for a banana. There were none in the refrigerator but I found some celery. I came back to the front room, waving my celery like a trophy. "Hold her down!" I ordered. "Spread her goddamn legs!"

Vicky didn't seem to believe I could do it. I'd show her! I grasped the celery and rammed it up her crack. She tried to hold herself shut, her muscles were tight. I rammed and rammed with all my might. I got it up her crack and kept on shoving. I shoved that celery so far up her crack I thought it would come out of her nose. I kept shoving and twisting. There was a demon inside me that could do anything. Vicky let out a piercing scream but I wouldn't stop.

The girls got scared. Somebody said, "Stop it, Cookie, you'll really hurt her." Somebody said, "You're going to get us all into trouble." Somebody said, "For God's sake, Cookie, stop it already. You'll kill her." They pulled at me. I let them drag me off her. The celery came out, still clutched in my hand, the last three or four inches dripping with blood.

I rolled over on my back and lay on the floor, panting. Suddenly a cold chill came over me. It couldn't be. I couldn't have done that. Not me. It was a dream. I tried to believe it hadn't happened. I wanted to turn the clock back to the time in the shower and just clean her up and let her go. I wanted to turn the clock back even further, before we'd written on her, before she'd taken her clothes off, before we'd locked her in Carol's house.

"Let her go," I said. "Give her her clothes and let her go."

Vicky didn't say a word. She didn't even threaten. She didn't even say that I'd be sorry. But she had that look about her, that martyred look, that told me she was looking forward to her revenge.

"You're okay now aren't you?" I asked. "You see, we only wanted to. . . ." I tried to act as if it had all been just a harmless joke, but I couldn't find the words. I felt guilty about what had happened; now I wanted to clean up and have everything forgotten.

"Go home now, Vicky, and don't tell a soul. You'll be all right, won't you?" I was hoping she'd smile and tell me all was forgiven. She said nothing.

We were all scared when she left. I tried to convince the girls that nothing would happen, that Vicky was far too frightened to tell anyone. We cleaned up the house, wiped up the egg and ketchup and lipstick, and mopped the floor. Then we went home. It was nearly seven, time for dinner.

I was good during dinner, really good. I ate with the family around the table in the kitchen instead of taking my chops and peas on a tray to sit in front of the television set as I usually did. I tried to be nice to everyone. I even planned to wash the dishes afterwards. Every time footsteps went down the hall past our door I jumped. Then the door bell rang. Ordinarily I'd have been the first to answer; this time my mother got up. I heard some muffled talking, then my mother called, "Danny!" My father got up and joined her. Through the open kitchen door I could see two burly policemen, giants towering over my parents. Then my mother came back to the kitchen, her face afire, and said, "Put your coat on, Cookie. The police want us at the station."

She had that special way of looking at me which meant, "Look what you've done now! Don't you know what you're doing to me?" I didn't say a word; I was almost in shock. We walked out to the police car and I got in the back between my father and my mother.

It was a small police station next to the neighborhood fire house. We went up some stairs to the sergeant's desk and then into a small room where the police talked to me and my parents across a big desk.

"A complaint has been made concerning a sexual assault on the person of Vicky Gordo . . . of a brutal and sadistic nature . . . allegedly involving your daughter and three others . . . the gravity of the situation . . . a juvenile. . . ." I heard only some of the words. When I was asked a direct question I denied everything. My mother was crying, my father was busy trying to soothe her. I wished there was someone there who could help me, someone who would listen to me and help me explain. I wondered where Carol and Bobbi and Hildy were. Had they been arrested, too, or was I the only one? Would I be kept in jail? I was lonely and terrified. Eventually I broke down and admitted everything. It seemed I had no choice. Then I saw Vicky walking out of a room with her mother. She didn't seem so badly hurt at all; in fact she was smiling—an evil little smile of contentment. My fear gave way to anger. The dirty little bitch! The nasty slut! How dare she rat on me.

They let me go eventually, around midnight. We took a cab home. My father sat silently; my mother kept firing away at me: "How could you do that? How could you do that to me? You'll never be any good, I always knew it. Look what you're doing to yourself. You're killing me!"

Neither of them went to work the next morning. My father went out early and came back with the morning paper, the *Yonkers Herald.* My story was all over the front page. They didn't mention Vicky by name but they had Carol's name and Hildy's; they were both over sixteen. Bobbi and I were referred to as juveniles—no names. It really made me mad. It was *me* that had done it and *me* that was going to get all the blame. I was really the star of the show. Now I was going to get the punishment without even the pleasure of publicity. But my parents saw it differently. "Thank God for that," my mother sighed. "At least people won't know about you. What you've done to me! What we have to suffer!"

The hearing was held in a small courtroom. It didn't look like anything I'd expected from television or the movies. The walls were painted gray. There was a raised desk for the judge and on the wall behind him was an American flag and some sort of official seal. I looked around to see how many spectators had come to my trial, but the room was almost empty; the only people there were those directly involved. We sat down at a long table; Bobbi was sitting at the other end of the table with her folks, the legal aid lawyer sat between us. I watched my parents and when I was sure they weren't looking at me I smiled at Bobbi and she smiled back. It was good having her there; I had company. If they put me in jail, they'd probably take her off, too, and then we could share a cell. It wouldn't be so bad after all.

I was the center of attention. The assistant DA had his say and then they read the medical report and our lawyer kept consulting with my parents and asking me questions. Each time one of the lawyers made a statement, the judge leaned down from his desk and asked me for my comments. The only embarrassing moment came when he mentioned the celery. Nobody had said a word about it before at the station house, or in the papers, or in conference with our lawyer. My parents looked at me in disbelief. I felt terribly sheepish. Celery! It all seemed so crazy. I couldn't understand it myself. Then the judge asked, "And did you place this . . . ahem, stick of celery in the . . . ahem, the private parts of Vicky Gordo?" and I had to suppress a giggle. Vicky didn't have to testify—we'd both admitted everything and, I guess, the court wanted to spare her any additional suffering as the phrase goes. But she sat there next to her mother, the picture of righteousness, pleased at the trouble she'd got us into, proud of her starring role.

Carol and Hildy were tried separately, as adults. They didn't appear at our trial and we weren't called in for theirs. Carol, I think, was sent away; Hildy's family moved out of their apartment on South Broadway. I never saw either of them again.

We went back to school after the first hearing. Bobbi and I were singled out like beings from another world. The kids looked at us and whispered about us but they kept their distance. I think the kids in my class were proud of me in a perverse way; they pointed me out to others. "There's Cookie!" I'd helped to put the class on the map. Officially, of course, no one was supposed to know what we'd done, but the news had traveled quickly.

A few days later, Bobbi and I were back in court for the sentencing. We sat in comfortable leather chairs in the judge's chamber together with our parents. No DA, no lawyers, no court reporter. The judge sat across from us at an ordinary desk. He seemed warm and friendly. It didn't look as if he'd throw the book at us. I wasn't scared of him; the only person I was really scared of was my mother. He gave us a long talk in what I assumed was meant to be an understanding tone of voice. He really seemed to care for me and what was happening. Maybe, I thought, I'll get away with it. Maybe he'll be so understanding that he'll just give us a lecture. Then he told us that we would both be put on probation for a year and that during my probation I would have to see a psychiatrist regularly. I was quite thrilled. Probation! Probation had status. Not everyone could say that they'd been on probation. It would make people respect me. And I had to see a psychiatrist, too. Even Bobbi didn't get that.

I really felt pleased with the outcome. I'd gotten away with it! My parents started being nicer to me. They *had* to be nice: Didn't the judge say I needed psychiatric help? My mother was afraid to provoke me. I knew she was afraid of me—and I took advantage of it.

As for myself, I was convinced I *was* crazy. Everyone knew I was crazy. There wasn't much point in changing or in acting good. Crazy Cookie, that was me.

I had to see the psychiatrist three afternoons a week after school, the probation officer twice a week. The psychiatrist had his office in a city building. I'd sit with him and he'd talk and try to probe into how I felt about things, but he obviously wasn't terribly concerned. I told him only what *I* wanted him to hear and lied like a trooper. I'd heard psychiatrists always start by talking about your sex life but this one wasn't even interested to know if I had a sex life at all. (At this time I was out almost every night screwing with men I picked up at the bowling alley or at Getty Square.) It didn't bother me that the psychiatrist didn't take more interest; I felt I was too far gone for anything so simple as a talking-to by a doctor to be of help to me.

The probation officer was even easier. I just had to go in and tell her yes, I was going to school and seeing my psychiatrist and home at nine-thirty every evening, and no, no problems—and I was done. She didn't want to be bothered too much by me, either, and everyone knew I was simply marking time until I was sixteen and old enough to leave school and marry Eddie. Once I was married I'd be out of everyone's hair and out of Yonkers and out of the state of New York.

My mother tried to forget the whole thing: The psychiatrist and the probation officer were taking care of me so she didn't have to worry. She didn't ask me where I went and she didn't ask me to stay home more. She knew that people were talking about us and that parents wouldn't let their kids mix with me, but officially at least no one knew and that was a blessing as far as my mother was concerned. As for making me content, she solved that easily by buying me clothes or underwear every now and again. That had always been her pattern: "I'll buy her a present or give her some money and then she'll be all right." She was a closed person who found it difficult to show her emotions directly.

My father said nothing. All he wanted was peace and quiet and his beer in front of the TV.

Eddie came home from Fort Dix for Christmas a few days after the trial. I was happy to see him, of course, but I wondered how he'd react to the news of my escapade. We kissed hungrily when we met, and in front of his family he acted as if nothing had happened. Then we went upstairs to his room. The moment he'd shut the door he started. He beat the hell out of me. "You've disgraced me!" he kept yelling. "You've disgraced my whole family!"

I cried and screamed so hard that eventually his family came running. His mother said, "Leave her alone, Eddie. She made a mistake, she paid for it. She won't do it again. Leave her alone, Eddie!" But Eddie kept on, and finally his sister had to pull him away from me.

Despite all my screams, he didn't really hurt me much. On the contrary, I felt that his blows were proof of his love; he really had to care for me a lot if he could work himself up into such a rage. His anger was exciting; I felt aroused. As soon as his sister had left the room we went into each other's arms and kissed and then we made love and everything was beautiful. He stayed for two weeks and it was like a honeymoon. He'd heard some rumors that I'd been screwing around with his gang—I denied it—and he slapped me around again and I discovered that he was enjoying the fight before the fuck as much as I did. After that he beat me almost every other day. I found he got angry if I touched him on the neck where he'd once had surgery, so I did it deliberately and then he'd slap me and we'd quickly get into a really violent fight that left me with black and blue marks. It got to the point where sex without being slapped was little fun and I'd beg him to hit me even in the middle of making love.

Nathaniel Hawthorne JHS wouldn't keep me any more. They saw me as a troublemaker and instigator. Bobbi stayed on, but I was transferred to Benjamin Franklin JHS in Park Hill, a black neighborhood, to which I had to go by public bus.

I'd never been much around blacks before. My parents had a real fear of them and so, in a way, had I as a result of a near rape by four or five black boys when I was at the Henry Street Settlement House a few years earlier. They'd been waiting for me in the girls' washroom and as I came out they all grabbed me and pulled up my dress and tried to get me back into the cubicle again. I screamed but there was no one around to hear me and I literally had to fight for my life to get away from them. At Benjamin Franklin, however, I discovered that blacks were quite nice. One boy in particular stood out: Albie, a very handsome boy, lovely brown skin, lead singer in a rock group. I liked Albie and so it was only natural, as far as I was concerned, that we fucked. We did it in the schoolyard after school before we went home, standing up against the wall, pretending we were just talking to each other, our coats around us against the icy cold. If anyone noticed they took it in their stride—I assume fucking on school premises wasn't an extraordinary event at Benjamin Franklin, though it was a very uncomfortable procedure.

I wasn't sufficiently discreet, unfortunately; I wrote a compromising note to Albie once which went astray and landed up in the hands of Eddie's mother, Alice. She came over to confront my mother with it and complain that I was screwing around—and not just with anyone but with a colored guy.

My mother asked me if it was true. She was really bothered by his being colored. I told her that it didn't mean anything, I didn't care for Albie, I was still in love with Eddie, and still planning to marry him. Her only comment was, "Be careful."

That was the second and the last time my mother had so much as hinted at sex to me. The first time was the summer after I'd turned eleven. We were away in the mountains and suddenly I found myself bleeding from my vagina. I was scared to tell her. I stuffed my panties with toilet paper and hoped the bleeding would go away; I thought it must be the result of screwing around so much with Stella's friends. Finally, after a week, I told my mother. She laughed—and gave me a slap in the face that caused me more surprise than hurt. I couldn't understand it. Why slap me? "It's a Jewish custom," she told me. "It's for good luck. What you have is called your period." I had no idea what she was talking about but she got me a sanitary belt and napkins. When I was still bleeding a week later, she took me to a doctor who bawled her out for not explaining things to me. "Does your daughter know what's happening with her cycle?" he asked, and then he told her to sit me down at home and teach me the facts of life. She did, too, in her own way. "You've got your period, now. You're going to get it every month. From now on you'll have to be careful." That was all: "Be careful." I had no idea what she meant or what I was supposed to be careful with. She certainly didn't say anything about contraception and she didn't tell me anything about fucking. And so, despite her mysterious admonition, I continued fucking and never used any contraceptives.

Eddie came home once again, for a long furlough prior to his transfer to Fort Campbell in Kentucky. He slapped me around over Albie, and then he slapped me some more over other incidents, and I made up some stories about having screwed with other boys that I'd never even been out with just to make him jealous and have him beat me some more. I thoroughly enjoyed myself the month he was home. And when he had gone off to Fort Campbell, I went back to the bowling alley and to Getty Square to find my nightly sex.

☼ CHAPTER SEVEN ☼

I got no presents for my sixteenth birthday and I had no party. Everything was being saved for the big event: my wedding that was to take place less than four weeks later.

But I did have a celebration of sorts and a present that was more precious to me than anything anyone could have given me: I left school on my sixteenth birthday. I literally danced out of the school ahead of my mother who had come to sign the papers. I pirouetted down the dingy corridors of Benjamin Franklin JHS, skipped away from teachers, principals, chalk dust, regimentation, and authority. I was an adult. My probation—such as it was—had ended a couple of weeks earlier; my probation officer was happy to see the last of me. (My visits to the city psychiatrist had stopped after only a few months.) I was free.

Our wedding was to take place at the Tropical Acres, a Yonkers nightclub. It was to be an elaborate affair with a band, liquor, and three hundred invited guests. (We made sure the guests knew we were flying to Fort Campbell right after the wedding and that if they were thinking of presents, we'd prefer something portable—like money. Bruce, Leslie's brother, was Eddie's best man; my sister Sandra was maid of honor and my cousin Lorraine was flower girl.

The date we chose for the wedding, February 16, 1958, turned out to be the day of the Great Blizzard. I woke up that morning with a flutter in my stomach and looked out of my bedroom window at the snow coming down, white snow covering everything, clouds of white feathers spiraling down like a flock of chickens being plucked in the heavens. Everything I knew was obliterated. It was a new world, a white world, a world I couldn't recognize, a world of the unknown. The telephone kept ringing all morning: The band didn't know if they could make it through the snow; the limousine mightn't make it; the minister mightn't make it; the guests were doubtful. I had to wear a coat over my white brocade dress, galoshes over my white patent shoes, a square of plastic over my veil and headdress. I knew how much time Eddie had spent pressing the paratrooper's uniform in which he was getting married and how much effort he'd put into spit-shining his paratrooper's boots that would be covered with snow up to the ankles before he arrived at the wedding. We made it, though, my father driving us in his car with the wheels spinning in the deep snow through the almost deserted streets, but the wedding started nearly three hours late to allow the guests and the band and the minister to arrive. The ceremony itself was brief and non-denominational. Then Eddie proudly turned to me with the ring, and I held out my finger to have it slipped on. We kissed and then I burst into hysterical sobs. Family and friends gathered around me, trying to comfort me, trying to calm me. "It's all over!" I sobbed. "It's all over!" They thought I was crying over the end of the ceremony and tried to tell me the ceremony itself meant nothing; sure it was over, but the dancing hadn't even started yet and all of my married life stretched ahead. I couldn't tell them I was crying for something else: for my childhood, for the past, for the good times I'd had or might have had, for the times when I could get away with anything. Now it was all over. All the fun and all the excitement and all the freedom. I was a married woman now, responsible for myself, no longer able to make excuses. Sandra, in tears, was the first to hug me. "It should have been you," I told her. "I wish you'd got married instead of me." I don't think she believed I really meant it.

Eddie and I drove with Alice and Poppi to their house so that I could change out of my wedding dress, but when we were ready to leave the snow was already too deep. Carrying our overnight bags, we trudged through the snow, down the middle of an eerie

Broadway that seemed as wide and unbounded as an ocean, struggling almost knee-deep until we reached the Van Cortland Hotel. It was only a few hundred yards from Bum's Rock and the only motel around Yonkers that I'd never been to.

We had a romantic wedding night. My mother-in-law had bought me a glamorous negligee that I wore for the occasion and I came to Eddie as a fresh new bride. We hadn't screwed for two whole weeks before our wedding although he was home on leave, and now we were man and wife, together for eternity, to have and to hold, to spend the whole night together and every night after that, legal, permitted, and blessed. We were tired from the exertions of the wedding and the long trek to our hotel room and it was well after midnight, but tiredness wasn't relevant. We were in no hurry. I'd never spent a whole night in bed with anyone before—not even Eddie—and now we had two whole days together with nowhere to go except to take our meals in the dining room and then hop back into bed. A new world lay ahead of me. Cookie Quinones, Mrs. Eddie Quinones, a child no longer. Only another few days in Yonkers to give us time to pack and to take in the pleasures of New York City's Broadway and Times Square, then I'd be gone from my youth for ever, away from Yonkers, away from my mother and my father, away from all the friends and neighbors. At Fort Campbell I'd be an Army wife; the Army would make a woman out of me.

We flew to Nashville when Eddie's furlough was over, then took the bus to Fort Campbell. Neither of us wanted to live on base so we moved to the nearest town, Clarksville, across the state line in Tennessee, a real Army town. We found a tiny apartment in the basement of an old frame house. At the time I thought it was darling, snug and cozy, a little doll's house of a home, but looking back I see it as probably the ugliest place I've ever lived in—and I've stayed in some really ugly places since! The rooms were minuscule and the furniture was huge and old-fashioned, with a high-backed sofa and ornately carved tables; what I found most attractive about it, I think, was the huge double bed.

The honeymoon soured quickly. Eddie was away at the base all day while I stayed home with nothing to do. We had no radio and no television. The other tenants in the building were hicks with whom I found it impossible to strike up a friendship. Our apartment was infested with huge flying bugs that terrified me and I used to sit outside most of the day to avoid them, waiting for Eddie to come home and make the apartment safe. As a housewife I was a failure. The only thing I knew how to cook was French toast; we had it for breakfast, lunch, and dinner. I could cook eggs—but only scrambled. I tried to make rice once, knowing how much Eddie liked it, but it came out looking and tasting like oatmeal and I burst into tears. Eddie ate it without complaints, but the look on his face told me more than enough. I'd imagined married life to be better than this.

One Saturday afternoon I made up my mind to make a real effort. I was going to make veal cutlets like those my mother used to make. I promised Eddie he'd have a real meal for a change, he'd see what sort of a cook his wife could be. I took the allotment money—over a hundred dollars—and went out to the supermarket. Going down the main street I passed some stores, a dress shop, a toy shop, a shoe store. I got to the supermarket and was just about to go in when a little devil whispered into my ear. I wanted to see those shops, just walk around them for a while, just see what they had. I hadn't walked around in a store for weeks, not since I'd stopped going to Getty Square. It wouldn't take long and it would be better to do it now than wait until later when I'd be laden with groceries and cutlets. I went back to look at the shop windows. I saw the clothes on display, all marked down to unbelievably low prices, incredible bargains. I stepped inside to see what they were really like. Three hours later I came home, loaded with blouses and shoes and dresses and a pair of black toreador pants with white scrollwork embroidery up the outside seams, the sort of pants I'd always wanted to get but which my mother had never let me wear. I also had a doll, an eighteen-inch doll with long hair and a huge hat and a crinoline skirt; I just *had* to have that doll when I saw it and I felt the fifteen dollars it cost was well worth it. I came home with everything except food. I'd spent all the money, every last cent of it.

Eddie was livid. He went at me with his hands, beating the hell out of me. I fell to the floor and he picked up a heavy chair and pinned me down with it, with just my legs sticking out, and as I tried to struggle out from under he kept kicking at my legs. I couldn't see what I'd done wrong. Finally I crawled away and into bed, hurt, bruised, and crying. Eddie came after me. He wanted to kiss me. I pushed him away. I didn't want him. I hated him and I hated myself and I hated Clarksville and our horrible little flat. Eddie tried to stroke me. I screamed. He threw himself on me and pinned me down and then he started taking off my clothes. I kicked and screamed and clawed. Eddie went right ahead. He was raping me. I didn't want him. I was being forced, brutally forced. And then suddenly I relaxed. I enjoyed the brutality of it, the animal smell of his anger, my own pain and humiliation. I opened my legs and let him enter and, still clawing and fighting to keep the sensations going, I let him take me and thrill me.

For the next three weeks, until Eddie got the next allotment, we subsisted on K rations that Eddie brought home from the base. We used each tea bag three times; we invited Eddie's friends to visit us for the evening so that we could bum cigarettes from them. Eddie wanted to take all the clothes back to the store and get a refund, but I persuaded him that the store had no refund policy. We starved for three weeks—but at least I was smartly dressed. On Monday, when Eddie was back at the base, I cut my hair very short and curled it with spit curls over my forehead, then I changed into my toreador pants, with a low-cut blouse and my padded bra and sat on the sofa in a seductive movieland pose to wait for Eddie. Eddie didn't like it—at first. He'd really loved my shoulder-length hair, so black that it was almost blue. But he found the new look in me irresistible. He kissed me and hugged me and stared at my clothes and got his hand down the front of my new blouse and his fingers on the tight crotch of my pants and within minutes he had my clothes off and we were screwing. I really enjoyed the way I could turn him on just by the way I looked and dressed. We had a really good screw and even Eddie had to admit that cutting my hair had been worthwhile. That night he got out his camera and flash and shot a couple of rolls of photographs, one roll with my new clothes on, one posing in the nude with only a towel strategically placed so that he wouldn't have any trouble getting the pictures developed.

As soon as we had some spare cash we moved to a new apartment where a lot of other Army families were living. I had friends at last and that took some of the loneliness out of my life and also took away some of the terror on the days when Eddie was scheduled to jump. I was sitting by the radio one of those days, clutching my doll for comfort, when I heard that an error in forecasting the wind strength had caused an accident at Fort Campbell: Five paratroopers had been killed and over a hundred injured. I called the base but they couldn't give me any news about Eddie. I got together with the other wives, all equally terrified. I called my mother-in-law; she told me they'd heard the news on the radio and were terribly concerned. Eddie came home very late that night, my first news that he was safe, with horrible stories of his friends whose shroud lines had tangled, causing them to crash to their death or mutilation. He had nightmares that night and woke up screaming.

I got pregnant in May. Eddie was in his glory when he heard, and we called our folks right away. My next-door neighbor, Sunny, also an Army wife, got pregnant around the same time. We went to the Army obstetrician together, we sewed clothes together, she showed me how to cook. We became close friends. We compared bellies every day; mine was always bigger and my breasts suddenly filled out, too. For the first three months I was sick. I threw up regularly, but the nauseous feeling stayed with me all day. I had to give up smoking because it made me feel so bad. I started overeating, eating all day, mounds and mounds of spaghetti. I gained forty-five pounds and could hardly waddle around. I felt ugly and ungainly and disgusted with myself but I wouldn't stop eating. I stayed in bed all day, getting up only an hour or so before Eddie was due, to make a stab at preparing some food. I told Eddie I'd been up all day but had felt too sick to do the housework and he'd have to do the housework after dinner—and press his own fatigues, too.

Our baby was born on February 20, 1959, two weeks overdue. Labor was unbearable agony. "I don't want the baby," I told the nurses when my labor pains became bad, "you can have it." I was relieved when he was born and it was all over, but I couldn't really love the baby, not until next day when they brought him to me washed and cleaned, a lovely little eight-pound baby boy with red skin and long black hair and the longest eyelashes I'd ever seen on a baby. I loved him then. I loved having a baby. I loved feeding him and holding him and checking all his fingers and toes. I saved the gown on which he threw up his first meal; I still have it, unwashed, with its yellow stains.

We called him Mitchell Todd. Originally I'd planned to call him Everett Mitchell. The Mitchell was after my grandfather, Murray. The last time I'd seen him was in 1956 when I'd gone down to Miami for the summer, but I'd acted up so badly—carrying on with boys, being rude to my grandfather's new wife—that he shipped me home after two weeks. It hurt me that I'd last seen him under such circumstances. I was really cut up by his death only a few months before Mitchell's birth. It's a Jewish custom to call a child after a dead relative, using the same name or at least the same initial, but not after someone living. I chose the name Everett after Eddie himself; since he wasn't Jewish it didn't matter that he was alive. But then Mike Todd—the current husband of Elizabeth Taylor—died in a plane smash, my idol. I'd worshiped Mike Todd, whose swashbuckling and romantic manner always reminded me of my grandfather. His death compounded my feelings of loss at Grandpa's death. So the baby became Mitchell Todd, and Eddie was relieved because he hadn't cared for the name Everett, anyway.

We were in Clarksville for only another month after Mitchell's birth. I devoted the whole day to my baby, fussing over him and worrying about him. I didn't breastfeed him because my mother had told me that this wasn't a Jewish custom. I fussed that Mitchell shouldn't be too warm or too cold, too hungry or too over-fed, too unhappy or too quiet. For a while, in fact, I made Eddie call the doctor almost daily for advice: Mitchell wasn't crying, did that mean that there might be something wrong?

Eddie was released from the Army in March. We packed our belongings and sent them to Yonkers via Railway Express, then we flew home to stay with Eddie's mother. They had a full house. George, Eddie's older brother, had come out of the Rangers a few months earlier and he was living there with his wife, Georgia, and their four-month-old son, little George. Almost as soon as we got there, Eddie's mother discovered that Mitchell had a deformed leg. We took him to a specialist who had the leg put in a cast and ordered special clamps that Mitchell had to wear for a whole year. I felt really shattered by this. I was sure it was my fault. I'd messed things up again. I'd had a chance to make something beautiful by giving birth to Mitchell, and now it turned out that his leg was deformed. It had to be because of something I'd done, some sort of retribution for my wild carrying-on, the Fates punishing me for all my past folly.

Eddie was out looking for a job much of the time. Georgia and I stayed home, playing with our children and chatting with George who didn't bother to even look for work. Alice cooked enough food for us all and my only chore was to help Georgia do some of the cleaning. I wasn't happy. I felt everyone was comparing Mitchell with Georgia's baby, blond and bouncy George, and I sensed that Eddie's stepfather resented me because of Mitchell and his leg, and because I was Jewish—Poppi was, after all, a German. I felt myself attracted too much to George and sensed I might be heading for trouble. Sometimes, too, Eddie stayed out late at night without explanation. I hated staying home with Georgia and George and I hated even more staying there by myself because Alice filled my head with stories of witchcraft and spirits and she had me convinced the house was haunted.

I spent a lot of my time at my parents' home. There, at least, I felt that Mitchell was welcomed. My mother could sense what was happening. "You ought to get out of that house," she told me, "young people need a home of their own. You don't have any responsibilities with Alice to take care of things and Eddie doesn't feel real pressure to find himself a job." It seemed a good idea.

Eddie finally got a job at the Anaconda Copper plant at Hastings-on-Hudson and we found a lovely apartment close by. My mother promised to lend us the deposit and the initial rent, and we were just about to sign the contract and move in when I discovered that the apartment had been converted from what had once been a funeral parlor—and nothing was going to get me to live *there.* Eventually we found another apartment, in Yonkers, not far from my mother's. Eddie's mother bought us a dining room set and a washing machine; Mom put up the money for the lease and for current expenses and gave us some bedroom furniture. We were all set.

My mother and father came over to visit us in our new apartment quite frequently, bringing food for us to eat. I didn't like housework or cooking and I let the apartment get filthy. I had little time for Eddie although I always had food for Mitchell. That made Eddie jealous and I stirred up more trouble by telling Eddie that it was his fault; he wasn't earning enough and the only food we had was what my mother brought over. We had a lot of fights. And we didn't even have sex to look forward to as a relief from our constant bickering. I'd lost all interest in sex when I became pregnant and it didn't come back after Mitchell was born. Being a mother was being woman enough for me; sex was a chore. I started staying up late waiting until Eddie had fallen asleep before I went to join him in bed, and when he asked me right out about sex I'd claim that I felt sick or had a headache. For proof I'd get the aspirin bottle and very loudly shake out a few pills, but I never took them—I had a great distrust of drugs in any form, even of vitamin pills when I was a kid. Eddie stopped believing my excuses after a while, but that didn't help him any; sex turned me off and there was no way Eddie could turn me on.

A friend of Eddie's, Larry, started coming over quite frequently in the evenings to play showdown, a poker-like Army game that Eddie had taught me. When Larry came over I cooked dinner for us; I wasn't a great cook yet, but I could make a good meal when I had to and I'd slimmed down since my pregnancy so that I looked attractive again. I liked Larry. I felt myself strongly drawn to him. I wanted him to like me as much as I liked him. While the three of us played cards, I played footsie with Larry under the table; Eddie didn't notice. Larry started to come over every evening, not just to play showdown. Eddie, tired from work, fell asleep in front of the TV. That was the signal for Larry and me to get together. Larry was tremendously handsome and tremendously strong. He'd grab me in his arms and press my back with his powerful hands so that I'd think he'd break it any moment. I felt myself going limp, feeling terribly small and weak and helpless in his arms. That feeling of vulnerability, of weakness, was more pronounced than the actual sexual pleasure I got from our necking. We went on like this for a few weeks, necking and hugging in a corner while Eddie was dozing or on the living room floor when Eddie was in bed. Then Larry started coming around during the day while Eddie was at work and soon enough our hugging and squeezing turned to fucking. We fucked only once or twice. I felt not the least bit of guilt—the pure pleasure of being held by powerful Larry made me insensible to anything as petty as guilt—but Larry, who didn't mind cheating on his wife, was concerned for Eddie. He stopped coming around during the day and he stopped coming around evenings even to play cards. I think Eddie must have sensed the tension that had existed, but he didn't question me about his friend.

Around this time I got friendly with the three Capri sisters, Terry, Annette, and Phyllis. I met them one day while shopping and they invited me up to their place. I'd known Annette from Nathaniel Hawthorne JHS. Now they formed a singing group, something on the lines of the Maguire Sisters, playing parties and nightclub dates in New Jersey and on Long Island. I got close to them, almost like a fourth member of their set, helping them to choose their clothes, listening to their exciting stories of life in show business. I saw them almost every day, at their home or at mine. They liked me, they asked for my advice, and they made me feel important.

Eddie still had his job at Anaconda—and we still fought steadily over almost everything. Once it was over Mitchell's table manners. He wouldn't eat his breakfast cereal; I picked up the bowl and emptied it over his head. Eddie didn't say a word; he simply picked up a bottle of soda and emptied that over *my* head. That was a little fight. Others were more serious, like the time we got into a fight in the living room. We were saying vile things to each other, hateful, spiteful things. I hated Eddie for what he was doing to me. I hated what had become of us. I saw his picture on a dresser, a smiling picture of Eddie in uniform with an inscription in the corner, "To Cookie—from your husband-to-be." I picked up the picture in its big frame, lifted it over my head, and brought it crashing to the floor. The walls had closed in on me. I was trapped in my marriage with Eddie more than I'd been trapped even in school. In my school days there was always a way out: I'd be grown-up one day and free. Now I *was* grown-up and less free than ever. "I hate you! I hate you! I hate you!" I yelled at Eddie. "I'm sorry I ever married you. I'd rather die than live with you." There seemed no other way out. I picked up a large sliver of glass and stabbed at my wrists. The blood came, but not enough—I'd missed the place. Eddie slapped me in the face to stop my hysteria, then he took me to the bathroom to wash off the blood and put on a bandage.

Sandra got married on Thanksgiving. Eddie was usher, I was matron of honor. It was a big splashy affair in the Bronx, bigger than mine. Her husband was Jewish, a baker, and they'd met at a dance. I was happy she was married at last—she was twenty-two and to me that was really old—but I thought it was a waste of a good education as a lab technician for her to spend her days selling cookies in a bakery.

Between Thanksgiving and Christmas, Eddie and I had another big fight. It wasn't over anything specific, just the buildup of months of anger and frustration on both sides. Eddie gave me a real pasting. In better times it might have led to excitement and the excitement to sex and the sex to another truce in our never-ending war. But now nothing could arouse me to love for Eddie, not even a violent beating. There was no way to respond to his anger. I ran away. I ran out the front door wearing only a thin dress, out into the night. The snow was thick on the ground. I threw myself into the snow and rolled in it. I wanted to bury myself in it. I wanted the snow to keep coming down and cover me over so that I could disappear. Eddie ran after me. I saw him as coming to smother me, to strangle me, to crush the life out of me. I wouldn't let him get near. I fought and struggled against him and screamed. He must have realized I'd gone mad. He kept his distance.

Later, when I was exhausted and my body was numb from the cold, he picked me up and carried me to bed. Then he sat there by my bed and cried. I felt tender for him, but I knew there was nothing I could do. I was past help. It was all over. I couldn't bring myself to live with him. He really loved me, I knew, but I was too crazy for him to manage.

I called my mother and asked her to take me and Mitchell home. Eddie walked out just before Mom and Dad came for me. During the week he went back to the apartment and took his clothes away. I stayed with Mom and Dad. Mom explained the situation to the landlord, the lease was canceled. Eddie's mother took half of the furniture, Mom took the rest, and the washing machine went to Sandra.

My mother took it all in stride. I told her that it had all grown out of Eddie's jealousy at the attention I was paying Mitchell; she said she understood, that was how many men reacted. I told her I wanted to stay with her for a while so that I could get myself a job and be a better mother to Mitchell and she said that was sensible.

☼ CHAPTER EIGHT ☼

I moved back into my old bed in my old room. Except for Mitchell's crib which stood in the corner where Sandra's bed had once stood, it was just like in the old days, a typical teenager's room with pictures of film stars on the walls. I played the role of mother to Mitchell as well as I could and I tried to adopt the role of homemaker for my parents. I did some shopping and some cleaning, and even cooked occasionally. Eddie came around once a week to play with Mitchell, and each time he left ten dollars. We nearly always ended up by quarreling, though, and after a time he stopped coming and his contribution stopped, too. My mother got in touch with Alice and between them they arranged for a legal separation. It cost my mother one hundred and fifty dollars, and then she started putting aside money to pay for a divorce when the time was right.

I had never really liked the name Quinones; now that I was legally free of Eddie, I shortened it to a simple Quinn. Cookie Quinn.

Living with my parents, I now had someone to mind Mitchell in the evenings, and so I was freer to move into the world of the Capri sisters. I became almost a fourth member of their group; I even looked like them and people took me for their sister. Tommy, their father and a carpenter, was an Italian of the old school; he was strict with them and kept them in line—no drinking, no dating. He acted as their road manager and chaperon. I really liked him. He treated me as a member of the family. He used to drive the four of us to the spots where they were singing. I helped carry the bags, then I went backstage and helped the three sisters dress for their appearance. While the show was on, I sat with their father at a table out front, sipping Coke and watching the reactions of the audience. Tommy and I were always the first to start clapping when a number was over, and the last to stop. Between numbers we all sat together, discussing new songs and new acts. They valued my knowledge of dance routines and I showed them various steps they could use with their songs. Eventually we started planning further ahead, trying to work out a new act that would combine much more dance and movement with their singing; I would do the choreography for that. I had a hope I didn't dare express—that their show might include a brief act for me, too.

I felt really happy in this new world of show business. This was the sort of life I'd dreamed of when I was a little kid on the Lower East Side, the world of glamor inhabited by Philip's Aunt Anne. This is what I'd gone to dancing school for all those years. Now I was part of this world. With the sisters to set an example and their father to lay down the line, I became quiet, demure, and responsible. My whole personality changed. My mother was proud of me. Sunday afternoons she sometimes had friends or relatives come over and she'd ask the Capri sisters to entertain. "My daughter is working with the Capri sisters," she would boast. She thought that the experience of being married had matured me and that now, at last, I was respectable and responsible. And, indeed, I was. No drinking, no dating, no screwing. I was every bit as demure as the Capri sisters themselves.

One afternoon at the end of March, I was wheeling Mitchell down South Broadway. A man smiled at me outside an Irish bar. He had black curly hair and blue eyes, he was attractive and he looked Italian. I smiled back and walked on. He called to me. I turned. He invited me into the bar for a drink. His name was Boris and I liked him immediately. For the first time since I'd been married—not counting Larry—I was aroused sexually by a man. I couldn't stay long because I had to go home and prepare dinner, but I gave him my phone number. My mother was pleased when he called that evening; she thought it was good for me to go out and start dating men again. Eddie could be forgotten.

We drove through Yonkers in Boris's car, parked in a dark street and fucked. Old times again. It was a good feeling. I could have my cake and eat it, could live the quiet life with my parents and Mitchell and still enjoy sex, be taken care of at home and be independent, too. He called for me the next night and we fucked again. I waited for more phone calls, but I heard no more of Boris. I passed the bar on South Broadway a few times and saw him through the window. I waved to him but he pretended not to see me. Finally I walked into the bar and spoke to him. He told me he was too busy to see me.

I missed my next period; instead, I started throwing up. I'd never used contraceptives, not even with Eddie; it just hadn't seemed important. I was terrified at the idea of being pregnant. Fortunately, I'd had sex with Eddie once after we'd separated, when he'd come around in the afternoon to see Mitchell, and I thought I might be able to juggle the dates and convince Eddie and my mother that it was his baby. But even that was little consolation; I didn't want another baby, whoever took the responsibility for it.

I tried every dodge I knew. I sat for two hours in a scalding hot bath into which I'd poured two cans of dried mustard. I came out looking like a lobster—but still pregnant. I tried stretching and reaching for high shelves, I tried tumbling and falling, I tried lifting heavy objects, I spent hours running up and down stairs. Nothing worked.

I confided in Annette Capri with whom I felt the closest. She'd known about Boris and she sympathized with me now, but she couldn't give me any concrete help. Finally I sat down with my mother one Friday evening while my father was away on his weekly outing and I told her the whole story. I was already two months pregnant. She was very upset. "You've done it again," she said. "We gave you every chance to make a new start and you've gone ahead and messed it up. You'll have to go and find this Boris friend of yours and get him to pay for the abortion. It's his child, after all, and he should be the one to pay."

I had a pretty fair idea what he'd say to me; I wasn't wrong. I bearded him at the bar where we'd met and told him about the baby. "That's too bad," he said. "It's not mine and you can't prove anything." He paid for his drinks and walked out, giving me a look of utter indifference.

My mother came through: A doctor gave her the name of a contact, a diet specialist somewhere out in Long Island. We drove there and got the phone number of another contact from him. There were more calls to one contact after another, and finally my parents were able to make the arrangements. Two thousand dollars, the sum my mother had set aside for my divorce. I knew that some people knew where to get three-hundred-dollar abortions, and I knew you could get cheap and safe abortions in Cuba and in Puerto Rico, but my mother never stinted when it was for a good cause.

The abortion was set for one Sunday afternoon in my twelfth week of pregnancy. My clothes no longer fit me. I saw my big stomach and my swelling breasts in the mirror when I dressed and I felt disgusted. I was ugly and awful and bad. I wanted to kick myself.

My mother and father drove me down to Manhattan on the appointed afternoon, parking outside a designated Schrafft's restaurant. A few minutes later a couple drove up in a new Mercedes. My father handed over a package and they made me get in their car. I sat in the back. The man was in his mid-forties; I assumed the woman was his wife. They didn't say a word to me. I was terrified. I looked around at the buildings disappearing down Fifth Avenue, then the woman leaned back over the seat and put dark glasses over my eyes. We stopped after a while in a quiet street. In the elevator they put a blindfold on me and made me keep it on until I was inside the apartment.

It was a luxuriously furnished place. They made me sit on a couch. In one corner was a kitchen table set up with surgical instruments.

"Will you give me an anaesthetic to put me to sleep?" I asked.

"There's no time for that," the woman told me brusquely.

She gave me a pill, perhaps an antibiotic, and then they told me to get on the table. The woman gave me ice cubes to bite on and the man started pushing his instruments inside me. I was trying to scream from the pain and she kept holding my arms and head and forcing ice cubes between my teeth. I could feel every touch of the instruments scraping and digging and pulling inside me. I was being torn open. The tears ran down my face and mixed with perspiration, and the woman kept wiping my face and putting another ice cube in my mouth. Through the partly open blinds I could see a patch of sky. To take my mind off the pain inside me, I tried to imagine what there was out there. Finally it was over. Where the pain had been was now only a yawning emptiness. They told me to get up and I stumbled to my feet. The woman handed me two sanitary napkins to put between my legs. On the floor was a steel tray, red with blood and what I assumed was the foetus. "What was it?" I asked. "A boy," the woman told me. I really felt bad.

They let me sit on the couch for five minutes while they gave me another pill and a bottle of antibiotics to take home, then they rushed me out. They blindfolded me again and drove me back to Schrafft's where my mother and father were still waiting in our car.

I think my friendship with the Capri sisters would have come to an end anyway. I had become jealous of them. I didn't want to be simply an accessory sitting in the audience while they sang in the limelight. I didn't want to be a family mascot; I wanted to be one of them. Being good and pure, abstaining from drinking and screwing, had made me feel for a while that I could belong to the *good* world, the world represented by my parents and the Capri sisters, but once I became pregnant I knew it would never work. It was the same feeling all over again that I'd had when I'd accidentally killed Major. Now—I'd killed my child deliberately. I'd seen it lying in a pool of blood. Whatever I did would always go wrong.

Without the Capris I had no place in life. I didn't belong with the grown-ups; I didn't belong with the teenagers; I didn't belong to the square world; and I wasn't ready to go out into the wild world. I was completely anchorless. I shut myself up at home and went into a deep depression. I sat for hours looking out the window at the apartment building that now stood on the site of the haunted house. I found it an effort to attend to Mitchell; I didn't want to feed him, I didn't want to change his diapers. I wanted to be left alone. When Mitchell cried I beat him. When my anger was too strong, I put him in his crib and shut the door on him to stop myself from doing something worse. I wanted to block him out of my life. I wished my life was different: I didn't care how, I didn't know what, I only knew I didn't want it to be the way it was. I hated myself. I stayed all day in my night clothes; didn't wash, didn't brush my teeth. I sat in front of the TV set or stared out of the window. I was supersensitive. If my parents said anything to me, I would break out into sobs or start to yell and scream. They became alarmed and took me to the family doctor. He prescribed some pills to wake up with in the morning, and pills to calm my nerves during the day and pills to help me get to sleep; he also recommended that I see a psychiatrist.

I felt good with the pills. I woke cheerfully and felt alive all day and full of pep. I did the housework and cared for Mitchell and looked after myself properly, and at night I could fall asleep without problems. The psychiatrist, on the other hand, seemed a waste of time. I went to see him twice a week in midtown Manhattan, thirty minutes each visit, thirty dollars paid in cash by Mom. He made me sit facing him across his desk and had me tell him about my mother and father. I couldn't relate to him. He seemed to be looking at his watch all the time. I could try to talk to him, but he didn't seem able to understand me. Sometimes, toward the end of the session, I would start to open up and try to tell him what was bothering me, but it seemed that every time I did so he would look at his watch and say, "Save it for next week, time is up."

The psychiatrist took over the prescription writing, and he kept me on the pep pills, the Miltowns and the sleeping pills, but the pep pills made me feel too nervous and I stopped taking them. Finally I put all the pills aside. I didn't like drugs; I didn't want to depend on pills to regulate my life, to get me to wake up, and to get me to wash. I thought I could do it on my own.

Both doctors suggested that I should find a job to keep myself occupied. My mother arranged for a baby-sitter to look after

Mitchell every day and I went to the telephone company to get a job as switchboard operator. They gave me a test sorting cards alphabetically. I had to run though the alphabet each time on my fingers to remember the right order and I knew I'd messed up the test. They told me to leave the application with them and they would get in touch with me. It was the first and last time that I'd look for a job, I decided. To keep my mother off my back I pretended to keep looking for a job, in Yonkers and in the city. It worked fine. I could walk around and be by myself all day and know that Mitchell was being taken care of.

We went to Miami again that summer, staying at the Hotel Corso on Collins Avenue. My parents thought it would give me new interests. It certainly did. I fell in love with a lifeguard—Art—dark, deeply tanned, with a body like Mr. America. We had a tumultuous affair, screwing whenever we had the chance—once even in the ocean. I was in love with him and I thought he loved me, too, but every day I'd see him necking with a different girl; that hurt me. Then I entered the hotel's bathing beauty competition and walked away with first prize. Now I had my choice of men, as many as I wanted. I was the prettiest girl in the hotel and I made good use of it.

I also got friendly with a part-time hooker, a blond, big-busted girl called Fred, who was a lesbian. She had a john whom she visited regularly at the hotel and I often met her at the pool. I was very impressed by her. She took me out to a few of the lesbian hangouts and gay bars in Miami. I found her style of life exciting. Before I left, Fred gave me a number where she could be reached in New York.

Back in Yonkers my depression started all over again. I had pills but I didn't take them. I'd stopped going to the psychiatrist. The baby-sitter had Mitchell during most of the day and I wandered around, pretending to be looking for a job but being bored and out of things.

Then I ran into Leslie, Bruce's kid sister. She was a young woman now, poised and grown-up. She asked me over to Lane's candy store and we talked about old times over a Coke. I told her about Eddie and Mitchell and married life and she told me that Bruce and Bobbi, my friends from school, were now married.

Bruce was a ladies' hairdresser. She herself was going to hairdressing school with her friend, Sally, who was also sixteen and who lived in the apartment building on the site of the haunted house.

I met them almost every day and almost every day I complained about the boredom and the monotony.

"Yeah, that's Yonkers," Leslie confirmed. "Yonkers is a drag. No wonder you're so depressed. You ought to come with us to Greenwich Village in the evenings, that's where the action is."

☼ CHAPTER NINE ☼

The center of the action was at Barbo's, a soda-and-candy store in the heart of Greenwich Village. It reminded me a bit of our old hangout at Little Caesar's, but it was more exciting and far more impressive. It seemed to be the hub on which the whole of Greenwich Village social life revolved—at least that part of it with which Leslie and Sally were concerned. It was a glamorous place frequented by lesbians and other exciting types, *real* people. It was the first time I'd been in on the adult life of New York; I was a country mouse come to visit the city.

We went to Barbo's almost every evening and became friends with Lynn, an attractive dyke who wore boyish clothes and had her hair brushed back in a DA. Lynn had an apartment over Barbo's. She was having an affair with Irene, a very pretty fem. I wasn't surprised that Lynn turned me on sexually—she looked a lot like a boy—but when I found myself drawn to Irene, too, I started wondering about myself. I discussed it with Leslie and Sally. Neither of them had had any lesbian experience, they admitted, but they were very knowledgeable about the scene.

"I'm really turned on to Lynn," I told Leslie. "I want to make it with her. What can I do?"

"Forget it, Cookie. She's going with Irene. You'll get nowhere with her."

If anything, that was a challenge. I started dressing in the fem style, pants, shirt but very sexy, rolling my hips, trying to let

Lynn know by my looks and my eyes how much she turned me on. I sensed she was turned on by me, too. We usually wound up in Lynn's apartment at the end of the evening. Leslie and Sally would sit drinking cough syrup to get high; I asked them to let me try some but they wouldn't let me. "It's bad for you, Cookie. You shouldn't get started on that." Lynn and Irene were beyond cough syrup. They were shooting up dope and Lynn was dealing in it, too. It fascinated me that I knew some honest-to-goodness dope fiends, that I was part of their little world, almost. Each time they got out their paraphernalia I experienced a little thrill, but as much as I wanted to I couldn't watch them shoot up; the sight of a needle going into skin upset me too much. I tried everything I could to get Lynn to take more interest in me but nothing worked. I thought perhaps she didn't think I was hip enough. I finally brought it up with her when the two of us were alone. "You're avoiding me, Lynn, and it bothers me. I'm in love with you, and I want to be closer to you. It isn't because of Irene, is it, that you're holding back?"

I could see that Lynn was torn. She liked me, that was obvious, or she wouldn't have been so upset by my approach. "No, Cookie, I like you, I really do. You're a good girl, too. That's why I don't want to get involved with you. I'm bad news. If you get involved with me you'll start into drugs and I don't want that to happen to you. I don't want to be responsible for ruining your life."

I started going to the hairdressing school about this time. My mother and our doctor thought it was a great idea. Leslie had a boy friend at the school, Max, a real strung-out dope addict. Leslie and Sally and I used to come home from school together in the afternoons and stop off at Getty Square to make the round of pharmacies. We copped a bottle of Robitussin opium-and-codeine cough syrup wherever we could, then we went up to my place and got high on the syrup. The taste was terrible but once you'd downed the bottle you got a lovely feeling all over, floating off without a care, your head sort of nodding, and a beautiful flow of color and pleasures going through your head and body. We listened to records while we nodded, especially Olatunji playing African drums. Sometimes we didn't even go to school and just stayed home drinking syrup and nodding. In the evenings we went down to the Village together and always ended up upstairs with Lynn and Irene, drinking our cough syrup while they shot up.

Leslie discovered that I still had most of the pills the doctors had prescribed. "Hey man," she told me. "You don't want to waste that stuff. It's worth something. And you should try getting your doctor to give you more prescriptions, too. Tell him you need them." The doctor didn't need much persuasion. He knew I was a lost cause; the drugs would help me function.

I didn't like the pills and gave most of them to Leslie and she, in turn, gave me powdered amphetamines that I used to drink in a glass of Kool-Aid. The amphetamines did strange things to me. I was a different person. I could spend hours getting dressed, looking at myself in the mirror and fussing over every detail. Everything I touched or did seemed to be endowed with extra meaning. I began to enjoy talking and could sit and talk for hours and hours; without amphetamines I'd been the silent type. I had enjoyed doing the housework when I was on the pep pills but on amphetamines it became almost an obsession. I spent a lot of time on my hands and knees scrubbing the woodwork. I had to keep busy. I became very sure of myself, very powerful, conscious of everything I was doing. My parents thought I was really getting myself together: I was so happy, doing so many good things around the house, just what they wanted.

With amphetamines I couldn't sleep so I had to take sleeping pills at night and then use amphetamines again to wake me up. Usually I woke with a terrible hangover. I would have to take two pep pills and then I had to see Leslie and get some more amphetamines from her. The amphetamines made me jumpy and edgy with excitement and I had to drink cough syrup to bring me down and help me relax. I really liked being down more than being up and therefore preferred cough syrup to amphetamines. On cough syrup I'd listen to Olatunji and lie on the living room couch for hours, letting the record play again and again and again. I was drinking about three bottles of cough syrup a day by now and one day, when I was at home nodding and listening to Olatunji, I looked up at the ceiling and saw a man sitting there in an armchair. He was actually *on* the ceiling reading a book, not looking at me, just sitting very calmly and peacefully reading the book. I stared at him in fascination and then he disappeared. I shook my head to clear it and then I threw some cold water on my face. I didn't go back in the room; I didn't want to get into any other hallucinations. I bragged about it to my friends. They thought it was very weird to have hallucinations like this on something as innocuous as cough syrup and I felt very proud that I had accomplished something so unusual.

When I realized that I'd get nowhere with Lynn, I turned to Sally. There was a special tension between Sally and me that didn't exist between me and Leslie. I knew that Sally was as interested in exploring the lesbian bit as I was. It came to a head one afternoon when I was alone with Sally, drinking cough syrup in her house. We walked into her bedroom, we stood for a moment and then, all so naturally, she approached me and I approached her and we got into an embrace and fell onto the bed. We didn't say anything. We started kissing openmouthed using our tongues. We rolled around and I got on top of her and started undressing her. I didn't really know what to do. I was waiting for a lead from her, and Sally, thinking *I* was the experienced one, was waiting for me to take the initiative. I stripped her down to her slip. My hand was on her crotch feeling her crack through her panties. Then suddenly we heard her mother walking in and we stopped. Sally stood up and pretended she was changing out of her clothes. I felt guilty and embarrassed, convinced that her mother could sense what was going on between us. I was really very relieved at the interruption because I hadn't known what to do next and feared that if I did something wrong Sally would know that I wasn't as worldly as I pretended to be.

I thought I'd fallen in love with Sally. She lived in the building where the haunted house had stood and I could see her apartment from ours. I spent a lot of time just staring at her out of my window. I longed to make love with her and I decided that I'd have to get some experience elsewhere so that I could come on with her competently. The lesbians at Barbo's were all heavy into drugs and were mostly fems. The only butch I knew was

Lynn and of course she wouldn't have anything to do with me. The next Friday I went to a lesbian bar that I'd heard of in Greenwich Village, the Tepee. I walked past the bar, fascinated by all the mannish-looking women there. In the back room I saw a very pretty girl, short, freckled with very short blond hair. Her name was Sheila. She reminded me of Fred, my lesbian friend from Miami, only she was younger, about twenty-one. She invited me to dance. We danced the grind, a dance popular in gay bars, where you dance close to your partner, rotating and grinding your hips into each other. Peggy Lee was singing "Oh My Man I Love Him So." Sheila kissed my neck and bit my ear and I got very excited. I asked her if she had a place to go to and she said no, she lived in Staten Island, but she had a car so I invited her to come home and sleep with me. We got to Yonkers about three in the morning. I was trembling with excitement. I was high on cough syrup, pills, amphetamines and I was thrilled with the idea of losing my virginity to a girl. Although I usually enjoyed undressing in front of men and turning them on, I felt too embarrassed undressing where Sheila could see and went into the bathroom to change into a robe. When I came back, Sheila had stripped to bra and panties. I don't know what I'd expected from her, but the bra seemed out of place for someone who was supposed to play the boy's role. And I found myself turned off by her slender thighs. I checked to see if Mitchell was sleeping in his crib, then got into bed next to her and switched off the light. She moved over to the wall. I followed. She took off her bra and panties and climbed on top of me, making movements as though she was fucking. It didn't seem to have much point; if I wanted to get fucked I would have had a man do it. I thought that she ought to go down on me, licking my cunt or get me to go down on her but she didn't seem to know what to do. She was supposed to be the butch and she should have made all the moves. I didn't make any overtures myself; I didn't as much as touch her. She put her fingers in my cunt but without any real feeling and I got no satisfaction from it. She obviously lacked the experience. After a while I told her that I was tired and wanted to sleep. I lay in her arms and smoked a cigarette, trying to stay awake so that

Mitchell wouldn't see us together in this position if he woke up. After a few minutes I stubbed out my cigarette, rolled over on my stomach and went to sleep.

My mother was always very kind to my friends, no matter what kind of degenerates I brought home. She was nice to Sheila when I introduced her in the morning, as if having a lesbian friend sleep over with me was the most natural thing in the world. Perhaps she was relieved that with a girl, at least, I wouldn't get pregnant.

Later that morning I drove with Sheila to her father's house in Staten Island. I went with her for a week, meeting in the same bar about every other day. We tried sex once more in her car, but it was pretty much of a flop. I found her unexciting. She was a faker. She wanted to pretend she was a lesbian and she enjoyed the lesbian way of life, but she didn't care much for the physical follow-through. I thought I was more experienced than Sheila and could make a far better butch. I decided that I'd be a butch from then on.

I had Sally cut my hair very short. I bought boys' socks and a tee shirt—this was quite a few years before boyish clothes for women became popular. I wore my shirt collar open to show the tee shirt underneath and combed my hair back. I thought I looked like a real boy now. I went back to the Tepee in this outfit, walking with what I thought was a male swagger, sat down at the bar and ordered a beer. The beer tasted terrible but I drank it—like a man. A butch came over and sat down next to me. I'd seen her there my first night when I'd met Sheila.

She said, "Hi! What are you doing in that outfit? The first time I saw you, you looked real pretty, with long hair. This isn't the real you."

"It's not how you look, it's how you feel inside that counts," I told her with studied nonchalance. "I could be with a fem and I could also be with a butch like you, but I'm still *me.*"

We talked for a while. She was twenty-five. Her name was Harriet and her friends called her Harry. I let her know I liked her, but she had a girl friend waiting for her in the other room and she had to play it cool.

I knew that I'd like to make it with Harriet one day, but I

couldn't do it as a butch and I didn't want to come to her inexperienced. First I had to make it as a butch myself with another fem. I already had a great reputation as a butch in hairdressing school. Many of the students—boys *and* girls—were gay, or playing at being gay. We did a lot of kissing and petting but little more. The girls were nearly all fems. Leslie was my buddy although she was going with Max, Sally was in love with me, Sissy had eyes for me, Dorothy wanted to be my girl. I was popular. They called me Bobby—it went with my butch role. I petted only so far with them, then stopped. I didn't want to get into something I couldn't handle.

Dorothy seemed to be the best prospect. I knew she'd had sex with men so she obviously had some idea of what was what. I took her down to the Tepee with me and there we met an old friend from Yonkers, Lois, who'd been involved with me when I smashed up my father's car. Now she was a boy—she called herself Lou—and lived in Queens. She had a girl friend called Anne. The four of us got together regularly. One evening, after we'd been together at the Tepee, Dorothy and I went off together to the Fairview Hotel, a really sleazy place, its lobby filled with prostitutes and dope fiends, just the right atmosphere for me to play my role as butch. Dorothy paid five dollars for the room and we went up in the elevators. It was a dowdy, dingy room with little more than a double bed: ideal.

I sat on the bed and gulped down a bottle of cough syrup. For my newest thrill I wanted to be even higher than I already was. Dorothy asked me to turn her on with syrup, too.

"No," I told her. "I can't do that. It's bad for you. It can ruin your life and I don't want to be responsible for that." I was trying to play my role properly; this part was pure Lynn. We kissed and petted next; I acted Sheila's role, biting her on the neck and ear, but I did it with more competence than Sheila had ever shown. Then I lay back on the bed and told Dorothy to come to me. I took off her clothes with dash and determination and stripped her completely. I kissed her openmouthed and fondled her breasts, then I put a hand on her cunt and started forcing my fingers in. She was breathing heavily and her excitement was turning me on. I felt powerful. I felt strong. I held her tight and manfully, pressing her back against me, squeezing her shoulders. I pushed her down on the bed and put my hand between her legs again. I kissed her on the mouth, deeply, as she moaned, and gradually I moved my tongue and lips down her body. I reached her breasts and took her nipples in my mouth. I kissed the soft flesh of her belly; my fingers were working in her cunt, sliding in and out of the moist tissues.

I was almost there—and I was scared. Going down was really quite new to me. I hadn't even *known* about it until one evening a few days after my wedding when Eddie suddenly went down on me and started eating my cunt. I didn't know what he was doing at first but then, once I'd gotten over my surprise, I'd really enjoyed it and the only question in my mind was why he hadn't done it before. I knew what it felt like having someone go down on me but I didn't know what it would be like going down on someone else. Yes, I'd blown Eddie a few times without much enthusiasm, but that was something else. Going down on a woman was new and I hoped I'd do it well.

My lips reached the first of the curly hairs. It tickled. Now or never! I took a deep breath and pushed my lips and tongue straight into her snatch. God! It was revolting! She couldn't have washed for a whole week! I couldn't stay there. I straightened up and gagged.

Dorothy was upset. "What's the matter, Bobby?" she asked. "Have I done something wrong? Don't you love me?"

"Sure I love you, baby," I told her. "It's something else. The cough syrup. You know I warned you about it. You get terrible stomach cramps from it when you've been taking it for a while. I'll have to go home."

I opened the window and leaned out to take in the fresh night air. The street was deserted. The rows of cars parked down below looked like little bugs. I felt stupid and disappointed. I'd failed in another role.

I kept seeing Dorothy at beauty school after this, but I tried to avoid her. Sally was jealous that I'd chosen Dorothy first—I didn't tell her about the fiasco—but she understood my need to get to know more of the gay life: I was the pioneer of our group.

Once I was an accomplished lesbian, she knew I'd introduce everyone to it, Sally first.

I wasn't bothered when my mother found my tee shirt hidden in the back of a drawer. It seemed to bother her a lot though, and that was odd because she hadn't shown any signs of upset when I had brought Sheila home. I told her I didn't know where the shirt had come from, and to show my complete indifference I threw it away while she was looking. I really didn't care. I'd had enough of my role as butch; now I could be a fem. I got one of the girls at school to bleach my hair and wash out all the gunk, then I brushed it in a feminine style.

The following weekend, very feminine, I went back to the Tepee looking for Harriet. I sat with Lois; Harriet was at another table with her girl friend. I told Lois how I felt about Harriet and she went over to Harriet—or Harry as she liked to be called—and let her know. Harry smiled at me and I smiled back. We made eyes at each other all evening long, until even Harry's girl friend noticed. I could see they were going to have a lovers' tiff. Harriet, acting tough, got her friend to shut up, then walked over to our table and invited me to dance. She held me tight to let me know her strength. I was turned on. Before we went back to our separate tables I slipped her my telephone number.

"I'd like you to call me, Harry, but if you want us to get together you'll have to get rid of that other woman. There can't be three of us."

She pressed my hand: "I'll take care of it, Cookie. Then I'll call you."

☼ CHAPTER TEN ☼

The following Friday I started on dope.

Leslie and Sally and I had made the arrangements coming home from hairdressing school in the afternoon. That evening the three of us met with Leslie's friend, Max. Max had brought along a friend of his, Paul, also an addict, who had a beat-up old car. Together we drove down to a construction site across the creek from Freedomland in the Bronx. It was just getting dark. The men sat in the front seat and we three girls sat in the back.

Max and Paul started preparing the drugs. I sat by the window and looked out over the water. I could hear rustling in the front and I could see some of the action out of the corner of my eye, but I wouldn't look directly. I was afraid of that needle. I could hear them strapping a belt around Paul's arm, then Max's. My heart was pounding hard and I hoped nobody could hear it; everything was so quiet in the car. It was the same type of nervous anticipation that I'd had at eleven, when Stella had arranged for me to get fucked for the first time by Ralph and George. It was a real step up for me. I had a fluttering in my stomach: I hadn't taken any cough syrup that evening because I wanted to be fresh for the dope.

I didn't know in which order we'd get the dope so I waited in fascination as each person took his or her turn. Leslie, who was sitting between Sally and me, took off her jacket and put her arm over the front seat. Max reached back and injected the dope just under the skin, not in the vein. I couldn't look at the needle itself, but I watched her expression to see if it hurt. She winced for a moment and then, as the needle came out, she sat back calmly and waited for something to happen. Max rubbed the spot and slapped it to stop it from swelling up. She looked very relaxed and calm, and then very naturally she put her jacket back on. I couldn't see anything dramatic happening to her, but I'd heard that it takes a few minutes for skin-popping to take effect.

Then Max said, "Okay, Cookie, you're next."

I took off my sweater and twisted around to present my arm over the back of the front seat. I turned my face away and covered my eyes with my left hand. Max bent over my arm and slapped it hard. I jumped—I thought it was the needle—and he told me to relax, the slap was so that I wouldn't feel the spike going in. I kept my eyes covered. Then I felt another little sting, just like the one I felt from the slap—and then it was over.

"Is that it?" I asked, surprised that it was so fast. I'd figured it to be more dramatic and I felt there should have been more pain with it. Now that it had happened, I felt important. It was a milestone, like having sex for the first time with a man, or making love to a lesbian, or being married and grown-up.

I sat back and waited. Perhaps a minute or two later a pleasant feeling suddenly swept through my stomach: hot and cold bubbles starting in my abdomen and working their way up into my head. I wanted to smoke and lit up a Salem. I had never smoked a cigarette that tasted as good as this one. I'd never really liked cigarettes before and just used to smoke as a habit, but now I could actually taste the flavor. My body felt more relaxed than it had ever been before. My eyes started getting heavy and I felt the need to close them, but I wasn't sleepy—quite the contrary, I was acutely aware of what was going on around me. My mind was awake but my body was asleep.

My nose started itching terribly, and after I'd scratched at my nose I felt the itch in another part of my face. As I went from one part to another, it felt like a little flea jumping from place to place and making me itch while I was trying to scratch. It surprised me that even this felt good. Everything I did suddenly felt good. I felt myself talking. My voice was slower and scratchy and very thick. I liked the sound of my voice. It was perfect. Everything was perfect: I looked perfect, I felt perfect, everything I touched was perfect, everything I said was perfect, everything I heard, and everything I smelled. I was floating through space on a timeless cloud and the whole world was coming together in one big feeling and I was going over the edge of that feeling, dropping away and being out of it and then becoming part of this one great feeling. The only thing that was irritating me was the itching all over my face and on my arms. I kept on scratching and scratching, most of all on my nose, smearing the makeup all over my face.

We drove off after a while, past Freedomland which was just being built, then on down to Manhattan to the Statler Hilton Hotel on Seventh Avenue, where a hairdressing convention was being held to which we'd been told to go by the school.

The radio was playing in the car as we drove down. The music sounded extraordinarily rich and seemed to have many dimensions. I kept my eyes closed and nodded. The nodding seemed a different type of nodding from the kind I'd been used to with the cough syrup. This nodding was the real thing. I kept lighting cigarette after cigarette but I didn't actually smoke. I didn't want to break the nod by bringing the cigarette to my mouth, and so I simply let it burn down to my fingers. My eyes were very heavy, but I was aware of every sound around me and everything looked sharp and clear.

My body was completely relaxed and at ease. My eyes opened, my eyes closed, it didn't matter. I could hear and smell and see everything, things that nobody else even knew. I was different from them. I seemed to be asleep but I knew they couldn't get at me where I was and I couldn't get at them. I was completely shut off from the world of reality; I didn't *want* to belong to it—I felt so good where I was.

The movement of the car reinforced the feelings of moving and floating along, and each time we had to stop for a light and the car jerked, I got pulled back from my feeling and became irritated. I took a drag of my cigarette only when we stopped for a light, and then I let the ash build up again until it spilled over my clothes.

We parked the car at last and walked to the hairdressing show. I had a strange gait, the typical dope fiend's walk, and I felt very proud of myself. I'd first noticed that walk on Max at the hairdressing school and Sally had told me that he was a dope fiend. He walked with a waddle and a tremble, hunched up into himself, his skin was pasty and colorless, and his face almost devoid of expression. Max was the first dope fiend I'd met and I'd been very impressed by that fact and thrilled that I knew a real-life addict.

Now I was using dope myself.

I watched myself in the mirrors as we walked through the Statler Hilton to the convention. My face had changed. It seemed blank and yellowish. I looked closely at my eyes. The pupils were tiny and the iris had changed to a pale brown, a yellowish brown, and I told myself how pretty I looked. I looked really pretty taking dope, I thought, and I was proud of my new appearance. I wondered whether anyone else could notice the change and if anyone else would know that I'd shot up on heroin. I felt grown-up, really grown-up again; more grown-up than when I'd walked out of school for the last time; more grown-up than when I'd become a married woman; more grown-up than when I'd become a mother. Really grown-up now, doing things that few grown-ups were willing to do. I was doing what I wanted to do, not what others wanted me to do. I was taking dope, and with my dope I could say, "Fuck you!" to the world and tell them all where to shove it.

We walked around looking at the displays and at all the models having their hair done and showing off new styles and dyes and hair pieces and cosmetics. Once I would have admired them. Now I just looked at them in their teased coiffures and thought to myself how square they all were. The whole world was square. The models were sitting there or walking around and pirouetting as if they were something out of the ordinary, but all I could see was how really square they were. "They think they have something to boast about," I thought to myself, "but they don't even know what they're missing. They don't know what *I* have."

We went into the ballroom to watch the hairdressers' competition, but it didn't seem real. It all seemed so terribly irrelevant.

After a while I looked at Leslie and at Sally and they looked at me and we smiled very knowingly, and without having to say anything we all knew we were in the wrong place. This show wasn't for us. It wasn't our type of thing. We were far more exciting than anything they could dream of. We walked out together and stopped off at a luncheonette for a Coke and then went back to the car.

The drive back was like the drive down. Floating, drifting, nodding, scratching. I felt good.

Usually when I came home to Yonkers at night I felt dead. But not this time. This time I felt alive and aware. I showered, brushed my teeth, and combed my hair. Then I sat up in bed in my pajamas. I just wanted to sit and enjoy the nodding and the beautiful feeling that went with it, and to relive the excitement of what had happened. I lit one cigarette after the other and nodded.

Finally I decided I might as well go to sleep. I could always recapture that wonderful feeling by getting some more heroin. I stubbed out my cigarette and lay down, and as soon as my head hit the pillow I fell asleep. But sleep wasn't the usual kind. It was more like a nod, deeper than the deepest nod I'd ever known from syrup, deeper than all the nodding in the car. I was hovering between wakefulness and sleep, but there was none of the terror that usually accompanied insomnia when I woke up at night and couldn't get back to sleep. Being awake was good now and being asleep was good, too, and going off the edge from one into the other was even better. I stretched out my sleep. Each time I dropped off it was like finding myself in Shangri-la.

My father woke me in the morning and drove me to my Saturday job as shampoo girl and manicurist. I enjoyed the work, but what I enjoyed even more was coming home in the late afternoon with tips and salary—about twenty-five dollars each week. I wasn't going to use my money for cough syrup this week. Oh no! I wasn't going to take anything else anymore. From now on it would be the real thing—dope.

None of us went to school on Monday. I dropped Mitchell off at the baby-sitter's, then Leslie and Sally and I took a cab together to Max's house in the Bronx at 241st Street. The first time we shot up had been on him, but this time we gave him the money to go out and get two five-dollar bags, one for him and one to be shared by the three of us. We shot up in his kitchen. Just as I started nodding, a few minutes after I had shot up, I suddenly felt a choking in my throat and a heaving in my stomach. I ran into the bathroom and threw up. The more I threw up, the more I felt myself getting high and my head spinning. I was surprised, but Max told me it was natural, most people have it when they start shooting up until the body gets used to the dope. I nodded, feeling as good as the first time. We sat around in the kitchen. Nobody ate anything. Sometimes one of us would talk coming up from a nod, but it wasn't a conversation. There wasn't any need to communicate; sitting around together was enough of a bond. We stayed until about the time we ordinarily left hairdressing school and then I went to pick up Mitchell. I was home in time to cook dinner for my father. After shooting up, I had no appetite. My father asked me why I didn't eat. "I've already eaten," I lied.

A few evenings later I met Harriet at the Bolero, a coffee shop that was full of drag queens and lesbians on Sixth Avenue in Greenwich Village. I let her know—quite casually—that I was shooting up. I wanted her to know I wasn't a child and wasn't just playing around—and, of course, I took care not to tell her I'd only just started. Harriet had been shooting dope for years, but she'd kicked five months earlier and now she was clean.

After a while we walked out of the Bolero. Harry put her arm around my shoulder as we strolled through the Village. At first glance we must have seemed a typical boy-girl couple: We were the same height, Harry wore boys' clothes, her straight black hair was cut short with a DA in back and a big wave over her right eye that bounced with each step. She had a hooked nose and very high cheekbones that gave her eyes a slanted look, thick full lips, and big teeth that flashed when she smiled. She walked with her shoulders slouched forward and with a little bounce in her gait. What gave her away as a woman were her breasts—not too big, but they sagged, and since she didn't wear a bra under her thin sweater they bounced noticeably as she walked.

After a while Harry paused and squeezed my hand. "I have a friend's place we can go to," she whispered.

It was what I'd wanted to hear. I said yes, and squeezed her hand in return.

She helped me into a cab and gave the driver an address at 174th Street and Grand Concourse in the Bronx. "I hate subways," she told me in an aside. I settled back for the long ride uptown. Suddenly she grabbed me aggressively and kissed me in the rough, tough way of a man. I played coy and shy. She kissed with her lips open; I made her force me to open mine. She pushed her tongue into my mouth; I accepted it passively. She wanted me to put my tongue in her mouth; I refused. She pushed my face away and commanded me to give her my tongue; I complied. She was masterful.

The apartment we went to belonged to a friend called Tom, a lesbian I remembered from the Tepee. Tom was there with her girl, Linda, and two faggots who shared the apartment with them. We sat for a while in the living room chatting about generalities, then Harriet took my hand and led me into Tom's bedroom. She shut the door but she kept the lights on. She pounced on me with the same aggressiveness she'd used in the cab, kissing me on the mouth, the face, and the neck. I started to take off my blouse and bra but Harriet stopped me. "No, leave it," she ordered. "I'll do that for you."

When she had my bra off she fingered my breasts and kissed them roughly. She undressed me gradually, still kissing but making no effort to undress herself. She pulled me to the floor and rolled on top of me, her fingers squeezing and kneading inside my cunt. It hurt—and it felt tremendously good. After a while she took her fingers out and stroked my breasts. Now she pulled at my hair, tugged, knotted her fingers in it, twisted. I moaned. She pressed her lips to my mouth and kissed, moved to my neck, my throat, my breasts. What a lover! Stronger even than Eddie's friend, Larry. We'd started in the middle of the room, then we were in one corner, then against a wall, rolling and sliding as she forced her love on me. Her mouth went from my breasts to my waist and from my waist to my belly and from my belly right into my cunt.

I'd been expecting it, I'd been anticipating it, I'd been hungering for it for weeks. But now that I had it the first thought that came to my mind was how experienced Harry was. She'd been with a lot of women. She knew what she was doing. I felt womanly, soft and terribly tender with her.

We fucked until two in the morning. Occasionally there was a pause as we sat up to light a cigarette, but she was down on me again before I'd managed to smoke mine to the end. My cunt was on fire with the painful pleasures she'd brought me. It felt as if this was the first time I'd ever been fucked. All my experiences with men were completely irrelevant; Harry was something else, Harry was an expert. She pulled me by the hair until my head hurt, she squeezed my breasts until they ached, she clawed at my cunt and bit and sucked until the blood came.

At two o'clock I was completely exhausted—and Harriet knew it. She became very soft and caring. She kissed me gently on the cunt now and worked her way up, soft as a feather, from my cunt to my navel and up to my breasts, ending with a long, lingering kiss on my mouth. She found my clothes that had been scattered all over the floor and helped me dress. Tom and Linda and the two faggots were still sitting in the living room; they went on with their conversation as if nothing had happened—which only heightened my sense of embarrassment. I felt so grateful to Harriet, so full of all that had happened to me. Only one thing bothered me: she hadn't gotten undressed. She didn't want me to see her body. What did she have to hide?

Harriet kissed me again in the cab home. I was sure the cabbie was watching us in his mirror. Did he recognize her as a girl? Did he know I was one of *them* now? I belonged to *them.* I was part of the group. I had always wanted to belong to a select group of select people who could thumb their noses at the rest of the world. Now I did and I could say *Fuck you!* to everyone else. I'd had my lesbian experience at last. It was another notch in my gun.

Harriet had the cab drop her off at her home on Allerton Avenue, not far away in the Bronx. Then she kissed me goodnight and gave me the money to pay the cabbie when I got to Yonkers.

I let myself in very softly. I was still floating with the memories. I had cookies and milk in the kitchen—as I did every night, then went to bed. I didn't wash. I wanted to keep the memory of Harriet on my body for as long as I could.

Next morning I was over at Harriet's home and we made love again—in the bathroom, because her father was sitting in the living room, and the bedroom had glass doors. We couldn't have privacy any other way. At times I sat on the toilet with the lid down, Harry kneeling between my legs so she could get her tongue at my cunt; other times we rolled about on the floor. We couldn't stay more than a few minutes each time because of Harry's father, then we'd have to straighten our clothes and go back in the living room to watch the television. Harry still refused to take off her clothes and she still wouldn't let me touch her body.

She came home with me in the afternoon—by cab, of course. On the way I picked up Mitchell from the baby-sitter. My mother did a double take when she saw Harry—everyone always did, not sure of her gender. I introduced them, and Harriet stayed for dinner. My mother came to the conclusion that she was really a rather nice girl.

We fucked every day that week at her house while her father watched television. I tried to sneak a look at her body while she was changing her clothes so that I could visualize her better while she was making love to me with her clothes on, but she was terribly shy and wouldn't let me see her naked. After a few days I asked her to come over to my place during the day. I wanted to have sex with her while I was high on dope. I knew that that would be something out of this world.

She came over in the morning when Mitchell was already at the baby-sitter's. She'd brought a nickel bag with her. Knowing that she'd been off dope for so long and having heard how difficult it was to stay clean once you'd been hooked, I felt guilty that I was getting her started again. She showed me the works: The cooker was a screwtop cap from an ordinary wine bottle, a bobby pin was twisted around it to serve as a handle. She tore the corner off the glassine envelope and shook the dope out into the cooker—about enough to cover a dime—and added a few drops of water. She laid out the spike. It was a glass eyedropper, the sort you buy for ten cents at any drugstore. The hypodermic needle was slipped over the tip, wedged in with a thin strip of cardboard torn from a matchbook cover. Now she lit a match under the cooker. In three or four seconds the water was boiling and the heroin had dissolved. She took a small plug of cotton and dropped it into the solution to soak up impurities that could clog the needle. She drew up some of the solution into the dropper, slapped my arm and popped the needle just under my skin. I felt the good feelings in my stomach immediately and then the nodding. She popped the rest of the dope into her own arm and we took off together. When she was ready, she cleaned out the needle in the kitchen sink and put her works away, then we went together to the couch in the foyer, facing the television.

She caressed me while I was nodding. It was a heavenly feeling. She kissed me. My head was spinning. Her lips came to mine, joined them, went through them, into my head, became part of me. My tongue was part of her. Our heads were merged in a cloud of love and beauty. She took my hand and led me into my room. She made love to me all day long. It was an exquisite experience, extraordinarily beautiful and intense. We were merging our bodies. I didn't know where I began or where I ended. Every touch and every caress was intensified by the dope, to the point where the excitation was almost too beautiful to bear. My thighs were around her, all over her, and with her. I was squeezing her into me. I held her head to me and whispered, "I love you, Harry. I love you."

I couldn't do anything for Harriet. Even when I tried to direct her head she got angry. "I don't need it," she told me, "I get my pleasure from pleasing you." After a while I believed her. She wanted nothing more than to give me all the pleasure she could, experiencing her joy through me. I no longer felt selfish. I was pleasing Harry by accepting her loving, and her reflected pleasures added even more to my own excitement.

We made love every day, in her house or in mine, or on a stairway after we'd made our connection. Mitchell went to his babysitter every morning. My mother gave me the fees for school, and pocket money, too, when I asked for it, and I spent it all on drugs for Harry and me. I still had the shampoo and manicure job Saturdays and that gave me extra spending money. Harry was jealous; she thought I might go for one of the hairdressing customers or one of the assistants. She told me she'd go crazy if she ever saw me with anyone else, man or woman. She became terribly possessive. Whenever I had a phone call she wanted to know who it was and what I wanted from them and what our relationship was. One day while over at my house, Harriet got jealous over something—I think it was the way I was doing my hair longer and more feminine. She thought it meant I had eyes for someone else. We were high at the time. She slapped me. I started to cry. That got her worked up and she started slapping me harder, a lot of slaps in quick succession. She screamed at me: "Bitch! Dirty bitch! You dirty bitch!" I tried to run away. She ran after me and held me tight. She got me to the ground. I got mad at her and struggled. She hit me harder. She caught me by the hair, yanking so that I couldn't move my head, and continued to cover me with stinging smacks. I was enjoying it in my own way, but I yelled and screamed to make her think she was hurting me. She called me every name under the sun. I enjoyed it all.

After perhaps fifteen minutes it became too much—for Harriet, not for me—and she stopped. She hugged me and kissed me, holding my face in both her hands and murmuring, "I'm sorry, I'm sorry. I love you so much." I kissed her back, burying my face in hers and sobbing from deep down in my heart. Then she undressed me and we made love. It was even greater than the first time. It seemed now as if everything was exploding. I didn't have to tell her I liked being slapped and enjoyed having her make love to me after she'd beaten and humiliated me. After that she hit me often. It added to our pleasures.

I got expelled from the beauty culture school. They'd found out about my affair with Harriet and guessed I was on drugs. Besides, I hadn't been coming to classes and I hadn't paid them since I'd first run into Harriet.

I told my mother they'd suspended me and she said, "Never mind, Cookie. We'll find you another place."

She got me into the Atlas Beauty Culture School on Eighth Avenue, a block north of Forty-second Street, the sin and sex center of New York City. I was excited by the new school, a real with-it place with with-it people, so much more real than the atmosphere of the Yonkers school. I loved walking along Forty-second Street or Eighth Avenue, surrounded by lesbians, homosexuals, dope fiends, and pimps. I felt at home there. The only discordant note was the tourists and businessmen who hung around the dirty book stores and the cheap movie houses, leering at the girls. All they wanted to do was fuck. The dirty, piggish, degenerate animals. I hated and mistrusted all men.

I went to school only two or three days a week; the other days I went with Harriet to cop our dope. I had my own set of works now; I'd bought the needle from Harriet's connection and the dropper from an unsuspecting drugstore. I'd learned to skin-pop for myself. I shot up at home before I went to school, nodded during the day, then took off again in the bathroom shortly before school was over. The ride home was great: It didn't matter whether I had a seat or not, the bumping and the jerking of the train only added to the great feeling, and even people bumping and rubbing up against me in the crush felt good. Standing or sitting, I could slump and nod and experience the motions of the train pulsating all the way inside me.

When I didn't go to school I went with Harriet to Lexington Avenue at 100th Street in Spanish Harlem. Our connection was a black janitor named Maurice. He let us shoot up in his apartment, and if his wife happened to be home we shot up in the boiler room. We usually bought a nickel bag between us and took off, then we went up on a rooftop to nod; though it was winter, we didn't feel the cold when we were high. We stayed up on the roof for quite a while, then we came down to hang around the block for another three or four hours and copped a few extra bags for that evening and the next day. It was a real community. Everyone knew everyone else by name. There were only a few white addicts there and most of the people were blacks or Puerto Ricans. Harriet and I were always together, just about the only white girls there. I felt at home, I was part of the community. At the time I was still rather pretty, innocent, and girlish-looking with my hair worn in two braids. The addicts treated me like the neighborhood mascot. They called me Cookie—or Baby.

☼ CHAPTER ELEVEN ☼

Harriet had got to know my other friends, Leslie, Sally and Max, and Max's friend Paul who had the car. We met them one morning after I'd dropped off Mitchell at the baby-sitter's and we got into the car.

Paul told us about a drug called Dilaudid that you could buy in a drugstore—if you had a prescription. It was a legal variant of heroin. You could get twenty or thirty pills for three dollars and each one turned you on like a five-dollar bag. He had a doctor's prescription pad and he asked me if I'd like to try and cop some Dilaudid for him. I was game; the idea of using a legal way to do something illegal seemed like fun. Leslie had told him that I had a gift for handwriting; I could imitate a lot of different styles. Max showed me on a piece of scrap paper what to write and I made out an impressive prescription for thirty Dilaudids and signed it with a medical flourish. Paul parked the car on Riverdale Avenue, three blocks from our house, a block from our local drugstore; then they waited while I went into the drugstore.

I looked very young with my short skirt and braids, and I had a very innocent face. There were butterflies in my stomach and their fluttering could easily pass for shyness on a face like mine.

"It's for my mother," I said, handing over the prescription. "She has kidney stones and she's in terrible pain."

While I waited for the prescription to be filled I skipped around the store looking at the displays. Then the pharmacist called me over and gave me the pills in a little white bag. "I couldn't give you the full amount," he apologized, "we're out of them. But I gave you twenty to get along with."

"That's okay. As long as I have enough for my mother until she can get to the doctor again."

I wanted to run and shout and let the others know how easily I'd scored, but I took my time and walked slowly out of the store. They were sitting in the car, looking in my direction. I made a signal, with my thumb and forefinger forming an O, and held up the white bag. I couldn't see their faces at that distance but I could easily see their smiles. I felt good. I'd carried it off.

"They only let me have twenty," I apologized when I got in the car.

"Twenty!" someone said. "Hey, man, that's cool." "Twenty! That's great, Cookie."

We drove to the usual place across the water from Freedomland. Paul dissolved the Dilaudid in the cooker and then we all took off. It was purer and better than the adulterated heroin we bought on the street. It hit me almost immediately, and the high was better and longer lasting. We stayed near Freedomland for a while, nodding, then we drove back to Yonkers. Paul, who'd provided the prescription and the money, kept the pills, but he gave me four of them for my help to share with Harriet. I didn't invite Max and Paul into my house; both had a habit and I knew they'd steal us blind if I so much as let them past the door.

We went out to cop Dilaudid almost every day. I was glad: I was feeling really down in the dumps now when I awoke in the morning, not wanting to do anything, but if I had heroin or Dilaudid I could take off and feel my old self again. I wanted to get high every day. I told myself it wasn't the physical need so much as the joy of knowing I was clever enough to be able to get Dilaudid. Max also got some prescription pads and once I was wise to it, I went to our family doctor, Dr. Tollman, and while he wasn't looking I stole some blanks from his desk. We went looking for Dilaudid every day, making the rounds of pharmacies in Yonkers and the Bronx.

Max and Paul had told me that it wasn't easy to get the stuff; most pharmacists were hip to anyone who looked even remotely like an addict, so I made a special point of looking young: No more jeans for me but short pleated skirts, bobby socks, bucks, and my hair worn with bangs and a ponytail. I affected a gawky manner and sang out "Oh, hi!" as I handed over the prescription, just like any clumsy teenager. It worked easily for a while because I had the confidence, but then I hit a run of bad luck. It must have started when we tried the same pharmacy a second or a third time. The pharmacist made some excuse saying they'd stopped carrying them or they had none left, and that made me worried I mightn't get them at the next place. Without confidence I couldn't carry off my innocence act properly. We'd drive around for half a day trying one pharmacy after another and I'd get more and more scared. Eventually we got to the point where we'd have to try perhaps ten druggists before we found one that would sell us Dilaudids.

The last one I tried was a drugstore just off the Grand Concourse. I walked in with a prescription blank from Dr. Tollman. I could feel the pharmacist's suspicion straight away. He looked at me very hard, then he took the prescription and went to the back. I heard him use the phone. He might have been checking with the doctor or he might even have been calling the police. My impulse was to run, but I couldn't run out and leave them the prescription because they'd be able to trace me easily through the doctor. I held my hands clenched. My heart was beating at double speed.

Finally the pharmacist came back to the counter. "Where did you get this prescription?" he asked.

I gave him the story of my mother and her kidneys.

He looked at me with narrow eyes. "How old are you?"

"I'm . . . I'm . . . ," I stammered. I was watching his moves. Out of the corner of my eye I saw that he'd put down the prescription on the counter for a moment. "I'm fifteen!" I said, and with that I grabbed the prescription and ran out of the store. My friends were sitting in the car half a block away. "Let's go!" I yelled. "Let's go quick!" They had the engine started and the door open and when I jumped in they were already in motion. It was the last time I tried to buy Dilaudid.

Harriet and I went back to copping in Spanish Harlem. We

met there almost every morning, made our connection, and shot up. If we didn't see Maurice we'd stand around, and soon enough someone would always come up and say, "Hey, Baby! I can cop for you." We'd give him the money for however many bags we wanted and we'd turn him on, sharing two bags between the three of us. Sometimes we got beat for our money: The cat would simply disappear or he'd bring us a few bags of milk sugar—known as dummy—and be off before we discovered our mistake.

On the whole, though, I felt I was among friends. "You shouldn't be shooting up," people would tell me solicitously—even while we were sharing together. They warned me I'd start hustling one day. I laughed. "Me? Never!" But I was glad they really cared for me. I didn't know they were simply trying to edge me away from Harriet who was watching over me like a mother hen. They knew that sooner or later every addict starts hustling and they wanted to be there once I got started.

I knew about hustling, but I thought I was a special case and I had a special strength that would let me stop whenever I wanted to. Harriet probably wasn't as convinced as I was. "If I ever catch you hustling, Cookie, I'll break your arm. I swear I will, Cookie," she warned.

I stayed at the beauty school on Eighth Avenue for only a month, then quit. They would have kicked me out anyway because I showed up so seldom and when I did I was always stoned and nodding. Now I could spend every day with Harriet. She was my man. I wanted to do everything with her and I wanted to be as much like her as I could.

I told Harriet I wanted to mainline, injecting the dope directly into the vein as she did instead of popping it under the skin. Everyone else was mainlining, too; it was much better. I was used to the needle now and in fact I enjoyed the sharp prick itself as a promise of the good sensations that always followed.

Harriet tried to talk me out of it. "You start mainlining and before you know it you'll have a habit," she warned.

I persisted.

The first time I mainlined was at Harriet's place in the Bronx, perhaps two months after Leslie had first turned me on to skin-popping. She took the belt off her pants and fastened it around my arm just above the elbow, to make the veins stand out, then she slapped my arm to stimulate the blood and make the vein even more prominent. I watched her as she pushed in the spike; I wanted to learn from her. She loosened the belt and squeezed on the bulb. The dope went into my vein. I got an immediate rush. She tightened the belt a moment and the pressure from my heart pushed the blood and heroin through the vein again and up the eyedropper. She loosened the belt and injected the mixture again. Again she tightened the belt and when she let go of the syringe bulb the blood and heroin rose once more. She did it a few times. Each time she squeezed the dropper I got the same rush, an unbelievably exciting feeling of warmth and composure. Addicts call this trick "booting"; it increases the pleasure of the first rush and spreads it out over what seems ages but is usually less than a minute. With popping I'd had the sensation first in my stomach; with mainlining it went directly to my head. It was everything I'd expected—and more.

On 100th Street they knew I was mainlining now. They warned me again. "You'll get a habit, Baby, and then you'll be hustling just like all them other chicks." We were the only white girls in the neighborhood who weren't hustling, the only girls who still had their looks. We still looked fresh.

I laughed at them. "Me a streetwalker? You must be out of your fucking mind."

"Yeah, Baby! You'll be strung out soon enough. Just you keep mainlining all that dope."

"But I can control myself. And Harriet would never let me get a habit."

Did I mean it? In a way I did. I wanted to believe that I could always stop myself before it got too late. And yet there was a fascination in going the whole way, tasting everything, knowing there was nothing I wouldn't dare to do. Did I really want control? Perhaps not. Perhaps I wanted to shuck off all responsibility. A habit was a hallmark of sorts, a license. A habit could excuse everything. With a habit I could throw off all restraints, be responsible to no one, not even to myself.

"How do you know when you have a habit?" I asked the

junkies on 100th Street. I wanted to be around when it happened to me. I wanted to be the first to recognize it.

They laughed and snickered. "A habit, Baby, is a habit. And when you have it, Baby, you'll know you have it. And if you want to know if you have it right now, try not taking it for just one day."

I knew I wasn't hooked. I could have stopped any time I wanted to. Sure I was taking off twice each day, but that was because I *wanted* to, not because I *had* to. When I woke in the morning I wanted to feel able to get through the day, so I shot up. I wanted to feel good at night, so I shot up again. And in between, I took off whenever I had the chance.

It wasn't easy finding the money for dope each day. I'd lost my Saturday job, and I could no longer tell my mother I needed the money for tuition at the hairdressing school. But occasionally I could wangle five dollars out of her for pocket money, and I could also—as I'd been doing since I was a little kid—snitch money from her pocketbook while she was asleep. One day, for some reason, I had no money and Harriet had none either. She'd stayed over with me that night in Yonkers and we had no dope to shoot up in the morning. I thought that maybe if I could wait until my mother came home at night, I could get some off her and then we could go down to the block and score. But now it was only noon and Harry and I were walking down Riverdale Avenue and the weather was chilly and windy and I felt just awful. Really terrible. There was a pain in my calves that got worse with each step. I was yawning like crazy. I shivered, the water rolling out of my eyes with each yawn.

"Harry," I said, "I feel real weird." I described my symptoms. "Is it a habit? Does it mean I have a habit?"

Harriet took it philosophically. "Yeah, baby. You got a habit. Ain't that what you wanted?"

I was thrilled. A real habit. An honest-to-goodness, high-flying, down-to-earth, real McCoy habit. Wow, man! I was a junkie. Jay-you-en-kay-eye-ee junkie. Junkie was something special, something big and important and heroic. Real wild. A name that meant something powerful and gutsy like Annie Oakley or

Wild Bill Hickok. I was as excited as I'd been that other time, coming home on the bus from hairdressing school with Sally and Leslie when Leslie had promised to turn us on to the real thing. That was a lifetime ago. That was . . . could it really have been only four months earlier? It seemed impossible.

If I hadn't felt so bad physically, I would have whooped it up. But I was feeling bad. Real bad. I wanted to get straight, get some dope into me so that I wouldn't be sick. Every step I took I felt worse. I really had to get straight. Harriet's mother wasn't home either, so she couldn't get money from her and she said her old man never gave her any. That surprised me; I'd always taken it for granted that she got the money for her drugs and her cab fares off her father.

"I know where I can get some money," Harriet told me. "It's always good for fifteen dollars. That'll get us straight."

We went to a taxi place just over in the Bronx where cabbies wait for calls. "I know one of the guys in here," Harriet told me. "I'll go up and see him and get some money off him. Wait outside for me; it won't take more'n a few minutes."

She came out after half an hour with fifteen dollars, just as she'd promised, and we took a cab down to the block and copped. I didn't want to think too much about the money, but it bothered me. I wanted to get straight, that was the most important thing, and I wanted some dope to take home so that I wouldn't be sick again. But was she . . . ? No, she wouldn't be hustling, I knew that. Then she must be friends with one of the cabbies. But why would he give her fifteen bucks just like that? She couldn't possibly be that friendly with a man. She'd told me she was a virgin, that she'd never had *anything* to do with *any* man, that she couldn't stand men, had an aversion to anything to do with men. I couldn't work it out. I didn't want to. Nothing made sense—not the sort of sense that I could accept.

I started questioning Harriet whenever she had money. "Where d'ya get it, Harry? You're not hustling, are you? I'd kill myself if I ever found out you did that." Harriet denied it. There was always some fabulous, way-out explanation that never rang true but always satisfied me enough to allow Harriet to turn me on with the dope she copped.

Then one day while she was over at my house I questioned her again, and this time I wouldn't accept her explanations. "It can't be true, Harry. You couldn't have got the money that way. You're lying to me. You don't want to tell me, I know, but you *have* to tell me the truth. Do you hear that? You *have* to tell me."

And she did. She admitted everything. She was hustling. She'd been hustling. That was the way she'd gotten the money right from the first time I'd met her, and even before.

My whole world collapsed. I went crazy. I screamed. I picked up things and started throwing them around the kitchen. I smashed things, I spilled them on the floor. I tore at my own body. I pulled at my hair. I couldn't take it.

"You lied to me, Harry! How could you! How could you!" I had a vision of Harry with a man. A *man!* It destroyed everything I felt for her. Everything that had happened between us. If a man had touched Harry's body, it was like having a man touch me. It made me feel sick to my stomach. It made me want to throw up. "I hate you, Harry. I hate you! Hate, hate, *hate* you!" I wanted to die. I wanted to kill myself.

Harry realized how cut up I was by her admission and tried to comfort me: "I'm sorry, Cookie. It's the only way. There isn't any other way to maintain my habit. You know I hate men; you don't think I get any fun out of it, do you? Do you know why I hustle, baby? It's so's to make sure you don't have to hustle yourself. I'm never going to let you hustle, baby, never! I'll never let any man touch you. That's the honest truth. If someone's got to hustle, I'd rather it was me. Let them touch me; I can take it. I don't feel a thing. But not you."

I could see she really loved me. She was doing it for me. I felt bad, ungrateful, unkind. I hated what she was doing but I couldn't reproach her. "Is that the honest truth, Harry? You only do it for me?"

"I swear to God."

"But you swore you'd never let a man touch you. You swore you'd never been fucked by a man, that you were a virgin."

"I am. I don't fuck them. I only give blow jobs."

It satisfied me.

I hated myself each time I let Harriet turn me on. I knew that it meant she'd been hustling for me. I hated myself and I hated her, but I had no choice. I didn't want to be sick; I wanted to get straight. There was no other way.

I was with her once when she was on her way to turn a trick with a couple of guys in an apartment in the Bronx. She told me to come up with her. It was freezing outside; I could sit in the front while she went in back to turn a trick.

They were surprised when they saw two of us. They were even more surprised to see me. They let Harriet know they'd rather make it with me. Harriet shook her head. "No good!" She made it clear she'd never let them get near me.

She went into the back room with them and I could hear them dicker, then they all came out and dickered some more.

"Okay," one of them said. "We'll pay you extra if you'll party together. We'll watch you partying and then we'll fuck with Harry."

Harriet told them I wouldn't party.

"Then we don't want any of it."

They had us in a bind there. They knew we needed the money, that we were desperate.

"All right," Harriet agreed. "Forty dollars and you can watch us party. But you're not to touch her."

"Thirty-five."

They put the money on the table and Harriet stuffed it into her jeans. We went into the bedroom. I unbuttoned my blouse and pulled up my skirt and took off my panties. Harriet went down on me. She didn't go into my cunt; she only pretended and I was grateful for that. I was stiff like a mummy. I watched their faces as they leered at us and I was filled with disgust. I knew I ought to pretend I was enjoying it, but I couldn't even pretend. I hadn't let a man get near me for ages and ages, for a year almost. I hated what they were doing to us. I wanted to spit in their ugly faces. They were mocking what Harry and I felt for each other. They were dragging us down into the dirt.

After about three minutes Harry sat up. We'd performed for them long enough. That was it. I got up, buttoned my blouse, and went into the other room. I wanted to throw up. Harriet stayed behind to finish them off. She came out after about ten minutes and said: "Come on, baby. Let's go."

Harriet cared for me. Harriet was everything to me: sister, mother, lover. She stayed at my house much of the time and became one of the family. My mother liked her and always asked after her folks: "How's your mother? And your father? And your sister, too. Give them my regards."

Harry slept in my bed. My mother raised no questions. We were quiet at night; our lovemaking was kept for the day. At night we took off before we went to bed and then we'd be too high for sex; lying close together, hugging, kissing, and nodding was enough for us.

It was different during the day when we were alone together; then we could have really wild sex. Harriet was terribly solicitous over me. She bathed me, she brushed my hair, she got me food—just like a mother monkey. She took care of my clothes, choosing what I should wear. I always looked clean and neat and fresh. And good. I was grateful to Harriet for protecting me, for letting me keep my self-respect. She was taking all the burdens on herself.

I enjoyed my love for Harriet and I enjoyed the power I had over her—especially when I was high. I could take off with her, provoke her into anger, make her beat me, make her love me, get her to prove how much she needed to care for me.

I always awoke sick in the morning, needing to take off and get straight to turn off the terrible pains and cravings. We always tried to keep back enough dope at night so that we could get straight in the morning. Then I would take Mitchell to the babysitter and we would go down to the block to make our connection. Harriet would hit me and then hit herself. We'd make love then and there wherever we were, on a stairway or on a roof, Harry finger-fucking me while we kissed—a delirious, lingering, space-tripping episode that lasted at least a half hour unless we were disturbed.

When we were high and had copped enough to last us through

the next morning, we could take the subway home—south on the Lexington Avenue IRT, change to the crosstown shuttle at Grand Central station, then get the Seventh Avenue local all the way to the end, at Van Cortland Park. I was high on the subway, and being high I used my powers. I only had to look at a man—or at a woman—for a second too long to provoke Harriet's jealousy. She was even jealous of the junkies we met on the block and tried to get me away from them as quickly as possible.

"You were making eyes at that cat, I saw you."

I denied it.

"You did."

"I didn't. I was looking at something else. That old woman with the bags."

"You were not. You were looking right at him. I saw you smile."

I couldn't stand it when people didn't believe me. I had no moral scruples about lying or about anything else, but on those occasions when I told the truth I wanted to be believed. When Harriet accused me of something I hadn't done—and there were many real things she might have accused me of—I got mad.

"You motherfucker! You don't trust me!" I always made sure I had an audience. I shouted to let everyone hear, on the train or at the station, especially at Times Square. "I hate you, you motherfucker!"

It always embarrassed Harriet. She would try to calm me and then I'd yell back: "Go away! Leave me alone, motherfucker. I hate you!" She might try slapping me and then we'd get into a big fight, but most of the time she just wanted to be saved from all the embarrassment and gave in to whatever it was I wanted. If she wouldn't give in, I could always threaten to throw myself in front of the train and once, on Riverdale Avenue, I actually ran in front of a car and Harriet had to run into the road and pull me back.

"What did you do that for, stupid?"

"Stop picking on me, Harry. For Chrissakes, Harry, stop picking on me."

I had so much power over Harriet when I was high. I could control her rages, turn them on at will, then make her show her love for me despite everything I'd done. And on the subway I could let go with my tantrums, knowing that I would always win; I could scream my loudest and know that Harriet would stand by me and take care of me.

☼ CHAPTER TWELVE ☼

Over the summer I came to see less and less of Harriet. She was too busy looking after herself; her habit took up much of her time. Often I didn't see her for days at a stretch. When she didn't come around to Yonkers I had to go down to the block and cop for myself. I'd wait until my parents were home and then, after dinner, I'd hitch a ride on Riverdale Avenue down the Henry Hudson Parkway to Ninety-sixth Street. Unlike Harriet with her boyish looks, I had no difficulty in getting a ride when I needed one—and I knew how to take care of myself when a driver got fresh. There was an underpass under the highway at Ninety-sixth that led to Riverside Drive, but that took too much time and instead I always dodged between the speeding cars on the highway to get to the crosstown bus that brought me to within four blocks of 100th Street. After I'd copped, I could take the more leisurely route home by subway.

I was deep into my habit now, but my parents didn't seem to notice. I might sit with them on the sofa looking at the television, milk and cookies in my hand while I nodded. My mother would say something and I'd jerk my head and the milk would spill all over the rug. She was scared to question me; she didn't want to have her fears confirmed. One time I nodded over breakfast and my face fell forward into the cereal bowl. My mother called me out of it and I lifted my face, all covered with Rice Crispies. No comment. I shot up in the bathroom, sitting on the seat for an hour or more while I nodded behind the locked door, and no one said anything. I could take hours over my makeup, applying eyeshadow and liner, nodding all the while, and my mother would just tiptoe past with a worried look on her face, checking to make sure I was okay but scared to make a comment. If I didn't have a cooker, I sometimes cooked up in a teaspoon; my explanation when she found it, that I'd blackened the spoon with a match so that I could use the soot for my makeup, satisfied her.

Most of the time I did little more at home than take Mitchell to the baby-sitter in the morning and pick him up in the evening. When I was high I could do things for him like feeding him, playing with him, or washing his face, but when I was sick, or even if I was straight but not high, I had no patience. His crying would make me mad and I would hit him hard and really hurt him. Sometimes I was so scared of what I might do that I shut him in his room for his own safety.

One morning, in September of 1961, I kept Mitchell home from the baby-sitter because he had a cold. I'd copped enough the evening before to keep me supplied through the day. I shot up in the kitchen, but it must have been purer stuff than I'd been used to getting on the block and I overdosed.

I woke up on the kitchen floor with Mitchell standing over me, screaming with terror. I looked at his face and tried to pull my thoughts together. My left arm was still strapped up, with the needle in place. I yanked at the spike, threw it across the room, then reached up my hands and pulled Mitchell to me.

I hugged him. He'd saved my life, the poor little kid. Only two and a half, how could he understand? We cried together.

I was really scared now. I couldn't go on like this. Overdosing is a constant risk for every addict, but I'd tried to put the thought out of my mind. Now I knew it could happen to me. And my habit was getting expensive. I was shooting three or four bags a day at five dollars each. They weren't kidding me on the block: I was hooked. Before long I'd have to hustle; Harriet couldn't take care of me forever. I really had to do something about my habit —soon.

I worried about it for a few days, then on Friday evening while my father was out I sat my mother down and told her I was hooked on dope and needed her help.

Her face was ashen. Her fears were confirmed. She could not longer hope that her silence would make everything unpleasant go away. "Yes, I knew something was wrong. You've been acting a little dopey and you had me worried, but I didn't know what to look for with drugs. You've been getting pale and skinny lately and kind of lifeless; is that from the drugs?"

"Yes, Mommy. You've got to help me. I want to clean up. I want to kick my habit. I need your help."

"Yes, Cookie, we'll do everything we can for you. We want you to get well again. You must know what you're doing to yourself. Aren't you tired of all this? Don't you want to make a proper life for yourself?"

I told her yes, I wanted to clean up, I wanted to get clean but I couldn't do it by myself. I needed her for support.

"You really want to?" She seemed happy. She wanted to believe that my troubles would soon be over.

"Yes, Mommy, I'll prove it."

I was still high. I felt strong, strong enough to do anything I set my mind to. I brought out my works and showed them to her. "Here you are, here's everything. Without works I can't shoot up." I took the needle and pressing it down on the kitchen table, I broke it in two. I smashed the dropper. I gathered all the pieces and flushed them down the toilet.

On Saturday I went through withdrawal, kicking cold turkey with no drugs to help me along. I threw up. I had diarrhea. I could neither eat nor smoke. I crawled into bed and my mother piled blankets on me, three blankets, four blankets, I was still too cold. Suddenly I was too hot. I threw off everything. I couldn't stand the heat. I screamed. My mother was distraught: "I don't know what to do for you."

"Leave me alone!" I yelled at her. "Just leave me alone!"

I kept shivering, throwing up, running to the bathroom with the shits. Then I thought of a hot bath. I ran it as hot as I could stand. I felt comfortable in the bath and relaxed. When I couldn't take the heat any more I got out and catnapped on my bed. Each nap seemed to last for hours but I know it was only a few minutes. Then I went back into the tub. The warm water let me relax and allowed me to nap for a few minutes at a time. It went on through the night and through the next day. I wouldn't let anyone near me. If they came close, if my mother or father so much as talked to me, I screamed.

By Sunday evening I knew I couldn't do it that way. I couldn't kick cold turkey. I needed help. I'd go to Dr. Tollman and ask him to give me something to help me. But Dr. Tollman wouldn't be in his office until Monday afternoon and I couldn't last that long.

I told my mother I had to get straight, immediately. I had to have enough dope to get me out of my withdrawal. She saw how bad I was and gave me twenty-five dollars out of her purse. I put on some old clothes, a pair of pants to keep me warm, an old wool hat on my head. I didn't wash, didn't brush my teeth, didn't comb my hair. I didn't have the strength to hitch a ride—and the way I looked I couldn't have got one, either. I took a cab. I felt terribly sick and threw up all the way, out of the window, down the side of the cab, inside the cab. The cabbie was angry. I promised him a special tip if he'd just get me over to 100th Street. I was desperate.

I copped a nickel bag but I couldn't turn on; I'd broken my works. I went up to the first junkie I met and told him, "I need your works." He knew I'd share my dope with him in return. We went up on a roof and he hit me and then he hit himself.

It was just enough to get straight. It wasn't enough to get high on, but I was feeling more like my normal self. I went back on the street and copped another bag and found one of the regulars who was willing to get high with me. I spent most of the evening on the block and copped a set of works and enough dope to last me through the next morning. In twelve hours I'd be sitting in Dr. Tollman's office, asking him to help me get off dope forever.

But when I left the block I didn't say good-bye to the junkies. . . .

Dr. Tollman was a short, thin man with thick dark hair, very distinguished looking. He spoke little and never so much as smiled. I had always seen him as someone who could listen to me and make my family aware of my needs. I trusted him.

My mother told him of my drug problem; her eyes were red and she kept wiping them. I sat by quietly, watching the expression on Dr. Tollman's face. It never changed—and that gave me confidence. He wasn't judging me; he understood. He seemed to know about heroin. "When did you last use a narcotic?" he asked.

"I'm all right, Doctor. I just shot up a while ago."

He gave my mother a prescription for Dolophine—methadone in pill form. He told her to ration it out to me, not to let me take more than the proper dose. Then he gave me a thorough examination and sent me home.

The Dolophine got me straight. It didn't give me a high, but it let me get through withdrawal without sickness and without pain. My mother sent Mitchell to stay with Sandra for two weeks and she herself stayed home to look after me.

I took the Dolophine for over a week. I was no longer dependent physically on heroin but I was becoming more and more depressed. I wanted to get back to the scene on 100th Street; it was the only life that meant anything to me, but I knew that if I went I would be right back on a habit and sooner or later I would be drawn to prostitution unless an overdose took me first. There seemed no way out.

I spent my days crying. At night I'd wake screaming from my dreams. I was talking to myself. I felt myself growing worse and worse. Hot baths helped. Hot baths always helped.

I went into the bathroom and ran the water. I was wearing a quilted robe, orange and yellow. I watched my reflection in the tub as the water flowed in. I dipped my hand in the water and watched the colors swirling around it, orange and yellow. I took off my robe and climbed into the tub. It was good. I lay back, let out some of the cold water and filled up with more hot water. The mirrors misted. The bathroom filled with whirling clouds of steam. I had to have hot water to cover me. I wanted to be comfortable in the hot water, covered and protected. I watched the water rising higher and higher. The soles of my feet were burning but the pain felt good. It was painful in a good way.

Suddenly I saw them. They were looking at me. Men! I pressed my hands over my breasts and crossed my thighs, then drew my legs up to my chest to protect myself. It didn't make sense. "But there's no one here to see me," I said loudly. I wanted to believe it.

I lay back. Suddenly I saw men's eyes all over. Dozens of them. They came in pairs, in all colors and all sizes, staring at me from walls and ceilings. Just eyes and nothing else. I didn't just see the eyes—I could *hear* them. I tried to crawl deeper into the water to get away from them. Then I shut my eyes and screamed.

I'd never really screamed before. I'd always strangled my cries somewhere to hold them back. Now I let go. I knew this was what I had to do. I went into my scream. I turned over, rolled up into a ball, became smaller and smaller and entered right into my scream. I *became* the scream. I'm told that my scream was the most terrifying thing my parents had ever heard, that it came with an unbelievable loudness that shook the walls. But I didn't hear it. I was right inside that scream. I was the scream and the scream was me.

My mother and father tried to get me out of the tub, but I kept rolling and thrashing about in the water. I terrified them and their terror communicated itself to me. My mother finally let out the water.

They put me to bed wrapped in wet towels, but I wasn't there. I had no body; I had only a voice, a voice that wasn't screaming anymore but had to announce its existence. My voice talked. It talked on and on. My mother sat by the bed and tried to listen to the voice while my father called the doctor. The voice talked on.

The doctor gave me sedation and the voice finally went to sleep. He kept me on sedation for a few days, then when I was coherent again he suggested to my parents that they take me to Grasslands Hospital, a mental institution in Westchester County, "for observation."

I was pleased with his suggestion. It would give me a way out. It would keep me from the temptations of 100th Street. Perhaps I could clean up for good and come out and start all over again. Perhaps I could get away from Harriet and her jealous demands on me.

My parents drove me out to Grasslands on a Saturday afternoon and signed me in as a voluntary patient.

I didn't like the hospital too much. The patients were all psychotics; there was no one there that I could relate to. I think I must have been the first junkie they had. I didn't actually say I was an addict; I told the psychiatrists who interviewed me only that I was fooling with drugs. They asked me a lot of silly questions: "How does it feel to use drugs?" "What do you do then?" "Do you have fantasies associated with using drugs?" I felt they were using me as a guinea pig. I was wasting my time.

I was clean, no dope, no methadone, I was no longer physically addicted but I still needed a regular high. They gave me sedatives and tranquilizers, which I saved up a few at a time, then swallowed all together. It wasn't like heroin, but it gave me the semblance of a high and that helped.

Every night I dreamed of shooting up. I wanted to feel that needle in my arm. I wanted to be back with my friends. I was with the wrong people; I didn't belong here. Harriet came to visit me after I was there a week. She was high; it made me jealous and I missed the old neighborhood and its junkies even more. Harriet urged me to get out as quickly as possible and come back to her. I knew I couldn't stay.

The medical board recommended that I remain for an extended stay of a few months but I was a voluntary patient and their recommendation wasn't binding. I called my mother, and my parents came to take me away after I'd been there only two weeks.

It was strange being home again. I didn't feel I belonged. I thought of the days ahead, at home, my parents, sitting in front of the television, taking Mitchell to the baby-sitter, spending my days putting on makeup and taking baths and getting dressed and picking up Mitchell and having dinner with my parents and sitting in front of the television. I could see the depression coming on again. I could see the fears and the unknown terrors.

"I'm going out to see some of the kids," I told my mother.

"You're not going to let them get you to use drugs again, Cookie, are you? Not after all this!"

I was hurt. "Mommy! How could you? Don't you trust me?"

I went downtown with a couple of dollars, straight to 100th Street. I was clean now and felt good; Harriet by comparison looked pretty strung out, all fucked up. I embraced her and we kissed. I was so happy. She introduced me to a Puerto Rican guy she was with, Franco. He was about thirty, had an olive complexion, black eyes, a small nose rather like my father's, and sensuous lips. Over his curly black hair—it was long for those times and must have looked sloppy to most people—he wore a little beret tilted to one side. He was thin and short—five feet seven or eight, about the same height as me—and he walked with his toes turned in. I wondered why I'd never seen him on the block before. He said he knew where we could get some good stuff.

Harriet was in too bad a state to hit herself. Franco hit her first and she nodded immediately. Then I rolled up my sleeve and Franco rubbed my arm to bring up the vein. I liked his touch on my arm. I found myself staring at his face and he caught my glance. I didn't want to admit it, but he was the first man who'd turned me on in well over a year and I tried to pretend he hadn't excited me; I knew I had to play it cool or I'd be in trouble with Harriet but she was nodding and hadn't noticed a thing. Then Franco hit me with the needle, only a small amount because I was clean and couldn't tolerate much. It was the moment I'd been dreaming about for over three weeks, ever since I'd stopped shooting up. It hit me with a wallop. Diamonds were tingling through my blood. My head glowed. I was high. Nothing threatened me now, not even my strange attraction to Franco.

Right away my life was back in the old pattern. I saw Harriet most every day and made out with her. I was down on 100th Street regularly shooting up. Soon I was back on two or three bags a day and within two weeks I had my habit again. My mother kept questioning me about drugs; I denied everything, but now that she was hip to me I had to be extra careful. I slept with my works hidden under the pillow, and I didn't dare shoot up in the bathroom when my parents were home.

I didn't like what was happening. I wanted to clean up, cut

down on my dependence, get back to the great feeling of starting off again at the beginning when a small dose was enough to keep me high all day. I knew Grasslands hadn't been equipped to help me, but there were places in Manhattan that worked only with junkies, and junkies went in there regularly to clean up for a while.

Primarily, though, I was worried about Harriet. She was destroying herself. I had to help her. She had to clean up before it was too late.

My mother had found out that I was shooting up again. I admitted it; I told her I had no choice. I couldn't face the depression I'd gotten into when I was off it, I couldn't take another psychotic break. "I'm going to be a junkie for the rest of my life, Mommy. I'm going to die a junkie."

✡ CHAPTER THIRTEEN ✡

My mother was happy when I told her I was going to Manhattan General Hospital to clean up and that I was taking Harriet with me. "It's not like Grasslands," I said. "In Manhattan General they really know how to handle dope addicts."

I asked her for some money to use in the commissary there, and then I met Harriet and we went downtown together, stopping off at 100th Street to shoot up on the money my mother had given me. It was October 31, Halloween, and kids were going around in outlandish makeup and fancy dress, trick-or-treating.

We got there around noon. Harriet had been to Manhattan General before and she knew her way around. The addiction department occupied almost half the building. I'd never seen so many junkies together as I saw in the waiting room, fifty or sixty of them sitting on the benches and on the floor. People were dealing quite openly and then went to shoot up in the bathroom. Some of the addicts were sick, some were straight and a few were high. The female nurses looked like butches, nasty and brutal; the male nurses swished around like faggots. It looked as if the whole hospital were run by the crowd from 100th Street.

I had always had faith in hospitals and doctors as dispensers of help if one really wanted it, but the people at the hospital didn't seem any better than I was, nor any better equipped to help. Nobody gave a damn.

We waited around for a couple of hours, then our names came

up and we went to the desk. They didn't have any spare beds, we were told. They couldn't take us. We'd have to go home. We could come back again early the next morning and sign in.

But I couldn't go home. I'd already spent the fifteen dollars my mother had given me and I couldn't face the hassle of having to ask her for more to get dope that evening. We walked around for a while near the hospital, then we sat down in Stuyvesant Park. I was getting desperate. Soon we'd be sick and then we couldn't do anything. We had to cop soon. The question was where to get the money. Harriet was too strung out to raise so much as a dime; her weight was down to something like ninety pounds and she looked lifeless, almost dead. No one would have paid her to turn a trick.

"Let's snatch a purse," I said. I'd never snatched a purse before but I'd heard people discuss it. I knew the principle: You seek out a likely person in a crowd, come up suddenly, snatch, and run as fast as you can.

Harriet agreed.

"Let's look around and see who we can take off," I said. I knew that I would have to do the job; Harriet was too dull and clumsy, she lacked any sense of coordination and she didn't have the strength if it came to a fight.

We walked around for a while. It was getting dark and chilly. Fourteenth Street was crowded with shoppers from Klein's and the schlock bargain stores. People were coming home from work, from the Con Ed building and the insurance offices and up out of the subways. Sixteenth Street looked much better. It was dark and quiet. There were small houses and a few apartment buildings and it looked like a fairly well-to-do block. I spotted my victim on Sixteenth Street, between Second and Third Avenue. She seemed to be in her early sixties, gray hair, thin, well dressed, fragile. She had to be well-off to live in a neighborhood like this. She looked too old to be working; perhaps she'd been visiting someone.

I looked at Harriet and she looked at me. I pointed to the woman and Harriet nodded. I told her to keep close behind me and keep an eye out in case someone followed. We were still close to Third Avenue. The woman passed an apartment building with a doorman standing by the lit-up entrance. I let her go on. Now she was in the shadows again. I shortened the distance. I was jumpy and scared. My heart was pounding. I focused my thoughts on her purse and the way she was holding it. I was praying that Harriet would do the right thing.

When we got to a fairly dark and deserted spot I stepped up behind the woman. She was holding her purse loosely in her left hand. I grabbed and tugged and ran off with the purse toward Stuyvesant Square.

I was five yards ahead of the woman before she realized what had happened and started screaming. "My purse! My purse!" she yelled. "Help! Help! My purse." She had a powerful voice for her size.

"Let's go!" I yelled to Harriet without breaking my stride. At the park I turned right, ran down one block with Harriet close behind, right again into Fifteenth Street and halfway down the block. We ran into a walk-up tenement and waited behind the door, out of breath. I emptied the purse out on the floor. There was nearly thirty dollars there, twenty-seven in bills plus some change. Nothing else of any value. We left the purse on the floor and took the Lexington Avenue subway uptown from Union Square.

We took off a few times on 100th Street and copped enough for the next day, then we went to Harriet's house in the Bronx to sleep. I told her mother that if anyone called she wasn't to say we'd spent the night there; I wanted my mother to believe we were already in Manhattan General.

We were back early next morning at the hospital. They interviewed us separately. I was interviewed by an administrator, a kindly looking woman who seemed to show a genuine interest in me. She saw I was young and presentable and she assumed this was my first time; I didn't tell her I'd cleaned up in Grasslands only a few weeks earlier. She let me know, subtly, that they were despairing of people who kept coming in just to clean up for a while so that they could go back and use drugs again. She let me know that she had trust in me, that she thought I'd go through my twenty-one day medical to the end and not come back again. She told me the rules: If you leave before your medical is up, you have a problem getting back in again. If you stay your full twenty-one days, the social workers will help you learn a trade, find a job, get an apartment, go on welfare—anything you need to stay off drugs.

Once I was certain of being admitted I went into the bathroom to throw away my works. It was still early, but the bucket in the bathroom was filled to overflowing with used tampons and works by the dozen. We were taken upstairs, searched, checked, searched again, examined. They gave us pink nightgowns and pink robes. Harriet and I got put in the same room with four other girls.

The women on our floor—about eighty of them—were mostly older. The majority were black or Puerto Rican. They were losers: lifelong junkies, physical wrecks, worn-out whores. I didn't want to be part of them. I felt I was a cut above them. I was young, pretty, alive. I still had a lot going for me.

The nurses treated us all like so much shit. They were nasty, mean, and spiteful, and never said a kind word. One in particular annoyed me. She was a tall, skinny, blue-eyed blonde in her thirties, ugly as sin, who seemed to despise me even more than she despised all the other addicts. She singled me out for her nastiness. I hated her guts.

Three or four times a day we lined up to get our methadone—in liquid form so that we couldn't store it up or trade it. You lined up, they checked your name off the list, and you drank it out of a little paper cup while they watched. No cheating and getting seconds, no taking it off into a corner. It had a nasty taste, like cough syrup. At night they gave us a sedative, chloral hydrate, also in liquid form. On the first night I watched one of the addicts snatch a cup of chloral hydrate while the nurse's back was turned. The second night I did the same, and then went up for my official dose. I followed it with a cup of hot water that was supposed to increase the effect, and it brought on a fairly good high. Physically it made me want to sleep, but emotionally I felt the high and I was able to fight off sleep. The more I fought against it, the more powerful the high.

Sex was rampant. Everybody was making out. There wasn't one girl among the eighty who wasn't at least part-time gay—

and that was the only thing about the place that made me feel at home. Two girls, both black, turned me on but I had to play it cool with them because of Harry. She and I used to make out together in the showers with the water running. It was good.

There was nothing to do all day. Sure they had what they called occupational therapy, but that was just arts and crafts. I poked my nose in there, once. A bunch of girls were sitting around in their pink gowns and pink robes making dolls and jewelry. It turned my stomach. When I got out and went back to the block I wanted to be able to say I'd been to Manhattan General, that would show I was a regular, I was tough. I didn't want to say I'd been at a place where they made dolls.

Most of the time the girls just sat around and rapped. Topics were limited to drugs and tricks. How long have you had your habit? How often do you shoot up? In which hospitals have you cleaned up? Who has the best dope? Where do you make your connection? How often have you been arrested? And tricks, of course: Where do you turn tricks? How much do you get? What do you let them do? Do you know any johns with way-out requests? Who's your pimp? I was the only one there, I think, who'd never turned a trick. I was an outcast. I had no stories to tell. I wasn't nearly as tough as I pretended to be. There was some card playing—but without money it lacked excitement, and so most of the time the addicts just sat and spun out the same worn-out stories of drugs and tricks.

Doctors came around occasionally to check on our physical health. Social workers advised us where to go once we got out. They held out their services as a sort of carrot: Stay the full twenty-one days and you'll get everything you need to stay clean. I knew already I couldn't stay in this snake pit for three whole weeks and I didn't pay much attention to them. The only member of the staff from whom I thought I could get at least some understanding was a woman doctor, a psychiatrist. She was fairly young, had oriental features, and she turned me on sexually. She had me sit in her office and got me to talk about my background, my family and my schooling. She listened to me as if I was a real person—which was more than anyone else did.

The food was terrible. Compared to this, Grasslands had been a resort. For breakfast we had oatmeal that was as mushy as the rice I'd cooked for Eddie when we were first married. For lunch they gave us fried baloney with gravy. For supper we had hard-boiled eggs or some other garbage. Fried baloney every day. God how I hated that baloney!

Harriet and I had signed in on a Wednesday. We had baloney for lunch on Wednesday, Thursday, Friday, and Saturday. On Sunday the mean blond nurse came around with the lunch cart. The girls came and grabbed their trays; I stayed where I was. She called out to me: "You there! Aren't you coming to get yours?"

I told her I had no appetite.

"No appetite! What do you think we run here?"

I told her I didn't want any, that I couldn't stand the food, it made me sick.

"That's too bad. This isn't a country club. Come and get what you're given."

She made me mad. I went to the cart and picked up my tray and threw it at her. The girls grabbed me while I was still aiming my throw. I missed and it hit the wall. I was going to punch the dirty bitch in the face but the girls—Harriet especially—held me back. "You motherfucker!" I yelled at the nurse and then I turned to the other nurses and called them a bunch of motherfuckers, too. "I'm getting out of here, you motherfuckers. I'm not going to stay with a bunch of motherfuckers like you. Fuck you!"

I let Harriet calm me a little, then I turned to her: "Come on, let's go. Let's get out of here. We don't belong."

As voluntary patients they couldn't keep us if we didn't want to stay, but the nurses claimed we couldn't check out on a Sunday. I made a big scene. Then they said they'd be glad to let us go if they could, but our clothes were locked away downstairs and they couldn't get them for us until Monday. I carried on some more. Finally I had my way: They sent someone down for our clothes, they brought out some forms and got us to sign that we'd left on our own and that they weren't responsible, then they told us that was it. "It'll be a long day before we let *you* back again," they told me. I didn't give a shit.

We went down in the elevator, walked through the lobby and out into the chill November air.

Then it hit me. What had I done? I'd meant to make a scene but I hadn't wanted to get thrown out. I knew we'd be in hell soon: When you turn off on methadone you get much worse withdrawal pains than when you turn off on dope. I felt especially bad about Harriet. I knew she hadn't really wanted to leave; she'd left only out of love and loyalty for me. If it hadn't been for the bitchy blond nurse, I think I would have walked right back and begged to be let in again and I think I could have carried it off: I was good at making scenes, I could have made them feel sorry for me and, hard-hearted as they were, they might have let us back in.

Long before we got up to 100th Street I was suffering from withdrawal pains in all my joints. My memory of what happened next is a complete blank. Somewhere, somehow, we must have copped some dope. The next thing I remember is being home. I was straight. No more pains. My mother was surprised of course. I described the hospital to her. "It's not for me," I said. "They treat you like dirt. I couldn't stay there." On the block that evening I'd heard of a hospital in Queens that was supposed to be good for cleaning up. They let you in without making you wait, they treated you as a regular patient, no special addict wards, no snake pits. I told my mother we were going there on Monday morning.

"You know best, Cookie," she said. "If that's a better place you ought to go there."

She gave me some more money and on Monday morning I met Harriet on the block. We shot up, then took the subway to Queens and signed in. It was everything we'd been told. They even gave us the methadone in pill form and the sedative came in pill form, too, so we were able to hide them under our tongues and take a few at one time for a better feeling. We stayed the full two weeks, then we went home.

The morning after I got out of the Queens hospital I got ten dollars from my mother so that I could go looking for a job. I met Harriet on 100th Street and we got high. We went to the block every day just as before, but now we needed to buy much less than usual to get the same high. That gave us more time to be together and make love.

I got to thinking back on the purse snatching. It had been so easy, something I had an obvious gift for. I could do it on a regular basis and then Harriet wouldn't have to turn tricks. I suggested the Lower East Side since I knew it well, and I knew I wouldn't be recognized there, not the way I looked now, six years later.

I stole a long kitchen knife from a friend and stuffed it up my sleeve; it was so sharp that I was afraid to bend my arm. Then we chose a dark spot on Ludlow Street and we waited. I don't know how many people I let pass before I spotted a middle-aged woman in her mid-forties, small, Spanish-looking, all bundled up in a hat, heavy coat, and boots. I had a strong feeling that she would bring us luck.

I signaled to Harriet.

Harry stepped in front of her and asked her the time. I dashed behind her with the knife in my right hand and hitched my arm around her neck to choke her. The knife fell down. My left hand covered her mouth. "Take it!" I yelled to Harriet. "Take it!"

The woman put up a tremendous fight. She got me down on the ground and pulled at my hair, but I was able to keep my hand over her mouth to stop her from screaming, and with my other hand I punched her as hard as I could. Finally she loosened her grasp. Harriet grabbed the pocketbook and ran while I gave the woman one last punch and jumped clear of her. I followed Harry down the street.

Harriet ran one way at the corner, I ran the other yelling, "Help! Help! He stole her purse! There he is!" People were running in all directions.

I caught up with Harriet on Allen Street. I asked her where the pocketbook was.

"It's all right," she said, "I've got the purse."

"No, where's the pocketbook?" Some intuitive sense told me the pocketbook was important. The woman had fought so hard for it.

"I dropped it back there. Don't go. You might get caught."

I went back anyway to find it, then we went into a house on Allen Street and climbed all the way to the roof. Harriet opened the change purse and said, "Oh, we got eighteen dollars. That's good. That's enough."

"There must be more," I said. "The way she was fighting there must be more." I opened the pocketbook and felt around. Nothing much. The lining was bulging, though. I reached in, found a slit in the lining, groped around, and came up with a roll of bills fastened with a rubber band. There were twenties, tens, fives, just a few singles. We started counting. Almost a thousand. A thousand! Just a few dollars short of a thousand.

We hugged each other. We laughed. We joked, we danced together on the roof, we threw the money up in the air and let it rain down on us. We were rich!

"I knew it!" I sang. "I knew it!"

It was my first real success in life. I'd made it at last. It had been all *my* doing. I'd planned it, I'd chosen the victim, I'd fought for it, I'd insisted we find the pocketbook, I'd finally found the money. All *my* doing. I wanted Harriet's approval. I wanted everybody's approval. I wanted everyone to know how great I was. I wished I could go home and tell my mother how great I'd been, that I'd made good at last. I wanted to be able to say to her, "There, Mommy, you thought I was a failure, but I got a thousand dollars and it's only the second time I've tried it."

"Mitchell is going to have a great Christmas this year," I told Harriet. I rolled up the money again in its rubber band, then I placed it in my bra. I wanted to be able to feel it. It was too late to do anything so we took a cab back to Yonkers. We had as much money as we needed. We were high on excitement, high enough not to need to get dope.

Next morning we went down to Greenwich Village. I spent two hundred dollars on clothes for myself. I bought a reversible cape coat with mandarin collar, one side black, the other brown and gray plaid, and stretch pants with straps under the instep. Harriet bought boys' clothes. We bought matching shirts to mark us as a couple. I spent seventy-five dollars on toys for Mitchell and bought presents for all my friends and relatives. We had so many bundles, we had to pile them in a cab to take us up to Yonkers.

I told my mother some far-fetched story about where the money had come from. She had no choice but to believe me.

We felt really rich now, Harry and I. We had enough money to set ourselves up as dealers and buy our dope wholesale—twenty-five nickel bags at a time for seventy-five dollars on which we could have turned fifty dollars profit. But each time it seemed so pointless to sell it when we could use it ourselves; we had so much, after all, and our money would never run out. So we shot up our stock and turned on all our acquaintances, too—for free. We went everywhere by cab. We were living in a junkie's paradise; the good fortune could never end.

✡ CHAPTER FOURTEEN ✡

Within two weeks all our money was gone. I needed money urgently. I took my new clothes to the block and sold them for enough to keep me in dope for another day. Then Harriet told me her aunt was away on vacation. She had a lot of jewelry, silver, and appliances: We could make some easy money that way.

We lined it up with one of the people from the block, a Puerto Rican—not Franco—who had the experience. We went to the apartment, in the Bronx, that evening. Harriet and the man broke in through a window in the back while I waited at the front door, then they let me in. It was as Harriet had promised: a big box of jewelry, silverware, a portable TV, a toaster, appliances—a good haul. We piled the small stuff into shopping bags we found in the kitchen, the man brought his car to the front door, and we took the loot down to the block straight away. A fence gave us sixty dollars for it—enough for a couple of days.

We didn't pull any more burglaries and I didn't snatch any more purses. I let Harriet take care of my habit whenever I couldn't boost enough money from my mother. Harriet was becoming very possessive. We quarreled a lot. We'd been together for well over a year now and I felt she was bugging me, she wanted to run my life. Franco had also joined our little world and we sat around together a lot, Harriet between me and Franco, my arm over Harriet's shoulders letting Franco know with an occasional squeeze of the hand that I cared for him, too. If I could somehow manage to get away from Harry. . . .

I tried to break away from her. I left the block at 100th Street and Lexington and went up the street to Second Avenue. There I met Grace, a pretty Irish girl with freckles and green eyes. She had a longtime habit and was in a bad way, but we had a lot of fun together. I used to pretend I was blind and Grace led me around with my hand held out and people dropped change into it—as much as two or three dollars an hour. It was a big joke, but it was too much of a hassle trying to keep a straight face for so long.

I thought of an easier way. Churches, I knew from my church-going days on the Lower East Side, always had well-stuffed collection boxes. We broke into one, a Catholic Church in an Italian neighborhood, and went straight for the collection box, but it was chained down and I found it impossible to force the lock. There was a huge golden crucifix on the altar. "Let's take that," I said. "We can sell it to a religious store in the Spanish section."

Grace had religion and was scared. I told her to keep a lookout and I'd do the boosting myself.

It was heavy. It must be solid gold, I thought. I took the crucifix and a statue; and Grace reluctantly took a couple of statues, too.

We tried to peddle the stuff in Spanish Harlem. The storefront churches wouldn't take it. The religious shops and herbalists were suspicious. Finally we found a shopkeeper who agreed to take them off our hands; he gave us five dollars for the loot.

In January I took up with a big-time pusher named Bimbo. He'd seen me around often with Harriet and had wanted to get together with me then, but I'd let him know that I couldn't do it with Harriet around. Now I met him in a bar and told him I'd broken with Harriet. He said he'd take care of me and set me up in an apartment he had on Ninety-ninth Street, between Park Avenue and Madison.

He was a flashy dresser—the Beau Brummell of Spanish Harlem. He was in his thirties, black, very fat, a lot shorter than me, and he had a gross face. He enjoyed flaunting me as his woman and I spent most of my time walking around with him where we could be seen or letting him make love to me in his apartment. He wanted to have sex with me almost daily although he couldn't get an erection most of the time; it may have been because he took a lot of cocaine. He disgusted me and I had to shut my eyes while I was in bed with him. He spent hours at a time with me, sucking my snatch, having me suck his dick, sitting up to smoke a cigarette, then going down on me again to suck. I found him disgusting.

The only redeeming feature was that he was keeping me in drugs. His specialty was cocaine which he carried in capsules inside his ear. He turned me on to coke and to speedballs—a mixture of cocaine and heroin. Cocaine perked me up, speedballs gave me a high with a kick to it, but I didn't really want the cocaine. I didn't want to perk up; I wanted to nod.

Harriet had been hunting for me from the moment I started breaking away and hanging out with Grace. Now that I was with Bimbo she was especially furious because she didn't think I should be interested in men. She used to call my home and ask for me; I stopped answering the phone when I was there and got my mother to tell her I was out. Friends on the block used to warn me when she was coming by so that I could hide. She'd told them she was going to kill me when she found me, and I believed her.

Bimbo had apartments all over the place and I knew he had a lot of girls hustling for him. I didn't mind so long as I had to have sex only with him; the alternative, I knew, was to become a whore on the street. This way I had only one man and I wasn't taking money for it, only drugs.

Then he started dropping hints: "I can't support your habit for ever." "You'll have to earn some money yourself." He was putting pressure on me. He wanted me to hustle, just for a friend, just for this guy. I knew where it would lead and I broke away from him.

Bimbo had helped me put distance between myself and Harriet. Now I felt freer to get in touch with Franco. He'd given me his phone number months before, when the three of us were still together, and I called him one Monday morning. The day before had been some Jewish festival; my parents had taken me to visit with their folks in Brooklyn and I had twenty dollars my aunts had given me. Franco also lived in Brooklyn, with his father and mother who both worked, and he gave me instructions how to get there on the train.

He had the drugs and everything ready when I came. He went into the kitchen to cook up, then he hit me and he hit himself and we took off immediately. That was what I admired about him: he was so forthright, so decisive, he knew just what he wanted and then went ahead and did it.

We made love while we were high. It was the first time in almost two years I'd had sex with a man I wanted and enjoyed. I fell in love with him as I'd never fallen in love with anyone before. I loved him, I worshiped him, I was willing to be his slave.

We spent hours lying together while he told me about his life. He'd started on drugs when he was twelve—and now he was thirty-one. He'd been in and out of prison for burglaries and muggings; he spent about as much time in jail as he was free—that explained why I hadn't met him on the block until after my stay in Grasslands. He had a brother, Hector, who was doing time in Elmira Prison in upstate New York, and another brother, Tony, who was a cop and lived across the street from his parents.

Franco told me that he had never known real love, that he had never had a woman who would stick with him. I knew I could give him as much as he gave me. I would give him love. I would stick with him.

I saw Franco almost every day. In the morning I'd get Mitchell dressed and give him his breakfast, then I'd put him on the bus that took him to nursery school. From there I'd go straight to the block to meet Franco; we'd shoot up, then go to his place and make love. I was comfortable with him; I knew I was loved. I was happy to have a man loving me again. Our love was gentle and caring: I didn't need him to prove his love by beating me. Neither of us could climax because of the heroin, but we could prolong our lovemaking for hours and hours. I always left in time to pick up Mitchell from the bus at five, to play with him for a while before my parents came home.

Harriet heard about us, of course. She'd been bothered when I was going around with Bimbo, but she'd come to terms with that;

she knew I was doing it only for the drugs I could get out of it. With Franco it was different. She knew I admired him. She felt threatened. I tried to avoid her but it wasn't easy. She knew I had to be home at five to pick up Mitchell and she waited around for me.

I really felt sorry for Harriet. She was the only person who really seemed to understand me. She knew what I was and what I needed. She was almost part of me. She *was* part of me. She was one side of my personality, the dark side, the tough side, the side that both fascinated me and terrified me. I wanted to be rid of Harriet and I wanted to keep her near me.

I couldn't avoid her. She was waiting for me when I got home. I couldn't throw her out. My mother had dinner for us. Harry stayed over and she slept in my bed. We made love. I couldn't tell her I was in love with Franco. We made love in the bathroom and we made love in my bedroom when my parents were asleep. After I'd taken Mitchell to the bus, we went down to 100th Street together and there I could meet Franco and take off with him on the roof, and then he and I could go to his house and make love and shut Harriet out of my life.

But when I got home in the evening, there was Harriet again, making demands on me, needing me, being needed.

The pressures and the emotional demands on me were becoming unbearable. I was torn between Harry and Franco. I couldn't cope. I needed them both. I could understand Harriet's jealousy but I rejected it. Her demands on me were increasing. I didn't know where to turn. I couldn't disown her and I didn't want to lose Franco—or Harriet. I found myself driven into a corner.

I couldn't take it. Every time I spoke I said the same thing: "Leave me alone!" I told my parents not to ask me questions. I asked Harriet to stop hounding me. I asked Franco to stop pressuring me. There were times when I didn't see Franco for days at a time. I'd go down to the block by myself to cop and then I'd go home. I didn't want to be with anyone. Then I was back with Franco and Harriet was calling me again and waiting for me. I couldn't take it. I was tired. I just wanted to be left alone.

I stayed home one morning. The telephone was ringing. I was tired. The telephone rang and stopped, and rang again and stopped, and rang again. I knew who it was. It was Franco and Harriet and Harriet and Franco. Everybody wanted me. Everybody was making demands on me. I couldn't take it. I was so tired. I just wanted to sleep. I just wanted to be left alone.

I went into my bedroom to look for my sleeping pills. There were sedatives and tranquilizers. A lot of them. I wondered which ones to take. I had them in my hands. I looked at them. "This will do it," I thought to myself.

I took a sheet of white paper off a pad and wrote on it:

> Dear Mommy and Daddy and Mitchell:
> I'm tired and I just want to sleep. Forgive me—and I really did love you all.
>
> Cookie.

I folded the note and put it in an envelope, sealed it, and wrote across the front "In case of death." Then I put it on my dresser.

I went into the kitchen with the pills and gobbled them down, three or four at a time.

I went into the living room and sat by the window, the window from which I used to look up at Sally's room after they built the new apartment house.

"This is my last look at the house," I thought. I remembered when the haunted house had burned down. Burned down and disappeared. Gone. "This is my last look at people."

I was curious. I wondered what dying would be like and whether I would know it when I was dead. I was getting a heavy feeling in my head, pleasant and very relaxing. I went over to the sofa and lay down. I started to cry. I cried for Cookie who had had such a tough life. I cried for Cookie whom nobody had ever understood. I was watching myself from the outside, I saw myself lying there on the sofa. I felt so sorry for this girl who was lying there, who was going to die so soon. I got deeper and deeper into the sleep and then I started calling out: "I don't want to die. I really don't want to die."

It was too late now. No one could hear me. There was nothing I could do. There was no way to turn back the clock. I had to die. I wanted to say I'd changed my mind but there wasn't anyone to say it to.

Then I heard the telephone ring. It was ringing for me. I wanted to reach out. It was a thousand miles away. My arm was made of lead, soft as butter. I reached out into a timeless space. My fingers closed over the receiver, grabbed, slipped. I tried again. I couldn't get the message to my fingers. I forced myself. I got the telephone to my ear. I heard Harriet's voice.

"Cookie, Cookie! What's the matter? I've been trying to reach you."

I sobbed.

"Cookie, speak to me. What happened?"

"I'm dying, Harry. I took a batch of pills. I'm dying . . . I'm sorry." I started sobbing again. I couldn't form words. The receiver fell out of my hands. It was over.

I woke up somewhere over on the other side. The living room was full of cops in uniform. They were slapping me in the face. They were marching around the room and trying to make me march along with them. They had to drag me around. They threw cold water on my face and slapped me. They talked to me. They told me to keep walking. I went to sleep.

The next time I woke I was in a cage of white. A bed. White sheets. A white cage over my face. White. I opened my eyes for only a moment and then I closed them because they were too heavy. When I'd rested my eyelids I tried opening them again. A long time later I turned my head. I was in a hospital. A nurse in white was sitting next to me.

"Mrs. Goodman!" A voice from far away. "She's coming through. She's opened her eyes."

Red eyes peering at me. Red eyes and red hair. My mother's face right close to mine. A smile through the tears.

I ought to smile. My face is like concrete. No smile. I can open my eyes but nothing else.

"Cookie! Cookie!"

Inside I want to smile. Inside I want to cry. But I can't do anything with my face. My lips. I can open them a little. My tongue is like a feather pillow, huge and soft and fluffy. "Where am I?" The voice comes from somewhere far away, from somewhere beyond the grave.

"At Cross County Hospital," my mother tells me. She asks me if I know what happened, if I know what day it is and why did I want to do it and do I feel better now.

The first thing I asked them to do, before I could even talk properly, was to take off the net canopy stretched over my bed. I felt like a trapped fish under it.

The nurse wouldn't let it go; standard regulations, she insisted. Dr. Tollman came, trusted, respected, understanding Dr. Tollman, neither a smile nor a frown on his face. He examined me and encouraged me, and when I asked him, he got the nurse to take off the nets—but only after he'd signed a note that he was taking full responsibility if I tried anything foolish or dangerous while the net was off.

I stayed at Cross County for four or five days, until I was over the physical effects of my near-fatal dose of pills. Then Dr. Tollman had my parents take me direct to Grasslands Hospital.

✡ CHAPTER FIFTEEN ✡

I clung to my parents when the nurse came to take me up to my ward in Grasslands. This wasn't like my first time there: Now I was sick; I felt weak and lost. I was saying good-bye to them, and the other world of Grasslands was waiting to suck me in, the world of the psychotics with whom I'd once thought I didn't belong.

Good-bye Mommy, Good-bye Daddy, Good-bye Mitchell, Good-bye Franco and Harriet, Good-bye Yonkers, Good-bye Cookie, Good-bye World.

I was very lonely and very sad. They took away my clothes and gave me some shapeless garments to wear: no belts, no buckles, no pins, no laces, nothing I could hurt myself with. They put me in a room by myself. It had mats on the floor but no bed; you can't hurt yourself falling off a mat. I wasn't allowed matches; I had to ask a nurse for a light and she watched me while I finished my cigarette. They kept me on medication. I was dopey, dreamy, far away. There wasn't much to do but sleep; when I was awake there was little I could do but brood.

After a few days they let me join the other patients. I was put into a cheery room with two other girls; it had sunlight and breezy curtains and real beds. I could sit with the other patients in the dayroom and talk, and play table tennis or watch television. They started me on a series of tests. I settled down with one psychologist, young and warm, who showed me a picture and asked me to tell him what I saw. He listened to me as if he really wanted to hear what I thought and I told him as much as I could; he nodded and seemed pleased and then I got some new ideas from the picture, so I told him even more. He made notes on a pad and when I couldn't find anything else to say about the picture, he put it back on the pile and gave me another one to describe. He seemed to like what I had to say and I felt he'd listen to me, whatever it was I said about his pictures.

They gave me other tests. I had to arrange blocks in a certain order while they timed me with a stopwatch. I had to pair up words in a list with other words that went with them. They gave me some simple math problems to solve and I was scared because I knew I wasn't very good at it, but they didn't seem to mind. They had psychologists and nurses fill in forms while they asked me questions. I began to enjoy all the attention and all the contact with new people. My days were filled. It seemed like a way of life, a routine almost as full as the life on 100th Street.

Then they called me before the psychiatric board for interrogation. There were perhaps seven or eight psychiatrists sitting in a semicircle in straight-backed chairs. I sat at the center of the circle, rigid with apprehension. Some of the doctors wore white coats, others were in business suits. It didn't seem real. Each one was hiding behind a cloud of smoke and when they spoke they gestured with their pipes. Two or three of them spoke with a foreign accent and every accent was different. I thought I must be crazy, really crazy. It wasn't happening to me. It was a dream: I was watching myself in a dream. In the dream I was a nut, a bona fide nut. The doctors were there to confirm it. They fired questions at me to prove I wasn't real. They were trying to trap me to prove I was crazy.

Only one doctor seemed to stand apart from them. He had an accent, too, and a pipe. He was short, he had fair skin and light brown hair and a little pug nose. But his eyes! They were blue, very intense, piercing. He said very little to me. He didn't try to throw me off with questions. He looked at me with his blue eyes and a kindly smile, and when I caught his smile he looked away in embarrassment and then I caught him smiling at me again and he held my eyes.

The next morning the nurse called me from the dayroom and told me to go to the office to see the doctor. It was the one with the blue eyes. Dr. Coro. Dr. Benny Coro. He told me he was going to be my personal doctor and that he'd try to see me as often as possible, every day if he could. He was interested in me, he said, and he would try to help me. He had many other patients, of course, whom he also had to see regularly, and I would also be seen by the psychiatric board.

I saw him regularly in his office. I also saw him frequently when I was in the dayroom: I'd look up toward the nurses' station, a glass-walled enclosure from which the nurses could observe us, and I'd catch Dr. Coro with his eyes fixed on me. I wondered how he was seeing me, as a woman or as a patient. It felt nice to have a man look at me as a woman but I wanted more than that: I needed a doctor to help me. I wanted Dr. Coro to take an interest in me as his patient, to be a doctor I could rely on to help me, not just a man who liked the way I looked.

Dr. Coro saw me in his office every day except Saturday and Sunday, for an hour at least and sometimes two. He had me sit facing him in a comfortable chair while he asked me questions. I expected him to try probing deeply—psychiatrists do that sort of thing—but he didn't. He'd ask me a question and when I'd answered that, he'd go on to the next one. He never tried to exploit my reply, he never seemed to go into the deeper meaning of what I'd said. I was disappointed. I wondered how much good he could be doing me if he didn't really dig deep like other psychiatrists.

Within a few days we'd established a degree of intimacy. Our daily sessions changed from medical interviews to personal conversations. Dr. Coro did less and less of the questioning as I began to ask him questions about his home in Italy, about Rome, about his friends and his family and his schooling. I found him to be an interesting conversationalist and I clung to every word he told me about his exciting life in Italy's capital.

Benny Coro had become personally involved with me. He no longer treated me as if he was the doctor and I the patient. I was looking at him and through him. I realized that I couldn't expect him to help me in a therapeutic way—but there was much I could get from him in other ways. I could use my femininity to get him to help me. I found myself taking extra care with my appearance when I knew he'd be watching.

I began to enjoy the doctor's personal involvement. I enjoyed having him in my power, and being able to manipulate him and working on him to get what I wanted from him. More than anything I wanted him to speak up for me on the psychiatric board, I had to have him in my corner, rooting for me. The board could send you to Rockland State. Nobody stayed long at Grasslands. Either there wasn't much wrong with you and they let you go after a few weeks or they thought you needed treatment and they sent you to Rockland State Hospital. Girls would come away from the psychiatric board and break down and cry. We knew what that meant: Rockland State. Siberia. They locked you up with nuts and threw away the key. It was a death sentence. They kept people at Rockland for years at a time. I'd have done anything to avoid being sent to Rockland.

I started calling Dr. Coro by his first name, but in his office only. And in the dayroom I used to check and see if he was looking at me from the nurses' station and then I'd parade in front of him, wiggling my ass, holding my head proud and my chest out —then suddenly turn my head to catch his stare. I'd sit in his office, hitch up my skirt, and cross my legs and uncross them while he looked at me with fascination and desire. I'd look at him across his desk and throw him a languid, sexy look and watch him melt. I had him completely in my power.

I told Benny that I loved him. "I want to be with you—alone. I want you, Benny. Take me away." We exchanged torrid kisses behind the closed door of his office. "I want more than this, Benny. I want *you.* I don't want to be always scared that someone might walk in on us. I want to meet you outside."

He told me the board was thinking of sending me to Rockland. He alone was speaking up for me; he'd do everything to help. When I got discharged—*if* I got discharged—I should try to learn a trade, find a job, continue with therapy. I must let the board know this. He promised to give me his number so that I could call him if I needed help once I was home.

A few weeks after I got there they transferred a new nurse to our floor. She was Dawn, a night nurse, five feet six, built as solid as a brick shithouse and fascinatingly beautiful. Her skin was the color of coffee beans polished to a high gloss. She had the darkest eyes I'd ever seen, and long, jet black hair. I felt the sexual attraction immediately. I wanted her. I wanted to make love to her. I wanted to take her in the way Harriet had taken me.

It didn't take much to make me realize that Dawn was attracted to me in return. When I made eyes at her she eyed me back. I smiled, she pouted her lips and curled the tip of her tongue over them. I could feel her eyes on me as I walked through the dayroom—and for her I assumed the strong, masculine gait of a butch.

She followed me into my room when there was no one else there, and we exchanged passionate kisses and furtive embraces. She helped me shower in the evenings, devotedly stroking my wet body and playfully pinching my buttocks. I stayed awake deliberately so that I could get up when all were asleep to go to the bathroom. Left, right, purposeful, strong, and masculine, I walked across the floor, my shoulders square, my hips decisive, my head thrust forward like a bull's.

Dawn calls down from her glassed-in station in a stage whisper, something between an intimate secret and a song of desire: "You! Get back to bed."

I look up, shut one eye in a mocking tease, and smile: "Come with me!"

She shakes her head, sadly: "You crazy or something?"

We both laugh. Mental patient and nurse, we're both crazy for the same thing.

During the day I dressed feminine, let my hair down, walked softly, smiled furtively, teased Dr. Coro. When evening came and I knew Benny was no longer around, I brushed my hair back, firmed my posture, hardened my smile, and became a butch for Dawn.

"You be sure and write a good evaluation about me, Dawn."

"You be sure and behave proper, Bobby." She called me by the name I'd gone under when I first started experimenting with lesbian sex. Behind the door to hug and kiss; into the shower to stroke and pinch. "Be sure and write a good report about me, and then when I get out. . . ."

Dawn brought me candy bars when she came on duty; Dr. Coro coached me for my appearance in front of the board. I let each know how eager I was to get out, how eager I was to do more than just kiss and hug.

My parents came to visit Sundays. "You should have been here on a weekday, Mommy. There's this doctor, Benny, he's Italian but he doesn't look it—he has blue eyes. He's crazy about me. He's really fallen in love with me. He's helping me a lot."

"That's good, Cookie. It's nice to know a doctor is interested in you and is helping you to get well. Do you have many friends?"

"There's Dawn, a night nurse. She's colored, but she's the most beautiful woman I've ever seen. And she's crazy about me too."

"That's nice, dear. It's good to know you're being helped."

I went before the board. Benny was there, trying not to smile at me. I gave all the right answers to their questions. I assured them I was cheerful, energetic, eager. No more drugs for me. A job, a career, regular therapy, good food, and plenty of sleep. I'd stay away from bad influences, seek out new friendships, mix socially. They had me wait outside and then I was called back and told I could go home. I smiled. Benny caught my smile and responded with his own.

I'd already exchanged phone numbers with Dawn. Now I gave Benny my number and promised I'd call as soon as possible. I called my mother at work and asked her to pick me up. Free again!

My parents didn't seem as happy as I expected when my father drove over to Grasslands that evening to bring me home. On the drive down the Saw Mill River Parkway I discovered why: Their apartment had been broken into that day while they were at work and everything of value had disappeared. Everything: My mother's fur coat, her jewelry which she used to hide in a pink leather purse stuffed into the bottom of a plastic garment bag in the closet, the money that my father kept hidden between his laundered shirts in a dresser drawer, appliances, a camera, suits. . . . The place was in a shambles when I got home.

I knew immediately that Harriet had something to do with it. Only she knew where my parents hid their valuables; I'd shown her once in a moment of foolishness. I was in tears. I felt betrayed. Addicts had to steal, I knew that, but why did she have to steal from *my* mother? Addicts weren't above robbing each other, even their closest friends when they needed money badly to get straight, but my mother had been so good to Harriet. It just wasn't right. And Franco? An icy lump in my stomach told me that Franco had something to do with it, too.

"I know those addicts," I told my parents. "I know where they sell their loot. I can get it back." I didn't tell them I suspected Harriet. I could hardly face the knowledge myself.

There wasn't much time to lose if I wanted to get anything back. My parents didn't want to let me go but I begged them to trust me. They could see I was too worked up about the robbery to think of anything else—even drugs.

I had my father drop me off at 100th Street and Lexington and asked him to wait in his car. I walked from junkie to junkie. "Have you seen Franco? Have you seen Harriet?"

"Franco? Harriet? Yeah, sure! They just pulled a score. Seen them around somewhere."

"If you see them before I do, tell them to stop selling the stuff. Tell them they better not sell it. Tell them I told you."

I walked from 100th Street up to 116th through the hot August night. I ran rather than walked, stopping when I saw someone I knew, asking after Harriet and Franco, repeating my warning.

I saw Franco on 116th Street. I recognized him from half a block away. He was carrying something. It was my mother's coat. "Give me that, you motherfucker!" I yelled when I got closer. "Give me that coat you fucking no-good bastard!" I tried to tug at it. I wanted to beat him. I was almost blind with rage.

Franco acted as if he didn't know what I was angry about. He steered me into a doorway and tried to calm me.

"That's my mother's fur coat you stole, you dirty rotten bastard!" I told him.

He was hurt. "I didn't know that was your mother's, Cookie, honest! Harriet took me there. I didn't know it was your place.

You know I wouldn't have robbed the place if I'd have known it was yours."

It was true that he'd never seen the inside of my home. Perhaps he really didn't know. It was difficult to believe that he hadn't guessed, that he hadn't suspected. He *must* have known, but I realized he couldn't have been sure and so he had no reason to let it trouble his conscience. Addicts need money; they have to take it where they can.

Franco gave me the coat; that was all he had, he hadn't sold anything else. He promised he'd hunt for Harriet and that he'd try to find the people she'd sold stuff to and get it back. He was really sorry, I could tell. I decided to believe his story. I wanted to believe it.

I went back to my father's car with the coat and we drove home in silence. I felt terribly guilty about the stuff my friends had stolen, it was my fault, my responsibility. But I was glad about the coat. I'd gotten it back from Franco. One thing at least. And Franco wasn't guilty; it was all Harriet's fault.

Dawn called me the next morning after she'd finished her shift. I asked her to come over as soon as she could and gave her directions. While waiting I showered, arranged my hair in butch style, and got dressed in shirt and pants.

She didn't seem quite the same Dawn when she arrived. She was somehow less enticing. Just someone else who wanted to have sex with me. She was available now, she wasn't hard to get, there was no longer any need to be furtive. It was too easy. We talked a while over Scotch and ginger ale, irrelevant talk that made me impatient and had Dawn panting breathlessly. I took her hand at last and guided her into my bedroom.

My first black woman. The first real woman that I was going to take as a woman. I guided her to the bed and had her lie down. I kissed her full lips and gently started unfastening her clothes. She wanted to help me take her clothes off; I stayed her hands. She wanted to strip me; I wouldn't let her. "No, baby. Today is *your* day. Your pleasure is my pleasure, that's all I want. Today you let *me* do it. I've been waiting for you for so long; you can't stop me now."

My left hand came to rest between her thighs. My fingers

curled. She was heaving rhythmically with her entire body and with each twist her crack opened wider and wider. My fingers slid in easily, two right inside, three playing along the sensitive tissues at the top and bottom end of her slit. I buried my face in the comforting fullness of her great bosom.

"Bobby! Bobby! What you doing to me!"

I was powerful with her and masterly. Masculine and determined. I roamed over the softness of her belly, stuck my tongue into her navel, slid my face down, pulled her thighs up and apart, and went down on her crack.

Her thighs closed around my head and squeezed. I was buried between her muscled thighs, squashed, secure. But squeeze as she would, push as she might, *I* was in control, *I* was calling the tune. I licked her and she sighed, bit her and she moaned, pinched her and she yelped with delight. My hands moved down together, outlining her buttocks, firming her thighs around my head, moving up on the outside of her thighs, over her hips, on top of her belly, then up to her breasts. I rolled her breasts in circles, I caught her firm nipples and squeezed. She moaned and writhed and closed her thighs even more firmly around my head and neck.

My tongue was inside her, licking, licking. I was drinking her in, all her womanliness, all her strength and softness, all her love and blackness. "Bobby!" she sighed. "Bobby! What you doing to me, baby! What you doing! Ooooh! Ooooh!" Her body thrashed, she threw herself around on the bed pulling me with her. And she came in a wild climax, a climax that put to shame those I used to simulate with Harriet.

She stayed with me all day. We made love in my bedroom and in the bathroom. I did for her everything that Harriet had ever done for me—except beat her. At five, I finally eased her out of the door with lots of promises and kisses, telling her I had to pick up Mitchell from the bus.

When she was gone I called Benny. Then I showered, sprayed perfume, brushed my hair into an alluring feminine style, applied makeup, and put on a sexy dress. I was ready for Benny when my mother came home.

"I won't be staying for dinner tonight, Mommy," I told her.

"Remember that doctor at Grasslands, the one who was so interested in me? He called just a while ago and asked me to meet him. I'll be having dinner with him."

My mother was really happy. Obviously I was well again if a doctor, a psychiatrist yet, would want to date me the day after I came out of the hospital. And I'd be mixing with better company now, none of those thieves and junkies who'd led me into so much trouble.

Benny lived in a walk-up building in Greenwich Village. The apartment was rather bare, as if he'd only just moved in. He kissed me in greeting, then poured out some red wine and had me sit down on the couch. He put his arms around me and kissed me. He started undressing me, my blouse, my bra, kissing my shoulders and breasts. Then he undid my skirt and pulled down my panties and had me lie on the sofa with my knees up and my thighs spread. He fingered my cunt for a moment, then he was on top of me and in me. Missionary position. He knew what to do without being very inventive, but he kept up his erection for a long, long time. He fucked and fucked, steadily, unwaveringly, driving his cock in and out with the same steady motion. I faked a couple of orgasms and then he had an orgasm himself, ejaculated and rolled off me.

After we'd finished screwing we went down to an Italian restaurant to eat; Benny knew I was crazy about Italian food. Then we went back up to his apartment and screwed again on the sofa. He was quite a nice person but not exactly great as a lover. I went home to sleep.

I told my mother next morning that I needed some money to go to an employment agency and look for work—and I went straight to the block to meet Franco and turn on.

The block was my life. I'd sworn off that life after my suicide attempt and during the long weeks in Grasslands, but the night I came out of Grasslands and went to look for the stuff Harriet had stolen—when I met Franco and spoke to all the other junkies, when I went back on the block—I found the old feelings coming back. It was my life, there was no getting away from it. I belonged to the block.

I could have got somewhere with Benny, a doctor, a bachelor,

Italian, handsome. He wanted me. I could have made it with him. I could have gone to see him every evening and spent week-ends with him, having sex on the sofa, going out for dinner . . . but it wasn't for me. It was a pointless life, square and dull and unexciting. Who wanted a man who'd let a patient twist him around her little finger? And Dawn's world was just as dull in its own way. I had achieved what I'd set out to achieve. I'd gotten out of the hospital. I'd mastered both the doctor and the nurse, I'd screwed them both. I had power any way I wanted to swing, as a fem, as a butch, or as a woman. I could do anything. I didn't need them anymore.

I was back with Franco, back on the block.

We were walking down 100th Street together when we ran into Harriet. She saw us, hesitated, and started to turn away. I headed her off. My fists flew up and I started landing punches on her face. I screamed at her in my rage. "How could you do a thing like that to my mother, you motherfucker!"

She tried to dodge me. "Honest, Cookie, I had nothing to do with it. It wasn't me." She had her arms up in front of her face to protect herself.

I could have taken it if she'd admitted it. If she'd told me how desperate she'd been I could have understood. But I couldn't take her brazen lying. I punched her and kept on punching hard, the way Eddie had taught me when I first joined his gang.

The dope fiends came running, first to watch, then to try and stop me. "Hey man, cool it!" someone shouted. "You'll draw a tip." I knew what they meant. The police left the block pretty much alone so long as there was only pushing and dealing and shooting up. But when there was a fight or someone created a scene they had to show they were still in charge and then they'd make things tough for everyone. I allowed Franco and a few of our friends to pull me away and I stood there, facing a frightened and bruised Harriet.

"I hate you, you motherfucker! I don't want to ever see you again. Forget my number. If you ever call my home again I'll tell my mother it was you that robbed her and she'll have you ar-rested."

That was the last I saw of Harriet. She disappeared from the block. She never called me again. None of the loot except for the coat was ever recovered. It wasn't insured and my parents were very cut up about it.

Dawn called me a few times. I was nice to her but I kept putting her off and eventually she stopped calling me.

Benny called me often. At first I made excuses. He kept pressuring me to see him again and after a while I stopped talking to him. When he called I disguised my voice and told him he had the wrong number; the phone rang again immediately and I wouldn't pick it up. He kept calling my mother, though, telling her that he cared for me and felt responsible and just wanted to know how I was getting on. Fucking liar! He was only after a piece of tail. He was just like every other man. Teacher, doctor, they were all alike. I had more sense than to expect a doctor to help me after all this. I was on my own. There was no one to count on except myself.

☼ CHAPTER SIXTEEN ☼

I was back in my old routine: prepare Mitchell's breakfast and see him off on the bus; hitch a ride down the Henry Hudson Parkway and take a bus along Ninety-sixth Street to meet Franco on the block; make a connection, take off, nod, hang around the block; perhaps go home with Franco to Brooklyn and make love; home at five to pick up Mitchell, play with him a while, put him to bed; nod in front of the television or go downtown to meet Franco again. Everything was the same as before except that I no longer saw Harriet.

Franco was my man, now, my lover. I trusted him—but I kept testing his love. "Tell me more about the girls you've known, Franco. Were they turning tricks for you? Did *she* turn tricks? Did you tell *her* you loved her? You wouldn't make *me* turn tricks, would you? Harriet never once let me turn a trick; she took care of me. *You* wouldn't let me turn a trick? Harriet never allowed me to touch a man, *any* man."

Was I only testing him, or did I want something else, too? Evil had a fascination for me; I wanted to experience everything. I wanted to be able to say there was nothing I hadn't done. Prostitution was one thing I wouldn't do—was I trying to get Franco to turn me into a prostitute, anyway? Did I want to manipulate Franco into taking the responsibility for getting me into something I had the desire—but not the guts—to get into myself?

I was testing Franco. I knew he wanted the money badly. We

were always worried about where to find the money we needed for drugs. He was doing burglaries and muggings but the money never lasted. One day he might turn to me and say, "What the hell, it's not such a big deal, the money is easy. Turn a couple of tricks and we can cop enough for tomorrow." I would have done it, I know, but I would have been terribly disappointed in Franco for letting me do it. He wouldn't, though; I knew he wouldn't. "No, Cookie, I'll never let you hustle for me," he always said. And since I knew he wouldn't, I kept provoking him with the suggestion until it was firmly implanted in his mind.

One evening, about a month after I came out of Grasslands, we were on Broadway near Ninety-sixth Street. We'd gone there to cop from a new connection. We were high now, just hanging around. A man approached me and smiled. Franco pulled me away. "A trick," he said with disgust.

I was excited. "I'd like to try it, Franco, let me try. Let me try it just for once and let's see if I can make some quick money."

Franco didn't spend much time thinking it over. "Try it if you want to," he said. "Ask for twenty dollars. Don't take any less. And make sure he pays you before you take off your clothes." It was all so matter-of-fact.

I strolled down the street, very casually, pretending I was looking in the shop windows. Franco followed a few steps behind. Another man stopped, tall, thin, kind looking, dressed like a business executive. He smiled at me. I smiled back. He walked up to me and said "Hi!"

I said "Hello."

"I have a place around the corner."

"I get twenty dollars." I wanted to apologize for the price. I knew most of the girls on Broadway were getting only ten or fifteen. I wanted to ask him if he was sure he could pay. It didn't seem quite right; sex was something I felt I should be able to give away, no one had ever paid me for it.

He agreed to the price without batting an eyelid. He beckoned and I walked at his side, across Broadway, down one of the cross streets toward Riverside Drive. Franco followed close behind to make sure the man didn't play any tricks. I had opening-night flutters in the pit of my stomach.

The man had a nice apartment in an elevator building. It looked too large for just one man; I wondered whether he was married and where his wife was.

"Drink?" he asked.

"I'll have a soda."

I finished the drink and he led me into the bedroom.

"The money," I said, holding out my hand. I tried to sound hard but I knew that if he said, "I'll pay you later," I couldn't have put up an argument.

He gave me the money, two ten-dollar bills, and I put it in my pocketbook. Wow! That was easy. I could have got out then and there. I was disgusted with myself for finally becoming a whore. But I couldn't have walked out without giving him what he'd paid for; that would have been dishonest.

He took off his clothes and shoes, keeping on only his shorts and socks. He put his arms around me to kiss. I pushed him away, gently. Kissing and petting weren't part of the deal. I could let him fuck me so long as he kept it impersonal, but I couldn't take any of the personal closeness he was pretending.

I took off my blouse and my pants and watched his cock go hard under his shorts. I took off my bra and panties and lay down on the bed. He lay down at my side. His shorts were off. I grabbed his penis and started to guide him on top of me. He was gentle. He kept his weight off my body on his elbows and he fucked with easy movements. He seemed to be putting some feeling into it. He let me know he saw me there as a person; I wasn't just a hole he was paying twenty dollars to jerk off into. I stroked his back, his buttocks, and his balls. I squeezed my legs around him. He was enjoying me as a person and I shared some of his pleasure in enjoying me. He came with a happy grunt. I was glad it was over. He'd gotten his money's worth and I felt proud.

"You're very good in bed," he told me when I sat up.

"Thank you."

"I really enjoyed it. I'd like to know where I can reach you again."

"I don't have a place."

"I'll give you my number and you can call me." So he didn't have a wife around. Perhaps she'd walked out on him. I took the slip of paper with his number and put it in my pocketbook. I didn't want to throw it away while he watched.

His come was getting cold inside me and dripping. I felt dirty and asked to use the bathroom; he gave me a fresh towel and I took my purse with me. I washed myself out thoroughly. Then I dressed and wished him good-bye.

The whole thing had taken about forty minutes. Franco was waiting for me down on the street. "I got it!" I told him. "It was easy. Twenty dollars!" I was as excited as I'd been the first time I'd copped Dilaudid. God, that was easy! I could do that any time.

Franco wasn't at all thrilled. "What took you so long?" He was angry at me. Or perhaps he was hurt and jealous.

"I didn't take long at all. I came down as soon as I finished washing. I couldn't have been any quicker."

"You were far too long. All you have to do is go up with them, take care of business, and get out. Don't let yourself get involved with your tricks."

We copped some more dope, then I caught the subway home to Yonkers.

Next morning I was back on the block. I felt as if I'd earned a postgraduate diploma. I could turn tricks now if I wanted to. I was one of the gang—but better. The other girls on the block were cheap whores, worn and tired and sick. They took ten dollars a trick, even seven or five if they couldn't get more. I was better than they were; I would never take less than twenty.

The regulars in the neighborhood—the pimps and hoods and shopkeepers—had been eyeing me for a long time. I don't know how many hundreds of propositions I'd turned down. They were all waiting for me to make the change; they were all waiting for me to turn pro so that they could get something out of me. I walked over to a gas station near 102nd Street. The manager had been watching me for a long time. I'd always avoided him but I thought he was quite a nice person. This time I went right into the gas station and started a conversation. It was a clear enough signal.

He cocked his head and said "How much?"

"Twenty dollars." The other girls were giving it away for half or a quarter of that, but I was fresh.

He didn't argue. "Okay."

We went into the storeroom in the back of the station. There were auto parts and tires on the walls, mufflers and radiators on the floor. I took his money. He pulled down his pants, I pulled down mine, and we had a quick fuck on the floor. Then he buttoned up, dusted off, and went back to work.

The gas station manager was good for twenty bucks every two or three days. It meant I didn't have to keep bugging Franco for money for drugs. The girls on the block started giving me professional tips: Always take the money first; don't talk money with anyone who looks like a cop—let *him* make the offer; charge extra for everything you can—to go down on him, to let him go down on you, to wear or do anything fancy for him, to let him go a second time; keep fucking while you're menstruating—why waste the time? A sanitary sponge from the drugstore shoved up your vagina will hold back the flow and if you hide the string in your ass he'll be none the wiser.

When I was on the block I fucked only with the gas station man. Others wanted to, but I wouldn't have them; they could go with the five-dollar whores. But there obviously wasn't enough money for me at 100th Street. Franco and I went back to Broadway and Ninety-sixth where the real money was. I turned two or three tricks a night there, but it wasn't easy.

"We have to get a hotel," Franco said. "That's the only way to make it up here."

I told my mother I was going to live with Franco. "Look after Mitchell, Mom. I'll come up to see him whenever I can."

"Do you have a place?"

"Sure, Mom. Don't worry."

"Where can I get in touch with you?"

"I'll call you. I'll try and call you every couple of days." My parents had been taking care of Mitchell more and more, especially after my suicide attempt. Mitchell seemed happy with them; he called my father his daddy. He was closer to them than to me.

"Give your mommy a kiss, Mitchell. Be nice to Daddy and Grandma." I packed a case with a few clothes and took the subway down to Ninety-sixth Street. Franco had taken a room near there in a hotel, right in the center of the best traffic. The hotel was filled with addicts and prostitutes. We had a kitchenette of our own, but we did no cooking.

We slept during the day. At five I got up, took off, nodded a bit, then got dressed. I had to look glamorous, like a film star. I modeled myself on May Britt: long blond hair with bangs, false eyelashes, lots of makeup, slinky dress, high heels. My beat was from Ninety-sixth to Ninety-second, down one side of Broadway and up the other, walking casually, pretending to be window shopping, my eyes darting to every man. I'd stand looking into a window, watch the reflections of men coming to stand next to me.

Franco was always within winking distance when I made contact with a trick. I'd look to him to check; if I didn't get Franco's approval I'd tell the man indignantly that I wasn't that type of girl. Franco could tell a cop a mile off and he knew intuitively if the trick was genuine or whether he'd give me a rough time. Soon enough I began to learn to distinguish good tricks by myself. Blacks were out; Franco said they were probably hustling themselves and they'd never pay me. He also disapproved of very young people. "They take too much out of you," he insisted, but I felt he was worried they might give me too much. He was jealous of my tricks—and I was glad he was.

"How much?" The men were usually very blunt. Few tried to make casual conversation first.

"Twenty dollars." Firm price. No argument. If they so much as started arguing I'd walk away; I didn't need any hassles. I knew I was good, clean, smart, glamorous, and sexy. I could charge more than the others. I had no problem finding a trick; it seldom took me more than ten or fifteen minutes from the moment I hit the street.

If he agreed to the price, I told him the name of the hotel and the room number. "Wait outside the room; I'll come right up." It doesn't do to be seen walking with a trick; it gives the cops something to pin on you if you're caught.

Franco followed close behind when we went up to the hotel,

and waited in the lobby. I turned straight tricks only, straight fucks. Give me your twenty dollars. Take off your own clothes and I'll take off mine. Get between my legs and fuck. God, how I despised those men!

Many wanted me to go down on them. I refused. If they wanted to go down on me I let them, and charged them the full twenty dollars. If they went down on me I wouldn't let them fuck me, too—that was five dollars extra, ten if I could get it. A second screw was also another ten. It disgusted me that a man could go down on someone he didn't know, someone he'd picked off the street, that he could eat her pussy that might be dirty or diseased, then go home and bring it to his wife or sweetheart. I took care to wash each time before I'd let someone go down and eat me, but they never would have insisted on it. Then I'd see them to the door, wash myself thoroughly, douche, wash myself again, put on makeup, powder, and perfume, get dressed, and go down on the street again, pausing to give Franco the money. I could turn one trick per hour without difficulty, but Franco still thought I was taking too long.

Our habits were costing us fifty to sixty dollars a day. All our money went for drugs. We had just one meal a day, in a luncheonette. Every two weeks or so, when the hotel manager started pressing, we sneaked out without paying the bill and moved into a new hotel. Sometimes I had to leave my clothes behind; that meant going out and boosting new clothes. I kept all my good clothes at home in Yonkers and went up once a week for a change of clothes and a clean, hot bath. I looked forward to seeing Mom, Dad, and Mitchell—my parents were taking full care of Mitchell now and either my mom or my dad was always home in the late afternoon to meet the bus from his school.

Gradually Franco and I ran out of hotels in that neighborhood. It had been quite a good place, busy but not too crowded, solidly middle class: young executive types, lots of sad singles, some elderly Jewish refugees, an art movie house, coffee shops, restaurants, a friendly crowd of prostitutes, and a good, quiet crowd of men who wanted to get laid and were willing to pay for it.

Eventually we had to move down to Seventy-second Street.

We got a three-room apartment in a residential hotel near Columbus Avenue. It was a much more commercial neighborhood, crowded with specialty stores, hotels, restaurants, prostitutes and addicts, and an international clientele. Seventy-second and Broadway was the local center of the drug trade, two blocks south was Sherman Square, a tiny triangle of grass and asphalt where Broadway and Amsterdam intersected, known more familiarly as Needle Park to the addicts who hung out there night and day. Every block had its specialty. South of Seventy-second Street, by the Embassy and Alamac hotels, stood the girls in fur coats and teased hair who operated in pairs and were driven off to do parties. North of Seventy-second on Amsterdam were the gay boys and lesbians. Black girls worked the side streets. Broadway was open to all.

Our rent was astronomical. The previous tenants of the apartment had left us their dog, a neatly trimmed black poodle I called Gigi. I bought her a rhinestone collar, fed her expensive foods, had her shampooed and trimmed regularly. I walked her on a leash when I was working; it gave me class and confidence: With a smart dog in tow I could ask for twenty-five and even thirty dollars for a straight fuck. It wasn't easy for anyone else to get that sort of money in this neighborhood.

We had to make at least a hundred dollars a day for rent, for drugs, for the dog, and for what little food we bought for ourselves. My beat was Broadway from Seventy-second to Seventy-sixth and along Seventy-second as far as Columbus. If I didn't make the daily quota I'd have to work my ass off the next day. When bills were due and I was desperate, I'd have to lower my price late at night and go with men I wouldn't have looked at ordinarily. Unfortunately it was the cheapjacks, the ten-dollar tricks, who always made the biggest demands, who wanted to draw out the fucking and wouldn't stop when they'd come, who wanted to rest and go again.

I didn't mix with the ordinary run of prostitutes in the neighborhood; I felt too superior. If a girl started walking up to a guy I was heading for, I never made an issue of it. She needed the money; I could always find another trick. I was pretty enough and sexy enough, I didn't have to quarrel over a trick.

I gradually built up a clientele of johns whom I'd met as tricks on the street. They'd taken my number or given me theirs and I had them listed in a little book. The phone would ring for me; a john asking if he could come over to fuck. Or, when I had free time, I might go through my book, call up a few johns, and arrange to go over and see one. I was good to the steadies. I didn't charge extra for house calls. I gave them more time than I gave to casual tricks. They liked me, I liked some of them, and I had to turn down quite a few offers from men who wanted me to move in with them. Most men, I discovered, have a strange missionary quirk. "You shouldn't be doing this," they'd say with two fingers up my cunt. "You're too good, you should give it up. A girl like you shouldn't be throwing herself away," they'd whisper as they shoved their cocks all the way up. "I'd like to help you make a new start in life." They'd come, get dressed, say good-bye and ask, "When can I see you again? And would you like to turn a trick with a friend of mine?" Ah well, their intentions were good.

My favorite john was Sam. He lived in a residential hotel on Broadway, the building with probably the largest number of illicit fornications per square foot per hour of any building in the United States. Sam was like a character out of Damon Runyon. He was a Russian Jew, about sixty-five, bushy white hair, bushy eyebrows, huge pot belly, and he smoked cigars. He spoke with a thick accent in a husky voice and reminded me of my grandfather, Murray. I really liked him. He was too old to fuck—in fact he couldn't get an erection—but I would give him a hand job and let him kiss me, and after a while he'd ejaculate a few drops of thin fluid. I charged him only ten dollars because I liked him, and soon enough we became really close friends. I sometimes spent a few hours just chatting with him in his room. When I had a lot of money I'd even go up and take care of him for free and when I was hard up I knew I could always rely on him to lend me some money to help out. Sometimes he paid me just to come up and talk and joke. He was a widower and didn't have too many kind words about his late wife "the bitch."

Franco was mad at me for spending so much time with Sammy. I tried to explain that I needed Sammy's friendship, that he was kind to me in a special way, but Franco didn't see it that way: "Don't get close with your tricks. You're a lousy businesswoman, Cookie, you shouldn't be in business."

Sometimes I spent the whole night up in Sammy's room instead of working the street. Sammy liked to fuss over me. "What's a nice Jewish girl like you doing in a business like this? A *schickse* I can understand; a *schwartze* I can understand. But you? Nu? Have you eaten? You look so thin anyone would think you hadn't eaten since Yom Kippur." Then he'd call down to room service and have them send up a steak, some soup, a good salad. "Sammy, thanks a lot, really, but you know I love Italian food. Can't you send down for some spaghetti or rice or something with meat sauce and spices?"

"Listen, young lady: You come up here, and you eat. You eat proper. None of that Italian stuff that just fills you up and makes you fat but doesn't give you any strength. You think I don't know what's good for you. I know. When you're here with me, you eat.

Sammy didn't like me to work on the street. "You're out there, you don't know who you meet. God forbid you should pick up a crook, a murderer, someone who's crazy in the head, someone with a disease, God knows. And all the time out in the cold weather and late at night. You don't want to stop—all right, who's forcing you—but at least stop working on the street. I have friends, I have connections, I'm friends with the barman, perhaps I can work something out for you."

He was as good as his word. I got taken on by the bar at Sam's hotel as a regular bar girl. I came in early in the evening, sat at the bar, and let men pick me up. Everyone knew this was a place to pick up girls. I'd let them buy me a drink, make them tip the bartender and take me upstairs. The rate for a trick was twenty-five dollars: fifteen for me, ten split between the bartender (who took care of the cops and the management) and the elevator boy (who arranged for an empty room we could use free of charge). I could see my regular johns before I started work and get in another five or six tricks a night easily. But I only did it for a week or two; it was too much like a nine-to-five job. I wanted my freedom. If I'd wanted to work regularly I could have gone across to another hotel on the other side of Broadway, a regular rabbit warren of single-occupancy rooms and horny men; I had so many regular johns there, I could have spent my whole day going from room to room.

In March of 1963 we had to give up our apartment. The previous tenants had returned to claim it. It didn't bother me too much; one place was as good as another to live. What cut me up was the poodle, Gigi. I'd become attached to Gigi. I'd come to see Gigi as mine, she was part of the image I was trying to project on Seventy-second Street. I told them I didn't want to give her up. I became hysterical. I tried to tell them how much the poodle meant to me. I told them about Major and Buttons. I offered to buy the dog. It didn't help. They took Gigi away from me. Franco promised to buy me another dog but I told him I didn't want it. I couldn't go through the same sort of loss a fourth time.

We moved out of the residential hotel and went to live with another couple on Eighty-second Street in a large apartment in a converted townhouse. The other people were big dealers. They were Cubans, the man's name was Jose.

☼ CHAPTER SEVENTEEN ☼

Franco was supposed to be a runner for Jose's operation; Franco did the actual pushing and I carried the drugs for him in the left cup of my bra. We took all the proper precautions: We never walked together while I was carrying and we only sold to people we knew. Since we didn't know the people on Broadway too well, that meant going back to the block, to 100th Street and Lexington Avenue. I'd sit in a luncheonette by the window and watch Franco as he made the arrangements with a customer. Franco would close the deal, point to the customer, and hold up a number of fingers. That was the signal for me to reach unobtrusively into my bra and pull out the designated number of packages. They'd be in my hand when the customer entered the luncheonette. He'd sit down next to me and we'd shake hands—or he'd simply brush past me—and when we pulled apart my hand was empty and his fingers were closed over his purchase.

We slept days and worked evenings. Every two hours I'd take a break from work, go into the john, and shoot up; my works were kept handy in my right cup, wrapped in a handkerchief. It was a good thing I'm pretty flat-chested.

The deal with Jose wasn't too profitable. We were using too much of the dope instead of selling it. Jose wanted his money every evening. We were desperate. I had to make money to cover our losses from our business fiasco and so I went back to turning tricks, not on the street but with my regular johns. In a pinch, when we were really desperate, I could always go up to Sammy at his hotel and score a ten or twenty off him.

One evening I felt sick. Jose and his woman were out. I couldn't go to work—not to carry, not to turn tricks. Franco went out by himself but left me a few bags to shoot up. I felt sick, the junkie's sick, the sick of when you've been too long on dope. It seemed strange. I shot up but I didn't get straight. I shot up again but I couldn't get straight. I kept shooting more and more. I couldn't bear the feeling of being sick. I had cramps and felt feverish and then I started throwing up. I lost control of my bowels and was soiling myself. I was sweating everywhere, my eyes were streaming, my nose was running, I was exuding fluids from every opening in my body.

Franco came home. He saw me writhing in pain. He didn't know what to do. I vomited all over him, I got diarrhea on him. "I think I'm dying, Franco," I told him weakly. He hit me with dope to try and get me straight and I threw up again. He put me into a warm bath and I passed out. He hit me again while I was passed out.

I woke up two days later in Metropolitan Hospital with tubes in my arms and legs. I felt small, terribly small, shriveled, an old woman, buried among the sheets. I wasn't sure whether I was alive or dead. I'd watched Joe Gandolfo, my mother's friend, dying of cancer, wasting away. That was me, now.

My mother hovered over my bed. It had all happened before. Was it a dream or was I dreaming it was a dream? Her eyes were puffed up. She wouldn't look at me. She couldn't bear to see my shriveled, old woman's face. She tried to stay with me but had to run out of the room. It was, she told me later, like watching her own mother die a second time.

I had drug contamination, perhaps something in the dope we got from Jose, perhaps some sudden change in my own body chemistry that wouldn't tolerate the heroin. It had caused acute dehydration. My weight was down to around eighty pounds. They'd given me a spinal tap while they were trying to diagnose it. It gave me terrible headaches. They had to treat me simultaneously for dehydration, shock, and withdrawal. They maintained me on methadone.

After two weeks they let me go. Franco came to get me. I still had a blinding headache from the spinal tap. I was so weak I could hardly stumble. I knew I had to take off, it was the only thing that would make me feel better. Franco supported me, half dragging, half carrying me from the hospital at Ninety-ninth Street and First Avenue. He had to get me to the block. I couldn't quite make it. I got as far as Second Avenue, then Franco propped me in a doorway to go and score. He came back a short while later, hit me, and we took off. I felt stronger now. My headache had gone. I could walk. We got back to Jose's apartment at Eighty-second Street by bus and I went straight to bed.

Our partnership with Jose didn't last long. Jose moved away and we moved into a hotel off Broadway. I went back to my regular johns and walked Broadway looking for tricks.

In June we decided to clean up. Our habits were becoming really big again. We couldn't continue much longer at our current level. It was time to cut back. Franco had been to the federal drug facility at Lexington, Kentucky a number of times. It was a place familiar to every addict. "When I was at K-Y, man . . ." was the way half the conversations among junkies always started. I felt inadequate never to have been there; I had no stories to share. I wanted to go to K-Y to clean up so that I could come back able to say, "When I was at K-Y, man . . . why, that place was no place, man."

We went to the New York City Department of Health and asked to be sent to Lexington. There were no beds immediately; they had to make arrangements. Then a bed came up for Franco and he went. My turn came a week later.

I was staying at my mother's, spending more time with Mitchell, going down to Broadway evenings to take care of my johns and then over to the block to score. My parents were happy that I was cleaning up properly, under federal auspices this time. I had visions while I was staying home in my own apartment and in my own room of coming back from Lexington six months later, cured, clean, staying clean. I'd get a job; Franco would get a job. It seemed unreal, but somehow possible, the pot of gold at the other end of the rainbow. My parents bought me a beautiful outfit as a going away present. They wanted me to be smart when I got to Lexington, I should make a good impression on everyone. People always liked me and wanted to help me; a good impression never does any harm. I had a set of matching luggage. My going away dress was black, very low cut, with lots of white trimming.

Mommy and Daddy and Mitchell drove me to Penn Station to see me off. I felt good setting off for Lexington and a new adventure.

I had lots of dope with me. Every half hour or so I got up from my seat and went to the john. The dope was in my left cup, the works in my right, both easily accessible through my low-cut dress. I shot up and went back to my seat.

The next day I was in Lexington. I walked off the train very smart, very proud. I looked like a well-to-do career girl. People must have been wondering whether I worked in advertising or in television. A cabby approached me: "Hey lady! You want a lift to the hospital?" He knew his customers.

The hospital was an imposing place, a huge palatial building set on a slight rise, surrounded by vast fields. There was a guardhouse at the entrance to the facility where we stopped while they checked my papers. Then we drove up to the building itself. From up close it looked more like an institution; it had bars on all the windows like a jail. I panicked. My God, I thought. Why did I want to come here? The cabbie knew just where to take me and let me off at the door.

As I got out of the cab I heard a voice from far above: "Cookie! Cookie!"

It was Franco! I could just make out a figure, high up by a barred window, waving to me. I'd written to Franco, telling him which day I was coming and he'd stationed himself above the patients' entrance, waiting for me for however long it took.

They gave me the most thorough shakedown I've ever had. They searched my hair, my armpits, my nose, my ears, my ass, my cunt, between my toes. "If you have a tampon please take it out and place it in this receptacle. You will be given a new one." You'd have to be foolish to bring anything into a place like this. I'd known about the shakedown, of course, and I'd used my last bag of heroin on the train and flushed my works down the john.

They put me in the detoxification unit for two weeks. I was given methadone, tranquilizers, sleeping pills, and vitamins and spent most of my time in bed keeping very much to myself. I was waiting to get out of detoxification and into population, the department where the rehabilitation program was administered. There I'd be able to get in touch with Franco.

Once I was transferred to population I asked to be sent to the dentist where Franco worked each time he made K-Y. It gave us the chance to be together for a few minutes, to talk, touch, kiss, and to exchange the latest news about ourselves and the institution. I went to the dentist as often as possible. Franco had a great voice when he wasn't on drugs; he was part of the facility's entertainment troupe and frequently came over to sing for the women. I soon picked up finger language from the girls and then I could rap with Franco across the yard that separated the men's section from the women's.

I'd been used to better company at Grasslands and better conditions; I wasn't in the same league with these girls here. Only a small proportion of them were voluntary patients like me; the majority were serving time for a variety of federal offenses. I had good clothes and I wore them proudly, a new outfit every day to let them know I wasn't just another hick. My mother had given me thirty dollars for the commissary and sent me more regularly; I was able to indulge myself in candy and I could hire girls who were doing time to do my laundering and ironing.

I had few friends at first and felt I was being ostracized; then I realized it was largely my own fault for trying to act the dainty lady. To get on at K-Y you had to be one of the girls. I started to look at the girls in a new light: They were an exciting lot, a really impressive bunch. They came from New Mexico and California, from Florida and Chicago. I'd never thought there could be such a variety. And I'd never thought there was such a variety of crimes you could be sent up for. They made me feel like a rank beginner.

Most of the girls had tattoos. I thought that if I had a tattoo it might make me more like one of them. I went to the leading tattooist, Rosa, a huge fat woman from New Mexico. She was a walking showcase of her art: she had names, pictures, butterflies, and mottos tattooed all over her. I chose a name and for five dollars in commissary tickets she tattooed "Franco" in very small neat letters on my left shoulder, using a darning needle and mascara. Tattooing was strictly against the rules and I had to keep my shoulder covered up until the scabs fell off; if anyone questioned me later, I could pretend I'd had the tattoo when I came in.

As soon as she'd finished the tattoo, I signaled to Franco to let him know. "I g-o-t a t-a-t-t-o-o," I said in finger language. He questioned me with his hands. I pointed to my left shoulder and spelled out, "F-r-a-n-c-o." He seemed pleased.

When the scabs had healed, I cut the sleeves off all my dresses —even the fine new ones my mother had got me—to let everyone see that I, too, was tattooed. The next Sunday I went to chapel so that I could show Franco my tattoo. The men sat on one side of the church, the women on the other side. It was the strangest service. The worshipers were busy with their fingers, not crossing themselves but rapping to their guys on the other side of the aisle. No one paid any notice to the priest or rabbi or minister or whatever he was. No one seemed to know or care which service it was or in which God's honor we were supposed to be there. The officiating chaplain did his thing as if he weren't there. He may have sung, he may have given a sermon; no one paid him the slightest attention.

As I might have expected, there were a lot of butches in K-Y. I was turned on by all of them, but a tall black girl named Mae excited me so much that I had desires for no other. She was doing five years for forgery. Unfortunately she was housed on a different corridor and so we couldn't room together or get together at night, but we necked a lot. I tattooed her initial just above my left knee, a tiny M just like the letters Rosa had made.

Somehow, word of my adventures with Mae got to Franco. Next time we rapped across the windows he let me know with an angry play of fingers how he felt about it. I was scared. What would happen when he discovered the tattoo? I broke off with Mae immediately and I didn't do anything with any of the other butches, either, but still Franco would have nothing more to do with me; he wouldn't even come to the window although I kept sending messages over asking the men to tell Franco I was there.

I fell in with a crowd of girls whose sole interest was trying to get high. Anything would do. We even stole mace from the kitchen, ground it, and put it in our coffee; it gave a sort of a high, better than nothing. One day we got into the medical department and stole a bottle of alcohol. I drank half the bottle and got stoned, really wild. They found that a bottle was missing and accused me and I became violent, thrashing and kicking and screaming. One of the hacks tried to pin me and I lashed out at her. Then all the hacks overpowered me and hustled me off to the bing.

I spent two days in isolation, an empty cell with a tiny barred window at the top. They gave me only plain food and I wasn't allowed cigarettes. When I got out I was called before a matron for a stern lecture.

"You are not ready for Lexington, Mrs. Quinn, and Lexington is not ready for you. We must ask you to leave."

I remembered the last time it had happened, in Manhattan General. I put on my contrite act: "I'm sorry, I really am. I don't know what came over me. It won't happen again."

It didn't wash. I tried my frightened little girl act: "I'm afraid to leave. I don't know what to do. I came in with my old man, I can't leave without him. This is my first time here; I don't know the place, I don't know how to get home."

It was starting to work on the matron. She sent someone over to the men's section to find out if Franco wanted to leave. Word came back that he was willing; he'd meet me outside the entrance. A hack walked me back to my room to pick up my belongings, I cashed in my commissary tickets at the office and got the money they were keeping for me; a few minutes before six that evening I had my walking papers, my matching luggage, my money, and walked out with Franco. I'd spent just over a month at K-Y instead of the six I was supposed to stay.

Our money was enough to get us bus tickets back to New York. When we got there we put our suitcases into lockers at the bus terminal and took the subway straight up to 100th Street. I'd planned to stay clean after I came out of Lexington but now I was so mad at them for kicking us out and for making me have to explain all the hassles to my mother that I felt I didn't owe them anything. Fuck them! I deserved some dope. We got a nickel bag between us, copped works, and took off. It was good being back in the old groove. From 100th Street we went to a hotel on Broadway to spend the night. Just the two of us, no tricks. We undressed slowly.

And then Franco saw my tattoo, the tiny little M on my left knee.

"What's that?"

"It's for Mitchell. An M. I was practicing: I wanted to see if I could tattoo other girls and earn some commissary tickets."

He slapped me across the face. "You're a dirty liar! You and your lesbian girl friend!" Franco was special to me; this wasn't how we'd loved each other. I didn't want him to hit me. But he beat me up anyway, until I was black and blue and sobbing and the people in the room next door had to bang on the wall for silence.

We made love after that, and it was good.

My mother got the surprise of her life when she came home from work the next evening and saw us sitting in the kitchen, smoking and drinking coffee.

"We couldn't stay there, Mom. That was no place for me. It was a jail. They had bars on the windows. Most of the people there were crooks who were doing time. Most of the girls were dykes; the hacks were all brutal bitches. That was no place for me."

My mother saw my point. It obviously wasn't a place for her daughter.

We stayed home for two weeks. Almost every day we went down to the block; there wasn't really anything else to do. I thought maybe I'd get back with some of my old friends from Yonkers but they'd moved away. Bruce and Bobbi had split up: Bruce had moved away and Bobbi had disappeared. Leslie was away somewhere. "I see her mother every now and again," Mom told me when I asked. "I don't know where Leslie is. Last time I heard about her she was in jail, for forgery I think, or was she in the hospital? I know it was one or the other. That's where she seems to be most of the time."

Our friends were on 100th Street. We rapped with them, we shot up together—there wasn't much else to do. In the afternoons we went back to Yonkers: I'd meet Mitchell at the bus and then we'd sit around until my parents got back and we could go out again. Within three weeks we were back on our old habits, really shooting up a lot again. We had only enough money in the morning to go down to Broadway to cop and get straight. Then I'd call the johns from my little book and arrange to see two or three of them so that we could go to 100th Street and cop enough for the rest of the day. At night I was back on Broadway, turning tricks. The old pattern was repeating itself.

I told my mother that we wanted to go to Miami, away from familiar surroundings. Down there we could get clean and really stay clean this time. I had good memories of Miami: my grandfather, the beaches, the sun, the sea. And since we had no idea where we could get drugs in Miami, we'd have no choice but to stay clean.

My mother gave us the money for our bus tickets, and an extra two hundred dollars in spending money so that we wouldn't have any problems when we got to Miami. We copped enough dope before we left to last us through the ride to Miami. We shot up in the rest room of the bus every hour or so, and were high all the way down.

We would kick later, in Miami, under the warm sun.

☼ CHAPTER EIGHTEEN ☼

Franco started feeling sick almost the moment we got to Miami. We were staying in a motel off Collins Avenue, a miserable place in which to have to kick.

"Let's go down to the beach," he suggested. It was good kicking there with the sun beating down fiercely and the heat getting right through to our bones. I kept on my shirt and dungarees, knowing that I'd soon be feeling the cold chills that come with withdrawal. The sun was my friend; I could sleep in the sun.

When the sun went down we had to go back to our motel room, to spend the night in pain and in terror. Sometimes when my nerves would jump me I'd be so agonized I'd try to beat my head against the wall. I wanted to punch something, beat something, show my pain and anger by destroying something. And sometimes I just screamed.

I couldn't stand the pain in my legs. Franco was as sick as I was and my pain made him feel even worse. He tried to soothe me. He massaged my back but massage wasn't enough. "Tickle my back, Goddammit! Tickle my back!" I screamed at him. It was the one thing that calmed me down at night—that and hot baths. Franco ran the bath for me and helped me in; it soothed me and he added hot water when the water got chilly. He did everything he could to help me in my pain; and I did nothing for him in return. A few times I threw up all over him.

It went on for a week: sleeping on the beach during the day, going through our terrors at night, eating almost nothing. I'd put on a lot of weight from the food at Lexington but now I lost it all and became thin and emaciated.

Then the withdrawal stage ended and we got into the shucks. I got an insatiable craving for all kinds of food and put back everything I'd lost. For a while we enjoyed ourselves. We ate expensively and spent a lot of money in bars—Franco was a heavy drinker when he wasn't on dope. Our money was going.

"Why don't you go out and get a job?" I asked him.

"Why don't *you* go out and get a job?" he asked me.

When it was all gone we looked at each other with a sort of "Well, what do we do now?" expression. I know what *I* wanted: to get high. And Franco clearly wanted the same. But how? I certainly wasn't going to turn tricks in Miami and I didn't want him to pull any jobs, either.

That evening I called my mother collect. "Mom! I'm in trouble. The cops are after us. They found the track marks on our arms and they've pulled us in. They'll put us in jail as junkies if we don't clear out of Miami right away. Can you send us some money through Western Union for our fares?"

We wasted no time once we were back in New York. From the bus terminal we took a subway straight to the block and copped. Then we went home to Yonkers.

I soon realized my mistake. I didn't want to stay in Yonkers. I really did want to make a new start, go back to Miami again, get a job this time, and clean up definitely, permanently. If I had something to remind me of my responsibilities, something to give me a real motivation. . . .

"Mom, if we took Mitchell with us to Miami, the cops might believe that we're going straight. They'd see us as a respectable family. If we had Mitchell along they'd probably let us stay."

So the three of us went back to Miami a second time, determined to make good. We got a cheaper place, a little apartment in the Cuban section. Franco found a job as busboy in a hotel. I looked after Mitchell.

It was the first time in my life I was really able to devote myself to Mitchell. I wanted to make up for all we'd missed. I tried to become a real mother to my son.

I took him for walks around Miami. "See, this is the house where your mommy's Granddad used to live. This is where your mommy used to stay with your Granddad and Grandma when she was a little girl. Here is where she once won a beauty competition; the judges said your mommy was the prettiest girl in the whole hotel."

"Mommy, when are we going home?"

"We *are* home, Mitchell. Our home is in Miami now. We're going to stay here."

"When are we going home to Grandma and Daddy?" He always called my father Daddy.

"We're going to stay *here,* Mitchell. Miami is a nice place. It never gets cold here and we can go to the beach every day of the year if we want to."

"I want Grandma and Daddy."

"They'll come visiting us soon. As soon as we're settled down and Franco's saved some money and we have a bigger apartment, Grandma and Grandpa will come to visit us here in Miami. They'll come to visit often. They'll bring you lots of presents."

"But why can't we go home, Mommy?"

There was so much to make up for with Mitchell. I felt ashamed of myself for having neglected him for so long. Now I'd make it up to him—and to myself. We went to the beach every day and romped in the sea. I built sand castles with Mitchell. I helped him dig for shells. I let him bury me in the sand. I tried to teach him how to swim.

"Mommy, when are Daddy and Grandma coming?"

"Soon, Mitchell, soon. When the summer is over we'll find you a nursery school here and Mommy will get a job and then we'll get a new apartment and Grandma and Grandpa will come to visit. Come, let's go home now and get dinner ready for Franco."

Oh, I tried! God, how I tried! I became a real mother, a real housewife: I took good care of our little flat, I always had meals ready for Franco when he came home, I was a good mother to Mitchell. It was all just as it should have been. It was all going to turn out well—at last. I knew I could do it. I didn't need doctors, I didn't need hospitals. All I needed was to get away from the past, to be given a proper chance to make a go of things by myself. It was going to work this time. It was going to work out great.

Then I got a painful kidney infection and had to stay in bed and we had to call in a doctor to give me injections of antibiotics. A few days later Mitchell got sick. It started as a cold, then he got a very high fever and convulsions. We had to call in the doctor again. Franco stayed home to look after us.

The doctor and the drugstore had taken the last of our money. My mother wired us the money for our return trip and we told the landlord to keep our apartment, we'd be right back.

From the bus terminal in New York we went straight to Yonkers with Mitchell. We didn't go to 100th Street this time, we didn't shoot up.

We stayed in Yonkers only a few days to make sure Mitchell would be all right. Then we got more money from my mother, stopped off at 100th Street to cop dope for the journey, and the two of us took a bus down to Miami for the third time.

Franco found a job as cabana boy at the Sheraton. Nearby was the Hotel Corso where I'd stayed sometimes with my parents when I was little. I recognized some of the people from years back—managers, desk staff, waiters—but I didn't tell them who I was and they didn't recognize me as young Cookie who'd won the beauty competition there three years earlier. When I was young I had envied the elevator girls and their glamorous blue and white uniforms; now I became an elevator girl myself.

Up and down, up and down on the late shift. "Going up!" "What floor?" "Going down!" The door opens on the main floor and I see myself sitting on one of the benches, a little girl in a pleated dress, trying to look older and sophisticated. Poor little twelve-year-old Cookie! What can she know? Little Cookie gets up, sweeps up the curving staircase in a dramatic exit. Up to her parents' room? Up to bed, with cookies and milk? I see her coming down the stairs again now, her ball dress stuffed with paper napkins to give the impression of full breasts. She's eighteen, a mother, a wanton, her hips swing and her eyes flash, her head is held proud. Cookie wants the world to see her, she wants every man to desire her. She walks down the stairs a step at a time, a step at a time.

"Going up? *Para arriba?*" There are many Spanish-speaking guests at the hotel. My accent fools them; they take me for a Cuban refugee.

"Que piso, por favor?" I'm alone in the elevator with a short, moustachioed man in his forties, smartly dressed, pearl stickpin in his silver-on-white tie, he speaks no English. He gives me a long look on the ride up, takes out a wad of bills, and flashes them to me. Money! We need money! There are so many things I want to buy to make our apartment look pretty. And I want new clothes: Every day I am surrounded by beautiful women wearing beautiful clothes. I want new clothes. Cabana boys don't make much money, even with tips. Elevator operators don't make much money—unless they have a lucky break.

Money! He's spread out his greenbacks like a hand of cards. I select four tens and pull them out of his hand. He smiles and puts all the money back into his wad. I bring up my wrist and point to the twelve on my watch. I'll be off at midnight. He tears a scrap of paper off a flight schedule and writes down his room number for me.

He has the money ready for me when I knock on his door. I take off my blue bow tie, my white blouse, my blue skirt, and fold them neatly over a chair. I've stepped out of uniform; now I can be a hooker. I take off my bra and panties, flop on his big double bed, and spread my legs. Fifteen minutes and it's over. He gives me an extra ten dollars on the way out and tells me, with gestures and Spanish, that he wants to see me again.

It was so easy, so free of hassles, so much fun to get so much money so quickly. I had found the way to solve our problem whenever we were pressed for money. Franco was lying on the bed when I got home, listening to the radio. I flushed the five crisp bills from my bra and flung them proudly on the bed.

Franco knew what it meant. He was furious. "Why did you have to do that shit? We don't need it. We're both working."

"But Franco, it was nothing. I made nearly as much in a few minutes on my way home as you make in a whole week."

"We don't need it, Cookie, do you hear! I don't want you to do this shit. Don't let me ever catch you at it again."

It was a very definite threat. I promised.

We never talked about drugs. It was one of those things from the past. We weren't going to have anything more to do with drugs; wasn't that what we'd come to Miami for? We didn't talk about it, but it was always on my mind. At night I dreamed about getting high. I didn't want to go back on drugs but I wanted to get high just once, to give in to those urgent dreams just once.

I finally mentioned it to Franco. I let it come out very casually. "Hey, Franco, what about rewarding ourselves for being good for so long with just a little shot of dope?"

I knew Franco had been tormented by the same desire. He'd been waiting for me to say something. Now that I had said it for him he could go ahead and do what he had also wanted. "Yeah, dope. That sounds like a good idea. I'll see where I can cop some."

He took twenty dollars and went down to the Negro section. I waited up for him expectantly, anxiously, excited. High again. Just once!

He came back at four in the morning. No dope. No one had trusted him. He couldn't cop.

He started going down to the Negro section every night, trying to establish himself there as a regular, trying to get to know how things worked in Miami, trying to find a connection. We talked about nothing but the dope we wanted so much. We were becoming desperate. I was talking myself into a new dependency on heroin, just one shot, just one time. We spent a lot of time and money in the Negro section; bars, restaurants, hanging around. Sometimes I was with Franco; mostly he went by himself while I waited at home. I was really desperate. I still had my works. I put a few drops of water into the cooker and cooked up. I sloshed the cotton around in the water to dissolve any grains of dope that might be sticking to it. After all, I'd been clean for a few weeks, I wouldn't need much to take off. I injected the warm water into my vein. That felt good! That felt really good. Just to feel that needle again, just to handle the spike again, just to watch the blood being booted in and out of the dropper. It was working, I told myself. I was high. Not very high, but a little bit anyway. It was good to have the needle again.

We were down to our last twenty dollars. Payday was still some time off. All we could afford to eat was Cuban fried rice, filling, tasty, and cheap.

"Let me try to cop this time," I said to Franco. "Perhaps they'll trust a girl by herself. Give me the twenty and I'll go down to the Negro section and see what gives."

On the way I stopped at a pet shop. They had a spider monkey in the window, a darling of a pet. I wanted that monkey. I wanted that monkey more than I wanted anything else. I wanted to have that monkey sit on my back and let me carry him around. I knew if I bought it there'd be no money for dope—perhaps that was why I wanted it. The shopkeeper told me the price: $19.95. Less than twenty dollars!

"Please don't sell the monkey yet. I'm going to ask my husband to let me buy it. I'll come back for it tomorrow, I promise!" There'd be money later for us to turn on; right now I wanted the monkey. I went home. On the way I stopped off for a container of fried rice.

I wanted Franco in a good mood when I broached the subject, a light and friendly mood to make him feel good and agree with me. I warmed up the rice and served it. I put on a sexy smile. "How do you feel about monkeys, Franco?"

Franco was used to my silly questions. He didn't pay much attention.

"I saw a darling monkey at the pet store, Franco. A really darling monkey. It'll be so much fun to have it around."

"A monkey?"

"Yes, a monkey. I left it at the store. I have to pick it up tomorrow." I wanted to present him with an established fact. He mightn't give me his permission if I said I wanted his okay first. I didn't actually say I'd bought it—but I didn't say I hadn't bought it, either.

"How much was it?"

"Only nineteen ninety-five. It really wasn't much."

He didn't even try to find out if I'd already spent the money or not. He was too mad. He threw the rice on the floor and started into me, beating the shit out of me, knocking me down. I couldn't believe his anger. I was blind to how he must have been feeling: After all, he'd let me talk him into coming down to Miami to get clean, he'd let me talk him into taking a lousy job, and just when he was used to the idea of staying clean and starting a new way of life I'd talked him into getting dope again. And then I'd pulled the rug out from under his feet, just as he was getting ready to give in to his hunger for drugs.

He kicked me in the face and punched me in the stomach. He grabbed me by the hair and pounded my head on the floor. I could have told him it was all a mistake, that I hadn't actually bought the monkey yet, but I felt I deserved what I was getting because I'd intended to buy that monkey. And I thought that if I told him I'd been teasing him, he'd get so mad at my trick he'd beat me up even more. He kicked me until I stopped moving and then he got up and stood over me, very controlled, trying to look very calm, bottling up all his rage inside.

Then it built up again. "A monkey! A monkey!" and he kicked and beat me again, until he'd exhausted himself.

I got to my feet when Franco let up. I backed away from him. I was by the kitchen cabinet. I opened the cabinet door and found a big kitchen knife. I held it in my hand, the blade pointing at Franco. Franco was about three yards away.

Franco looked at me, disbelief in his eyes. He didn't think I could do it. I held up the knife and took a step forward and then I realized that I couldn't do it. I loved Franco. I really loved him. He was a good man; it was me that was bad.

"Franco!" I said. There was a message in that word. It meant: *You know how much I love you* and *I'm no good for you* and *You deserve better* and *I'm sorry for what I've done to you* and *I've always loved you.*

He heard me. He heard everything I had to say in that one word. Then I twisted my wrist and shoved the knife into my belly right up to the hilt.

I fell over on my side immediately. "I've stabbed myself, I've stabbed myself," I kept saying, but I couldn't believe it; it couldn't be happening to me. There was no blood, but every time

I tried to move my body a wave of sharp pains raced down my back.

Franco collapsed on me, sobbing. "Don't die! Don't die!" He kept repeating it over and over again. He'd once watched a girl die from an overdose, a girl he'd been going with on and off for ten years; he'd been in constant terror of my dying on him.

The police arrived with wailing sirens. I passed out in the ambulance.

Two days later I regained consciousness. Two detectives were waiting by my bed. "What did he do to you?" "How did he stab you?" "He was trying to kill you, wasn't he?" "We want to get a statement."

They told me Franco was in jail. They were going to throw the book at him. All they needed was my statement.

"He didn't do it. It was an accident."

"Sure, lady, we understand. You had a fight and you really love him. But you got to tell us the truth. He tried to kill you and he very nearly did. The doctors thought you wouldn't live. Why don't you tell us what happened."

"It wasn't his fault. He didn't do it."

"We're doing it for your sake, lady. Next time you won't be so lucky. We have our job, you know; we have to take care of men who try to kill their girl friends."

They kept up their interrogation for the rest of that day and well into the next one. The detectives would ask me a few questions and then the nurse would shush them and after I'd rested or had my medication they'd be back again: "Tell us just how it happened, lady."

"It was an accident. I was coming out of the shower. I was wearing my shower shoes and I had the silverware in my hands and I tripped on a rug with a knife I was trying to put away. I tripped over my shower shoes with a knife."

"Okay. Now tell us what really happened."

They would have put me in the loony bin if I told them the truth. "It's like I told you. Franco had nothing to do with it."

"Your neighbors say they heard you fighting for nearly an hour. They said you were screaming and yelling at each other and it sounded as if he was beating you up. Your body is black and blue with the bruises."

"I tripped over the rug with a knife in my hand."

They realized in the end that they couldn't get anything out of me that would implicate Franco. "We'll have to let him go if that's your story, but remember, it could happen again and next time you won't be so lucky."

They let Franco out of jail. He came straight to see me. He collapsed on my bed and we sobbed in each other's arms for half an hour. He hadn't slept for three days, he hadn't shaved, he'd hardly eaten. They'd been interrogating him nonstop, trying to wring a confession out of him. They'd told him I was dead and he'd believed it.

"Don't ever do it again, Cookie. Don't ever do it again. Promise me you won't, promise me you won't die on me."

I loved him so much, my man. I loved him so much. I didn't know how I could ever have done it to him.

They had Rosh Hashana when I was in the hospital. A rabbi came round the halls, a big man with a bushy white beard, a white cap on his head, and a white shawl draped over his shoulders. I was still dopey from the sedation. He came into my room and blew on the ram's horn, an eerie lament rising and falling and breaking into a series of wails and staccato sobs and ending on a long stirring upnote. I found myself strangely moved. My skin tingled and my blood ran hot and cold. It was a call to me, Moses calling from the wilderness with a message from God—and then he was gone. A Jewish ceremony, the only one in which I had ever participated.

They kept me in the hospital for three weeks. I called my mother collect, and told her I had injured myself falling on a knife. She wanted to come down to be with me but I told her there was no need. When the doctors let me go, Franco packed our bags and gave up our little apartment and we returned to my mother's home in Yonkers.

"It didn't work," I told my mother. "Nothing's going to work for me." I let her see my scar, a giant gash from ribs to navel where the doctors had cut me open to repair the slashed organs. I let her see the tattoo on my shoulder and the tattoo above my knee. More marks, more disfigurements to add to the old scars on my legs where my mother had hit me with a stick, to the stab marks on my wrist, to the needle marks on my arms. I'd never liked my body, anyway: too tall, hips too wide, chest too flat. I hated it. I didn't want it. Nothing mattered any more.

"I'm a loser, Mom, and I'll always be one. I'll never change. Nothing will ever help me."

☼ CHAPTER NINETEEN ☼

Nothing would ever help me, nothing was any good. I'd had my fill of hospitals, I'd had my fill of doctors, I'd listened to enough psychiatrists, a bunch of fucking shitheads the lot of them, full of long words and smug sentiments. I'd tried leaving home and that hadn't cured me either. I was past help.

Junkies don't live long. If dope doesn't kill them—if they don't die from an overdose or from contamination—they'll die soon enough from disease or accident or violence. I'd never really expected to live long, I'd never expected to live to twenty-one. Perhaps that was why I'd tried to cram so much life into my teen years.

And then I realized I *was* twenty-one. This was October, October, 1963. I'd turned twenty-one in January. Where was I last January twenty-seventh? Turning tricks on Broadway? Walking Gigi along Seventy-second Street to go and see one of my johns? Having a long rap with Sammy? It was such a long time ago. . . .

So I'd actually reached twenty-one without noticing! I was living on borrowed time; there wasn't much time left for me to live.

Poor Mitchell! I wanted to be a mother to him but it wasn't possible: I was irritable and spiteful when I was around him too much, I wasn't good for him. He called me Mommy, but it was his grandmother who had the mother's responsibilities. I had only the name.

Poor Mitchell! He'd be better off without me.

And poor Cookie, scarred, sick, sad, disgusted with her life, disgusted with her body, with nothing to look forward to but the needle and the sudden rush. Poor Cookie living on borrowed time.

We stayed on in Yonkers, Franco and I. We were both still clean from Miami: Ten dollars was enough to keep us both high all day. My mother gave me the money without complaint: She'd given up any hope of my reforming. I don't know if she knew how I used to get my money; her ten dollars a day was a small price to pay to keep me off the streets and out of further trouble.

We slept through the day, got up in the afternoon, and left at four-thirty just before my father came home so that I wouldn't have to stay and cook dinner for him. From Yonkers we went to the block, copped, took off, then stayed around to rap with the other addicts. By ten we were home and then we slept through to the next afternoon. On Saturdays and Sundays my mother was home to cook. We didn't have to rush out; we could stay in Yonkers until after dinner.

On November 3 we went down to 100th Street after dinner. It wasn't easy to cop: The block was crawling with plainclothes narcos. It wasn't safe to shoot up there and we decided to go up on the roof of one of the projects at Lexington and Ninety-ninth —not usually a good place because of the Housing Authority guards who roamed the buildings, but since it was Sunday evening they probably wouldn't bother themselves too much. There were three of us: Franco and me and a friend of his. We took the elevator up to the top floor and walked up one flight. We tied up behind the door, sheltered from the wind that howled over the roof. Franco's friend took off first, Franco hit me and then himself.

We didn't hear the housing guards. They came up on us, two men in blue uniforms, guns drawn. We had just finished taking off.

"Okay, you! Don't anybody move!"

Franco and the other guy were off before they'd finished their warning. One of the cops held his gun on me and the other one went on the roof and flushed out Franco and his friend. They collected our works and brought us down to the housing police office, then they took us to the police precinct station on Lexington Avenue.

They have a saying on the street: "Once you fall you keep on falling"; once you've been busted you keep on getting busted. My luck had finally broken. From now on it would be downhill all the way. The only lucky break in the whole situation was that I didn't have a habit; I wouldn't have to go through the agonies of kicking in the police cell without help and without medication. At least I was clean.

They fingerprinted me. A policewoman examined me thoroughly, mouth, nose, ears, ass, and vagina. I was charged under Section 3305—possession of narcotics—and with loitering in a place where narcotics were being used. I knew they'd have a hard job pinning possession on me: The only heroin I carried was flowing through my veins. They'd probably find some traces of dope in the laboratory when they examined the cookers and the spikes and the glassine envelopes, but they'd have to prove they were mine. Franco had told them right from the start that the works were all his; if he stuck to his guns they wouldn't be able to convict me on the major charge.

They interrogated me for hours. I denied having shot up. I insisted we'd all three gone up just to rap. I insisted I was clean. I told them I'd just come out of the hospital in Miami after a serious operation and showed them the scar and told them of my other stays in hospitals to explain my track marks. I could hear Franco off in the cage where he'd been locked up, insisting loudly—probably to give me a cue for what to say—that I had nothing to do with it, that I was clean, but since they'd already booked me, they obviously weren't going to mess up their records now by letting me go.

The paddy wagon that picked me up in the morning already held a few girls, more got in at each stop until we reached the Criminal Court building, and there I was locked in a big cell with perhaps twenty girls, all in on drug or prostitution arrests. I was the only white girl among them and the only one who wasn't suffering from the onset of withdrawal.

After an interminable time my name was called. A woman attendant took me from the bullpen and brought me into the courtroom. I'd been allowed to make a phone call to my mother some time after my arrest; I saw her now, her red hair standing out among the rows of spectators, and I signaled to her. Franco and the other junkie were waiting at the defendants' table below the judge's dais, together with the two cops who'd pulled us in. The prosecutor rattled off the charges. Franco and his friend admitted they'd shot up but said I had nothing to do with it. The prosecutor was willing to drop the possession charge against me but said I was still being charged with loitering. My mother had left her seat to stand beside me. When she sensed a pause in the ritual, she spoke up.

"I'm her mother, your Honor. She's never done this before. I don't know what to do, she's never been here before. Is there anything I can do? Can't you let her out on bail; she's just been in the hospital after an accident and she ought to be home with me."

The judge seemed quite fatherly. He leaned forward in his chair while he listened and then asked a clerk to advise my mother. The attendant took me by the arm and took me back to the bullpen; on the way I gave a final wave to Franco and my mother.

When they'd processed a large enough bunch of girls, they loaded us all in a paddy wagon and we were driven off, rattling uncomfortably over the cracked pavement. Suddenly, over the noise of the van, I heard a familiar rustling. I looked up. One of the girls had hidden a few bags of dope inside her vagina; she wouldn't be able to sneak them into the House of Detention so now she shared them. The other girls all had habits and really needed it so I didn't take any for myself, but when she insisted, "Come on, baby. You, too," I helped myself to what was left. We snorted the dope up our noses because no one had works; it wasn't as good as shooting up but it helped me arrive high at the Women's House of Detention. I got fingerprinted again, searched, put under the showers, examined, photographed, and then I was taken to the hospital section for observation because of my recent stay in the hospital. They put me to bed, gave me a shot in the buttock that hurt like hell, and then I nodded and fell asleep.

I woke up to the tune of "Downtown" sung by Petula Clark. That's where I wanted to be: downtown, uptown, anywhere in town, anywhere but here. They served some food that made Manhattan General's fried baloney seem like a banquet. Before I'd finished downing the garbage, a uniformed hack, a real nasty butch type, called my name: "Quinn! Quinn! Let's go. I have no time to wait. You got bailed out." She seemed mad that I was out of her charge and tried to rush me down the stairs. My leg was hurting; my ass was one big sore from the shot they'd given me. "Quick, Quinn, hurry up! I don't have all day." They gave me my clothes and took me out to the rotunda where visitors were lined up to arrange bail. I ran up to my mother and hugged her: "Oh thanks, Mom! Thanks for bailing me out. I'm really sorry."

She seemed impatient. "Come on, Cookie, let's go. Daddy's waiting. He took the day off to look after Mitchell; let's go."

Franco stayed in jail. I couldn't ask my mother to stand bail for him. On Friday, November 22, we were both back in court for a hearing. I arrived early with my mother and a lawyer she'd hired. They rattled off a litany of names and charges and every now and again someone stood up in the body of the court and shouted "Yes" or a lawyer answered "Ready to go to trial." My name came up and I went to the front. My lawyer conferred with the prosecutor for a minute or less and then the prosecutor turned to the judge and mumbled something that ended with ". . . permission to dismiss the charges," and the judge said, "Dismissed," without looking at me. The lawyer took my elbow and led me back to the seat next to my mother. I told her I wanted to wait for Franco.

They brought him into the court after about an hour and had him sit on a long bench with the other prisoners. "I love you," I told him in finger language. "Come out quick. They let me go." He smiled and waved back. An attendant had him get up and face the judge.

"Court will recess for lunch," the judge said, looking at his papers. He picked up a bunch of files and walked out. Franco and the rest of the prisoners were taken back to the cells and the spectators rose and walked out the main door.

There was a long wait after lunch. People were whispering, clerks walked in and out, doors opened and closed. Franco was brought to the bench and I signaled to him, and then he was walked out again and a while later they brought him in once more. More waiting.

Then the judge appeared. He looked like a very tiny man, a very sad man. He stood behind his big chair, a little figure in black robes. His face was ashen and he had obviously been crying. He opened his mouth as if to say something. A clerk called for silence.

The judge spoke. "We have just received very bad news that . . . that. . . ." He had to stop to wipe his eyes. "We have just heard that our President has been shot." There was one loud gasp in which everyone seemed to join.

"Silence!" the clerk shouted.

"This court will recess and resume again on Monday." Then the judge turned and left the court.

I looked at Franco and Franco looked at me. Our hands were still. There was nothing we could say. The attendant beckoned to Franco and he walked through the door to his cell.

I was stunned. They were gone. John F. Kennedy and Franco, both gone. People were crying all around me. We took the subway home. I spent the weekend glued to the television, crying for my double loss, my double sadness.

The day after the President's funeral we were back in court. Franco had pleaded guilty at his first hearing; now it was only a matter of sentencing.

"Six months," the judge said.

Six months! Six months away from me. I wouldn't believe it. I started screaming. An attendant looked at me harshly, my mother squeezed my hand for moral support and led me out of the courtroom.

We went around the block, to the entrance to the Tombs—the Men's House of Detention—and I asked how I could get to visit Franco.

"Only relatives."

"But I'm his girl."

"Sorry. You got to be married to him."

"We're living together. We planned on getting married."

"Common-law wife? You gotta bring proof. Next. . . ."

The next day I was back. I had bills and receipts from when we were in Florida and where we'd been living together on Eighty-second Street. It satisfied them.

They had Franco stand behind a thick sheet of plate glass. He pressed his face to the glass and I kissed his lips a half inch away. He couldn't hear me; we had to converse through a pair of telephone receivers. "What am I going to do?" I said over and over. "What am I going to do?" I wanted to reach him. I wanted to smash the glass. I became hysterical. Franco tried to calm me but I wouldn't listen to his voice crackling over the telephone; his wordless gestures on the other side of the glass only made me more hysterical. I got up and left, without saying good-bye to him.

It was cold outside. I sat down on the curb directly opposite the visitors' entrance to the Tombs, and sobbed while people walked past me and around me. A chill wind was blowing and the drizzle turned to sleet as I sat there and looked up to where I thought Franco's cell might be.

It was dark when I finally got up, chilled to the marrow. I was in a daze, I walked on leaden feet. On Canal Street I met a man I could recognize as a junkie. We talked for a few minutes and he asked if I knew where to cop; he had the money, so I took him up to 100th Street and he turned me on. Once I was high I took the subway home to Yonkers.

Next day I was down on Broadway to see some of my steady johns. I stopped off at a coffee shop on Broadway at Seventy-eighth Street. A black man was sitting there at a table, very smart, two-hundred-and-fifty-dollar suit, alligator shoes, heavy ring on his finger.

I looked at him. He looked at me. I looked at him. He picked up his coffee and sat down at the counter next to me.

"Are you hungry?" he asked. "Would you like to eat something?"

"No, thanks. I've eaten." I didn't know what his bag was but he was obviously into something that brought him lots of money and if I worked my cards right, I could probably work something with him.

We got to talking. He told me his name, Marcel. I told him mine, Melody, the name I worked under.

"My old man got busted."

"Gee, too bad. How long for?"

"Six months."

"Tough."

"Yeah. I feel lost without him. We've been together nearly two years."

"You don't live around here."

"No. I'm with my folks in Yonkers."

"Come down here every day?"

"Yeah. When I'm working."

"Working?"

"I'm a working girl." There was no harm in letting him know I was a prostitute.

"Long way to come. You could come and stay at my place. I have a friend, you can stay with us."

I had another cup of coffee and then I walked over with Marcel to his apartment in the Lucerne Hotel on Seventy-ninth Street and Amsterdam Avenue. His friend, Rosalie, was a woman in her early forties. She reminded me of something out of an old Joan Crawford movie. She had platinum hair that was piled high on her head and came to a point over the front. She wore enough makeup to sink a battleship. She looked—and spoke—just as I'd always expected from a madam. She was very friendly and the three of us had a long chat.

"Why don't you lay up with us?" Marcel asked, looking at Rosalie for approval.

"Sure," she said. "We have plenty of room."

"I'd have to go home to get my clothes."

"Is that the sort of clothes you have?" Marcel asked, indicating the clothes I was wearing, tight sexy slacks and sweater.

I nodded.

"If that's the sort of clothes you have at home, forget it," Rosalie said. "They aren't good enough for where we work. You'll have to get some new clothes, anyway. All you have to do is turn a few tricks and then you'll be able to buy whatever you need."

I called my mother to tell her I wouldn't be coming home that night. "I've just run into some old friends. I'll be staying over with them."

☼ CHAPTER TWENTY ☼

Rosalie had me take a bath and then she made up my face with thick layers of pancake makeup, explaining the steps as she went along. "You'll have to learn to put it on yourself, Melody," she said. She worked in highlights here, created shadows there, brought out my cheekbones, softened my eyes. When she was done she'd created a new face, a delicate china doll, smooth and perfect, that bore no resemblance to the real me. I asked her about my tattoos and she looked at them closely and finally decided they wouldn't need covering up, they were too small to be noticed in subdued lights but she applied rouge to my nipples for emphasis. Then she lent me some expensive underwear, a smart dress, high-heeled shoes, and a chic camel's hair coat in wraparound style that came to below my knees.

We sat around over coffee while she gave me instructions: "You'll have to look very good for the sort of people you'll be meeting when you're with me. Class, you know; you got to have class. Keep your mouth shut. Let them do the talking and just smile and make as if you're listening—they'll think you're really bright if you let them do the talking. And don't get yourself involved in the arrangements or the prices or anything; I'll see to that."

We took a cab down Broadway to Columbus Circle and then walked along Fifty-ninth Street, across from Central Park where all the big hotels are. When we'd gone about a block, as far as

Seventh Avenue, a man accosted Rosalie. I kept a few paces behind them while they talked and then we all went into the bar of a hotel and had a couple of drinks. He was waiting for a friend, he said, and then he made a call and came back; the three of us went up to his room.

Rosalie was fast; she really knew the business. She had her clothes off almost before he'd turned on the light.

She had me lie on the bed first and he fucked me while she sat behind him, rubbing her breasts against his back, kissing him, and playing with his balls. He climaxed and almost immediately she rolled him over on his back, grabbed his cock in her mouth and started blowing him, telling me to squat over his face so that he could eat my cunt.

In fifteen minutes we were out of there with our hundred dollar fee and a sizable tip. We continued our elegant stroll along Fifty-ninth Street. A few men stopped to talk with Rosalie, but nothing came of it. At the end of Fifty-ninth Street, Rosalie pointed to a huge palace of a hotel. "This is the Plaza," she announced. "We're going to do a lot of work here."

Hey, I thought to myself, *I'm going to work here!* It seemed unbelievable. Right at the top of the profession! It was like being an actress and having my name in lights on Broadway. I'd hit stardom; I'd really arrived!

A man accosted us just outside the Plaza. He was in his early forties. He hailed a cab and we went to his apartment on the upper East Side. We fucked, sucked, balled, and were out in fifteen minutes with another hundred dollars plus tip to complete the night's take. Rosalie astonished me, such a superb businesswoman, direct, fast, and deliberate. My impulse would have been to play with the trick during the cab ride to give him a good time. Then I would have sat in his apartment, rapping, perhaps making coffee, and I wouldn't even have stepped out of my dress yet in the time it took Rosalie to get us through the whole double act, dress, and be on our way home.

Next morning Rosalie took me to Saks Fifth Avenue. I tried to boost a couple of blouses. She got mad at me. "You're crazy! Do you want to get busted? We can make much more money, as much as we need, we don't have to steal." It had seemed the natural thing to me; in fact I couldn't remember the last time I'd *bought* clothes for myself. I saw no point in buying clothes if I could simply boost them, leaving my old clothes behind and walking out in the stolen ones or stuffing a few small items under my sweater or coat. Rosalie had a good eye for elegant fashions, nothing flashy, just expensive good taste: two dresses, a cashmere sweater, a well tailored cloth coat, good shoes, neat underwear, all terribly correct.

She introduced me to a different world, poles apart from the one I'd known with Franco, the one bounded by 100th Street and twenty dollar tricks. Rosalie introduced me to elegance: dinners outdoors at the St. Moritz facing the park and the elegant crowds; exotic dishes picked from a menu written in French; dinners that cost as much as a whole day's supply of dope. I guess it was a good investment; we picked up many of our tricks over dinner.

Our best pickups were at the Plaza. We used to sit in the lobby, reclining on one of the circular banquettes that surround the pillars, two elegant ladies chatting, glancing up occasionally to catch a man's almost imperceptible glance. We'd glance back as if unaware, rise slowly off the banquette, smooth our dresses, stroll off toward the coffee shop with a look back for reassurance. The arrangements were made over coffee, then the trick went up to his room and we followed a decent two minutes later. Quite a disappointment for me, those Plaza rooms: dowdy, dull, old-fashioned without being antique. I'd expected some superlative elegance to match the reputation, the opulence of the lobby, and the wealth of the guests.

Marcel and Rosalie were good to me. They wanted me to enjoy the pleasures of the good life; they had dreams of making me over into fashionable elegance. When they found out I was on dope they were disappointed; it was a waste of my youth and my money, they thought, and they tried to get me to stop. Rosalie wanted me to impress her customers as a fresh young teenager, and when I was high I couldn't convey the correct look of eager interest; when I wasn't high I found it difficult to bring myself to turn a trick. The two of them were always bugging me when I went out by myself: "Don't waste your money on drugs, Melody. You could be using it for better things."

I rejected their distorted sense of values. If all I wanted out of life was food and clothes, I could have stayed home in Yonkers. I didn't turn tricks because I enjoyed it or in order to buy luxuries; I did it only because it was the easiest way to support my habit.

One day Rosalie was sick and I went to the Plaza by myself. I was high all the time. I did much better without Rosalie. I seemed to spend the evening going up with trick after trick. Also, for the first time I could really enjoy myself with my tricks. I no longer had to play Rosalie's elegant lady: I could be myself and jump on the bed and joke and giggle and take my time. It was a hilarious evening.

From the Plaza I went up to the block to stock up, and then I finished off the evening with a cup of coffee at Broadway and Seventy-eighth. I had over three hundred dollars. Marcel and Rosalie would expect only a hundred; the rest I could hide and keep for myself. It was mine after all, I'd earned it, they had no business telling me what to do. Why should I work my ass off for them?

I let myself be picked up by an enormously tall and handsome Negro. His face was a golden tan, his hair had been straightened and formed a wide sweeping wave over his forehead. I liked him. We went up to his room in a dingy hotel on Eightieth Street, just around the corner from the Lucerne where Marcel and Rosalie stayed.

Steve was gentle and warm with me. He called me Princess. He made me stand on his bed while he walked around me to admire me and slowly stripped me, garment by garment. He bathed me, then powdered and oiled my body. He adored me and I felt proud to be loved by such a handsome man. We spent three days together making love. I told him I was working. He said, "Well that's your thing." I told him I was an addict and he said I ought to stop, it wasn't good for me.

On the fourth day, Steve very politely suggested I had spent too much time indoors; it was time I got back to working. I didn't see the point of working, not with so much money still stashed in the lining of my coat, so I went to the block to cop some dope for the next few days, hung around to rap, and then I came home and gave Steve fifty dollars, telling him I had earned it from tricks. When my money gave out I made the round of my old johns, keeping just enough money for dope and giving him the rest.

Steve really loved me, he really wanted me to clean up. He took away my clothes and hid them with a friend, then he locked me up in his room, trying to get me to kick on pot. It was awful. I was sick. I needed to get straight and all he'd do for me was get me to smoke. I couldn't explain to him about the hot baths I needed and smoking pot only made me sicker.

He went out late one night to get me some more pot. I couldn't take any more of his "cure." I wrote him a note: "Sorry, it just won't work" and signed it "Princess." He'd left me my coat and my purse and I found a pair of his rubber sandals. I forced the door and tiptoed down the stairs. It was well below freezing outside and I was completely naked under my blue cloth coat. I ran to Broadway, the huge sandals flapping as I ran; sometimes they fell off and I had to run after them in my bare feet. A cab took me, shivering, to 100th Street. I copped, got straight, then copped some more to last me a few days. I took another cab to Yonkers and had the cabbie come up with me to collect his fare from my mother.

I stayed home, secure and warm. Finally, on Christmas Eve, my dope ran out. I had to cop. I went to the block hoping to cop enough to last over the holiday and then go home early to be with Mitchell and my folks. The block was deserted. I wandered around like a lonely orphan, my pockets bulging with money, but no one was around to give me what I needed. I was cold through and through. I felt lost and lonely, deserted by all my friends. I was sick and in pain. There wasn't even anyone to talk to, and the gas stations were closed so that I couldn't warm myself at the heaters. Finally, close to midnight, I ran into a junkie. He sold me one bag, just enough to get straight. I shot up on a roof, then went home on a lonely subway. I awoke sick on Christmas morning and went down to the block again. This time I was lucky and I was able to cop enough.

The day after Christmas I went back to the Lucerne. Rosalie and Marcel had left; they hadn't left a forwarding address. In the lobby I met one of the residents, Lemmy, tall and thin like a rake, as black as the night, as ugly as sin. He was dressed in an orange knit suit with a natty black hat. He'd seen me there before and recognized me. I asked him about Rosalie and Marcel; he invited me to stay in his apartment.

Lemmy got me Dilaudid, as much as I needed. I went back to working my old johns and Lemmy brought me some more clients. He allowed me to keep as much money as I wanted to spend on myself and he bought me all the Dilaudid I wanted. When there was no Dilaudid he got me dope. I never had to hustle for dope myself. He didn't pressure me, either; I was free to come and go—he even had a set of keys made for me.

Lemmy introduced me to a variation of the Murphy game. We worked this on Broadway around Times Square. I stood by a corner looking sexy and seductive while Lemmy, a few yards off, looked over the passing tourists. When he spotted a likely looking hick, he'd proposition him, pointing to me and praising my sexual skills. When the trick seemed hooked, Lemmy named the price and told him the building and the apartment number where he could find me, then he made a sign and I'd walk off, with the hick following.

Lemmy would stop him. "Hey, man! You can't go up just like that. You don't know those broads. You go up there with your money and they'll rob you blind and not even do the job. Give it to me and I'll pay her later when she's given you a good time." Sometimes, when Lemmy was really persuasive, he could get the man to entrust him with his wallet for safekeeping.

I'd go up in the elevator all the way to the roof, cross over to the next building, and come down. By the time the victim found out he'd been tricked we'd be far off, perhaps trying it on someone else. I found the game fun, but when the excitement had worn off I realized the thrill wasn't worth the risk and we stopped.

Lemmy then got me into a house between Sixth and Seventh Avenues, in the Times Square area, run by a madam called Margo. Margo was a short, fat, jovial woman in her early fifties, a female Santa Claus who waddled when she walked. She was probably of Jewish or Italian origin and looked as if she'd spent her whole life in the profession. Her house was really like a home, a two-and-a-half-room apartment in an old brownstone directly over a cafeteria, warm and friendly and comfortable. She had girls working for her in shifts. I worked from two or three in the afternoon until eight or nine at night together with a hooker called Pat from Buffalo. Pat had shoulder length auburn hair and was older; I guess she was about twenty-five, only three years older than me, but I saw myself as an eternal teenager and everyone else seemed old to me. Pat was an itinerant hooker; she moved around the country from house to house, and when she was in New York she always worked for Margo.

Margo was a proud mother to us. She had the place warmly decorated. There were flowers everywhere, plenty of food, beer in the icebox, and a pot of coffee was always kept going. Pat and I used to sit around wearing housecoats over our underwear, talking, smoking, and drinking coffee. Sometimes Margo sat with us; our conversations were mostly about clothes and about kooky customers we'd known. Customers might call Margo and make reservations or she might go down to the street or to the cafeteria to bring up customers during the slack periods. "These are my girls," she'd say, proudly indicating Pat and me. We'd get up and let the men walk around us to look and make their choice. Touching was strictly forbidden and we weren't expected to unbutton our housecoats, either, but Margo would lift my chin and say, "Look at that face!" and squeeze my body and say, "Look at that body! Look how young and pretty!"—like a poultry man showing off his broilers.

The standard fee was twenty-five dollars. The man would make his choice and walk off with one of us to the bedroom. In the hall there was a cookie jar into which we'd put the money from the customer; Margo took half and the rest was shared evenly between Pat and me, irrespective of how many clients we had. On a busy day I might have as many as ten customers, on a slack day only four or five. For fifty dollars, a man could have Pat and me together, either to party for him—doing a fake sixty-nine job—or to fuck us in turn. I always washed my tricks' genitals carefully when they came in, then oiled and powdered them. If they wanted special service I charged extra—"Around the World" was one of those and that involved licking his balls and asshole. If they were regular customers and knew Margo well, I'd have to give her the money, otherwise I'd make the customer promise not to tell Margo and then I could keep the ten or twenty dollars extra for myself. One of my specialties was the Hollywood job, a trick I'd learned from Rosalie: a blow job with my mouth filled with hot water. The Hollywood job was always worth at least ten dollars extra.

Lemmy had warned me that Margo wouldn't tolerate drugs. I had to take off before I left home and during the evening I'd have to sustain myself on Dolophines that Lemmy got for me. Margo couldn't risk drugs on the premises; she had elaborate arrangements with the cops—and that didn't include narcotics.

The plainclothes vice men were the hardest customers to satisfy: they felt they had the right to come up whenever they pleased, they demanded the best of everything and took the longest time and they never left a penny—not even a tip for us girls. Margo had a good reputation; customers felt safe about going to her house. They knew they'd get their money's worth, they wouldn't be robbed, and they wouldn't catch a disease. We had our share of kooky customers, of course, who demanded special ways of getting their kicks. One I remember in particular was a Jewish guy, a nervous little man in his thirties who came up regularly. Mama had told him it was bad to go with girls because you could get a disease, so he'd come up with a rubber hot dog he'd bought at the five and dime: He "fucked" me with his hot dog while he jerked himself off. Once I tried to help him add to his fun and I grabbed his cock to do it for him; he shrank back as if I was going to kill him. Other customers were less kooky but almost every one of them would insist on having us wear garter belt and stockings—and often high-heeled shoes—while they were fucking. My bill for stockings was astronomical!

Lemmy took good care of me. He'd bring me down by cab in the afternoon and pick me up in the evening; we'd go right back to his place so that I could shoot up and get high, and then we'd go out for dinner. He told me one day that he'd seen some beautiful boots for me in a shop on Broadway. Next day he bought them for me. They were gorgeous. They were made of lizard, a greenish-gold color, on a high chunky heel and zipped slinkily to just below the knee. This was a few years before boots became universally popular and I was right in the forefront of fashion. There wasn't another pair of boots anything like them and people used to stop on the street and admire them as I passed.

Then I got gonorrhea. I didn't know I had it at first. I had a burning pain with a feeling of pressure especially when I urinated, and thought it was my old kidney infection again. Then Lemmy got gonorrhea and he took me to his doctor and I had to stay away from the house for a week while I got injections.

I didn't go back to Margo's when the gonorrhea cleared up. The work had been getting too hard, I found it physically painful to spend so much time without dope, and I was fed up. I explained it to Lemmy and told him that I was getting a longing for Franco, who'd been sent to the city jail on Rikers Island. Lemmy gave me enough drugs—heroin, Dilaudid and Dolophines—to last me a while, and I had also put away a few hundred dollars for myself. I went back home to Yonkers.

I'd been writing to Franco almost every day, but I hadn't seen him since that terrible day at the Tombs. Now I went to South Bronx by bus and subway and got the prison ferry over to Rikers Island. My works and a supply of dope were stashed in my bra. As before, there was a glass screen between us—mandatory for prisoners in on drug charges. Franco had shaved off all his hair as a precaution against vermin but he looked round and healthy; he'd obviously had plenty of food and rest. I told him to hurry out; I'd make sure there'd be lots of dope waiting for him.

On the ferry back, crossing Long Island Sound, I caught a chill. Next day I had a temperature of almost 105 degrees and became delirious. Doctor Tollman diagnosed pneumonia and had me taken to hospital. When I came out I went back to the block. A few days later I overdosed. The addicts who'd shot up with me left me in an alley for dead. Someone ran off with my coat. Eventually someone found me and I was taken to Metropolitan Hospital and when they'd got me out of the overdose, I was taken to Bellevue psychiatric ward. It was full of psychotics who walked around muttering to themselves or screaming; I believe I was the only addict there. We weren't allowed to eat with anything more lethal than a spoon—and that had a very round bowl that was supposedly safe but made eating difficult. No shoe laces or belts. Nothing to do. There weren't enough beds and they had to put mattresses out in the hallway at night for people to sleep.

My mother came to visit me. I told her I was going crazy; I begged her to try and get me out. I'd been legally committed this time and they wanted to keep me for two weeks for observation, but with a lawyer's help my mother got me out in three days.

A few days after I got out of Bellevue I met a young kid on the block—Joe, about nineteen years old. I'd seen him there often over the years—he lived on the block—but now he was in business, dealing. He wanted to be grown-up and important, and showing me off as his woman helped him project that image. I went to live at his place. There were nine kids and his parents in the three-room apartment. We shared a bottom bunk in a room with four other kids. Joe was tall and healthy, very black, with a baby face. I had long blond hair, which he liked. His folks were from the south and treated me as one of the family; they taught me to dig soul food.

I saw that Joe could be of help to me; he would keep me in drugs and later he could become the source for the little nest egg I wanted to prepare for the day when Franco came out. Joe was only snorting; I told him this was kid stuff—he ought to skin-pop. When I had him skin-popping, I got him to start mainlining.

I didn't have to hustle for dope while I was with Joe but I was able to take some money off the fresh-faced kids who came around to the block with New Jersey license plates on their cars, usually on Friday evening, loaded with wages and enough spare cash to buy drugs for a week. Mine was one of the few white faces on the block and they felt somehow that they could trust me. "Hey man, you want to be careful around here," I'd warn them. "Some of those crazy junkies would as soon kill you for your money as give you the time of day. You're lucky I met you. I know the people; I'll take you to a safe connection."

I took them up on a roof where an accomplice was waiting.

He'd press a knife to their throats and I would go through their pockets and take their money and anything of value, then we'd run off. We knew the kids couldn't complain to the police.

Joe was now mainlining dope to keep up with me and to prove himself grown-up. He wasn't strung out yet; and so he would almost always fall out and become drowsy immediately. I seized the opportunity once when he was nodding and told him to go lie down. Then I grabbed a small bag of pure dope that he had out ready for cutting and packaging, put it inside my bra, and left his apartment on tiptoes. Once outside I ran to the subway and went home to Yonkers. I knew that was the end of the block for me: If I showed my face there just once again, Joe or his friends would rub me out.

I had the equivalent of perhaps two hundred nickel bags of dope worth a thousand dollars retail. I stayed home. I luxuriated in a hot bath every night. I took Mitchell for walks along South Broadway and on weekends I went with my parents visiting their friends and family. Franco was let out of jail and came to live with us in Yonkers. We were a happy family. We had plenty of dope to keep us going.

When our dope gave out we went to a new place to cop, one that Franco had heard of during his stay on Rikers Island. It was in Washington Heights, at the northern tip of Manhattan. We copped the dope on Broadway and then went up to the roof of a tall building. We'd just taken off when two narcos in plainclothes came up on us, guns drawn.

I screamed. It wasn't just an ordinary scream. It wasn't anger. It wasn't fear. It came up from low in my belly and gathered volume in my chest. The words I tried to form were "Oh, no!" but it came out of my throat as a bellow of anguish that summed up all the despair in my life.

The emotion communicated itself to the narcos; they couldn't remain uninvolved. "Okay, lady, we won't take you. We'll just take him."

"No, you can't take him," I screamed at them. "He's only just come home. He's been away from me so long."

"Okay, lady. We understand. We won't take you. Only him."

They couldn't understand me. They wouldn't understand me.

Nobody would ever understand me. I ran for the parapet. I had one foot over and I screamed.

Franco broke away from the narcos, ignoring their guns. He ran for me and grabbed me. The narcos helped him pull me back. They stood there and watched as Franco hugged me to his body and sobbed. They put their guns away and watched in silence. The shorter one of them finally spoke: "Okay, we won't pull you in, either of you. We'll let you go this time. But get out of this neighborhood. Don't let's ever catch you here again."

I threw my arms around him and hugged him. "Oh thank you, thank you!" and then I hugged the other one. I was so happy, so relieved.

After that we went to the Triangle, at 112th Street and Lenox Avenue, just north of Central Park in the heart of Harlem where Franco had friends he'd met at Rikers Island. We scored easily. Then we met up with George, one of the big dealers, and started to push for him. George had eyes for me and was always trying to get me alone. That made me feel safe. I knew that the next time I was in trouble I could go to George and have him take care of me. My only regret was that I hadn't met him earlier, while Franco was in jail.

We took a room on Broadway, in our old neighborhood. George got the dope delivered to us and we pushed it. Soon we were using up all our profits and I had to take up hustling again to cover our debts to George. I had a book fat with phone numbers now, and I spent most of my days taking care of my johns and my evenings hustling on the street. Sometimes, when I felt good and looked good, I went back to the Plaza; that could earn me a hundred or even two hundred dollars in a night, but I couldn't do it often. My looks were going, my teeth were rotting, and I was beginning to look worn and haggard. I was covered with scars. I had boils and abscesses all over my body. I went to Dr. Tollman regularly to have him lance my boils, but when he'd cleaned up a boil on my buttock I'd immediately get another one on my thigh. There was a huge crater on my arm, the scar of a baseball-sized abscess that I got after Joe's brother injected me with salt solution to pull me out of a near overdose in his pad. All in all, I was a mess.

☼ CHAPTER TWENTY-ONE ☼

It was November, 1964 and time again for one of those regular let's-clean-up-the-sex-and-be-moral interludes for the city, so the cops clamped down on hustlers on the Upper West Side. Franco and I were living right in the heart of the area. I could still take care of my regular johns in my room, but for hustling new tricks I had to go downtown to the Times Square area.

I took a working room in a small hotel on West Forty-seventh Street. My beat was along Seventh Avenue; much of the time I stood with a bunch of working girls outside the big Woolworth's at the corner of Seventh Avenue and Fiftieth, just a few yards over from Broadway where the passing throng of lonely men could look us over clearly in the lights from the store. When someone likely looked at me I smiled back, walked down to the corner, and let him follow. My fee was now fifteen dollars. If he wouldn't pay that, I'd agree to ten—but no less, although I was often desperate for the money. Whatever the price, they got the same service. I'd even blow them for no extra charge. I had no interest in my tricks; I had no desire to talk to them or to please them. I just wanted it over quickly so that I could get back to Seventh Avenue and turn another trick. I wore my gold lizard boots the whole time; it was amazing how they helped me pick up customers.

It was the end of November. That afternoon Franco and I had gone out and I had bought my very first Christmas tree. We had the bulbs and the decorations. I promised I'd be home early so that we could decorate the tree: a tree to light up our room; a tree to come home to at night; a tree to twinkle through Thanksgiving and Christmas and into the new year; a tree that would let me know that I'd never again go through the loneliness of the previous Christmas Eve; a tree to mark our first real Christmas together.

I wanted to turn a few good tricks, take my money and get home early. I started out at Woolworth's and walked up Seventh Avenue to the Americana Hotel. It was still early in the evening. As I walked into the lobby of the hotel and sat down, a man smiled at me. He was very handsome, in his early forties, silver running through his black hair, distinguished looking, fatherly. I had a strange feeling about him. A cop? Obviously not, he was too well dressed.

He smiled, walked down some steps, looked back and cocked his head. I followed him outside. I suggested we go across the street for a cup of coffee. I never did that with tricks around Times Square, but I thought that over coffee I could sound him out and see where he was at.

He didn't allow for too much conversation over the coffee. "How much?" he asked me right out.

"Twenty dollars."

"Okay. I have a room. We'll take a cab." He finished his coffee, paid, and we left.

He got his key at the desk and we went straight up to his room. It looked too neat and too tidy, as if no one lived there, although he'd told me in the cab that he'd been in town for a while. As soon as he turned on the light I knew that I'd let myself be taken in by a cop.

He locked the door and pocketed the key. "All right. Empty your purse."

My face fell. "Oh, shit! I felt it. I should have known you were the Man. I knew I shouldn't have gone with you."

"It's too late now."

"Come on, man. You don't really need me. There are thousands of girls out there. Why don't you leave me alone and let me go?"

I kept thinking of the tree. The tree was the most important thing in my life right then.

"Look, man, let me go. My man just got out of jail. This is going to be our first Thanksgiving together."

He went through my purse, found the booklet, and leafed through it.

"My, you're a busy girl. What are you doing on Broadway?" I couldn't help feeling a little embarrassed, streetwalking on Broadway with a book like that.

"Nothing. Things got bad. I had to turn a few fast tricks."

"Can I see your arms?"

I rolled up my sleeves.

"It's a shame a girl like you, ruining yourself, killing yourself. Sit down, I want to talk with you."

I had hopes for a moment. Perhaps he understood me. Perhaps he'd just give me a lecture and let me go. He talked to me a long time, very fatherly. He made it sound as if he was really trying to help me. "It's a real pity. A pretty girl like you should be doing something better."

I told him all about Franco and the tree.

"Do you have any drugs on you?"

"No."

"Look, I'm not after drugs; that's not my department. I'm from the vice squad, not narcotics. If you have anything you'd better use it up now."

"I don't have anything."

"If you have drugs, go in the bathroom, lock the door, put a chair against it if you like. I don't want the drugs; that's not my department. Go in there and use them before I take you in."

I saw that I could trust him. I went in the bathroom, propped myself on the floor with my feet against the door, and shot up all I had, two bags. Then I broke the works and flushed them and the empty envelopes down the john.

"What's going to happen to me?" I asked him when I came out.

"Oh, you probably won't do any time. This is your first bust for pross."

He helped me on with my coat and locked his arm in mine so

that I couldn't get away, then he took me down in the elevator and walked me to the Seventeenth Precinct station house, just across Lexington Avenue on East Fifty-first Street. He gave me a cup of coffee while he went through the paperwork of booking me and gave me another long talk. He wasn't just fooling, he really cared. By the time he left to pull in his next hooker we had become very friendly. He had me call him by his first name, Marty.

I was sick and throwing up the next morning at the Criminal Court building, just like all the other girls. The only encouraging feature was the Legal Aid lawyer who came to the bullpen to discuss my case: He advised me to plead guilty and get the business over quickly; since it was my first arrest for prostitution the case would be thrown out and they'd let me go home.

This time they had the prisoners shielded from the public; I'd called Franco and asked him to be in court to arrange bail but I could neither see nor hear him. I had no idea what was happening. Girls walked past the judge with their arresting officers, hardly pausing, walking in and out. Cases were being tried one after the other. The prosecutor, the judge, and the Legal Aid lawyer were talking about this, that, and the other thing. Then they talked about me. The judge asked me how I pleaded. I told him guilty. There was more talking. Marty was at my side in civilian clothes with a police shield on his lapel. I felt I was in good hands. A lot of big words. I wasn't listening to those; I was waiting to hear the magic phrase, "Case dismissed," so that I could go. I heard the judge say, "Ninety days," and I looked around to see who he was talking about. My lawyer was busy on the next case. Marty took me by the arm and walked me over to the bench where the girls were sitting. I asked him: "What happened?"

"You just got ninety days. I don't know what went wrong, the judge must have been in a bad mood."

I had to tell them that they'd made a mistake, it wasn't me, it wasn't happening to me, they couldn't do this to me. I collapsed or fell or threw myself down a flight of stairs. Marty picked me up and carried me to the bench and had someone bring me a glass of water. Even hysteria no longer worked for me as it had the last time, with Franco, on the roof. I didn't think of asking him what I could do now. I didn't think anyone could do anything for me. He walked away when I seemed to have recovered, saying, "You take care of yourself, now," and muttering to himself, "I just can't understand it. I just can't understand it."

At the Women's House of Detention we were taken to the tank for decontamination and locked up two to a cell for four days. I was sick and threw up. I was in agony and wanted to die. My cellie was Barbara, a quiet girl with a kind face who was also doing ninety days for prostitution. Barbara kept me sane. She just wanted to get her time over without trouble and without hassles. I followed her lead. Barbara lived outside with a woman who passed as a man, but she didn't mess with any girls in jail and I didn't either.

They'd taken away all my clothes—including my golden snakeskin boots—and they gave me a starched dress that tied around the waist, a torn blue sweater that was held together by safety pins, ugly anklet socks, and sneakers. At night the mice nibbled at everything left on the floor, and by the light streaming in from the Greenwich Village streets below, I could see bugs and cockroaches crawling over the walls, the ceilings, and the bedding.

The doctors, most of whom were foreign, treated us all like dirt. I don't know how often they poked me in the ass and the vagina; they really loved that, they were callous and brutal and reduced us to the level of cattle.

I was quiet. I kept to myself. I really behaved myself. I spent hours mopping down the corridor and shining the cell bars. The mop was heavy and gave me calluses, but I felt compelled to keep going down that corridor with the mop, mopping the floor, mopping it over and over again.

I couldn't eat the prison food. I wrote my mother that I was in jail, without telling her what I was in for. She sent me money for the commissary and I gave my commissary tickets to the girls who worked in the kitchen and they made me scrambled egg sandwiches so that I wouldn't have to eat the prison food—but I had to wait until the end of the day till they could bring it down to me. I put on fifteen pounds in three months from the starchy prison food.

Barbara was my confidante. After I finished my mopping and polishing I used to wrap myself in a blanket and sit with her against the steam pipes, talking about Franco and the tree we didn't get to put up and what I hoped to do when I got out. I was in jail over Thanksgiving, I was there for Christmas—the Christmas dinner was the highlight of the year with a *whole* slice of ham for each inmate. On New Year's Eve the other girls sang and celebrated and went wild; I lay quietly on my bunk and cried, looking out of the window over Greenwich Village at Whelan's drugstore where I used to hang out with Harriet, at the flashing neons from the Howard Johnson's where I used to shoot up in the john. I was in jail over my twenty-third birthday, too.

Franco called for me on the day I was released. I had my own clothes again and my gold boots and I felt, at last, like a woman, a person, myself. We had a cup of coffee at Whelan's and I looked back up at my cell and swore I'd never go back; I'd kill myself before I'd ever let them lock me up again.

Back in Yonkers, my first act was to draw a bath. I soaked in it for hours. I scrubbed myself until the skin was bruised. I rubbed and poked and scratched, trying to get out the dirt and grime of the Women's House of Detention, poking and digging into my ears and nose and vagina as if to scrape out the cockroaches I still felt crawling inside me.

The water couldn't wash away my disgust. The roots of my hair had grown out black, my face was covered with pimples and blotches, two teeth had been yanked out by the prison dentist and another one at the front had simply fallen out. Franco tried to get me to take care of myself, but I didn't want to. He was fussing around me like a solicitous mother; I felt he was bugging me. I didn't want to have to live up to anybody's demands. He and my mother seemed to be in league against me.

I went with Franco only a short while after I got out of jail, then I went to 112th Street by myself to cop directly from George, the big dealer, and let him know I'd be his woman. He was married, but he arranged to have me live in one of his apartments in another building.

Franco knew where I was. He came up to the door and knocked, he waited outside for me, he ran after me in the street. He wanted to talk to me, to knock some sense into me; all he did was preach at me: "You're fucking yourself up, Cookie. Don't you know what will happen? Don't you know what these people want from you?"

I knew, but George hadn't made me turn tricks for him—yet. I just wanted to be able to live in George's place, get my dope, not be bothered by anyone. Franco kept wanting me to be better, to pull myself together, he was too square for me. I didn't want it. I didn't want to raise myself again. I wanted to sink and sink and sink. It was going to happen sooner or later; I was too tired to fight it. I felt sorry for Franco. He was pleading and crying for me. He really wanted me and cared for me, but I had given up on myself and couldn't care for myself, and I couldn't bear to be around anyone who wouldn't just let me be and go where I had to go.

George cut back on my dope and I had to start turning tricks. I had to avoid Franco who was waiting for me on the street. I had to find tricks, seven dollar tricks, five dollar tricks, anything they would pay. Do anything for them they wanted, get fucked, get abused, get a few dollars for dope to keep away the pressure.

Franco was harassing me. George found me a dingy room in a midtown dive just off Eighth Avenue, a few blocks away from the Port Authority Bus Terminal. I turned tricks at the terminal. I wore my boots, their heels all worn down. They were my good-luck fetish; they helped me get customers. I sat in the mezzanine waiting room, trying to smile through my cracked face and my rotted teeth, picking up foreign sailors, soldiers on the run, laborers from New Jersey, degenerates from Forty-second Street. Ten dollars, seven dollars, five. Take them up to my room, then back again to the bus terminal. I had no wash basin in my room; I used the facilities at the terminal. George came up to my room occasionally to fuck, but he wasn't getting any pleasure out of it. I wasn't earning him money: The little I made all went on rent and dope and just enough food to keep me from starving. He offered to set me up in a better place and supply me with better customers, but I wouldn't have it. I didn't want up, I just wanted to stay down.

It was May. Too hot for boots. I bought a pair of cheap sandals and carried my golden lizard boots back to my room. I hung up the coat that Rosalie had bought me at Saks and went down to the terminal intending to pick up another trick. I never got there. I couldn't face working. I was sick from not having any drugs, I was sick in my body from hunger and malnutrition and from years of abuse. I wasn't dying, I was already dead.

I dragged myself into the subway and went home to my mother, shivering and cold and utterly, utterly miserable.

I collapsed in my mother's arms and sobbed. "Help me, Mommy. I can't go on. I have to stop. Help me, just help me."

The fight had gone out of me. I'd tried everything and now, in final desperation I turned to my mother once more, ready to accept her help, ready to accept her love.

☼ CHAPTER TWENTY-TWO ☼

My mother paused only long enough to calm me and reassure me, then she took me right over to Dr. Tollman—and she stayed home the rest of the week to nurse me. She made sure I ate properly, she doled out the Dolophines, she made me take the doctor's vitamin pills, and she brought me to his office every day for a check.

Again and again I had an urge to go back to my old room downtown. I wanted to pick up the coat that Rosalie had bought me and the gold lizard boots from Lemmy; I was attached to those boots, they were part of me. Each time I got ready to go I saw that room, I saw the tricks I used to take up there, I saw George coming up with the dope to fuck me, I saw the needle in my arm, I saw myself waiting at the bus terminal. If I went back for those boots, I'd be back in that room, back in that world, all the way back.

I stayed home with my mother.

I'd come home on Tuesday evening, May 4, 1965. On Friday afternoon I went to see a movie at the Park Hill Theater on South Broadway. I'd seen a write-up about it in that morning's Yonkers paper, Eartha Kitt in *The Synanon Story.* The papers had said it was about the rehabilitation of drug addicts; I didn't believe there was such a thing as rehabilitation, but I was curious to see what they made of the addict's life.

The movie was a revelation to me. They showed this place in

California that wasn't just a bunch of goody-goodies or self-important officials setting out to tell the addict what he should do, but something run by real addicts who were trying to help themselves. They showed Chuck Dederich, a onetime drunk who'd started the whole thing; his wife—played by Eartha Kitt—had been an addict, a thief, and a whore and then she'd come to Synanon and straightened out, and Chuck had married her.

I experienced a strange sense of elation. It seemed I was part of that movie; somebody had understood me and reached out to me, had offered to let me be part of something big. Something new could happen to me now, something new that would give me the sense of belonging I'd always looked for. I came home to my mother bursting to share my excitement with her. I tingled with the anticipation and the joy of having it happen to me. I'd had that feeling a few times before: when I was eleven and preparing to get fucked for the first time, when I was eighteen and about to go down on my first woman, when Leslie invited me to take dope for the first time. But this time there was more to it: It wasn't simply a new thrill to experience, it held the promise of life and hope.

My mother got caught up in my excitement. She neglected the Friday evening dinner she was cooking and got on the phone. Synanon!

But how do you find Synanon? I didn't even know how to spell it. My mother found the paper and we got the spelling out of that: S-Y-N-A-N-O-N. She tried the telephone directory but it wasn't listed.

"It's a place for dope addicts," my mother explained to the operator. "My daughter is an addict and she wants to get cured. It's very important." After much searching, the operator gave us a number to call in Westport, Connecticut.

My mother spoke to them first. Yes, it was Synanon. They asked her a few questions, then they had her put me on. They asked me about my habit and how long I'd had it and where I'd heard of Synanon and what made me want to become part of Synanon.

"I need help," I told the man at the other end.

"Come on Monday, before one. We'll see if you really need

help." And then he added, very bluntly: "If you're not here by one, forget it."

I was stunned by his directness. "If you're not here by one, forget it!" He didn't even know me; what right did he have to speak to me like that? Supposing something happened and I couldn't make it until a while later, would they really turn me away? He'd sounded so brusque, so determined, so sure of what he was saying. I had to believe him. No one had ever spoken so directly to me before about important things. I felt it was something I had to obey. He had that demanding, assuring way about him that I'd admired at one time in Harriet and later in Franco, but theirs, I had realized later, was just a pose and it soon enough turned to pleading and then to whining. I couldn't imagine the man from Synanon pleading or whining. He meant it for real.

I made up my mind I'd be in Synanon on Monday, *before* one.

I called Franco at his mother's home to tell him the good news: "They can help me, Franco. They can help you, too. Please go there and join them. Get your mother to call them and ask them for an appointment." I wondered who else would like to go to Synanon. Harriet? I wanted to call her but I couldn't face the thought of speaking to her after all that had happened since we'd parted. I thought of Leslie, but my mother told me she was in trouble, in the hospital, or perhaps in jail.

Saturday I spent washing my things and packing for Synanon. Sunday my mother gave me some money to go and meet Franco downtown, telling me not to get lost, not to miss my appointment. She didn't have to warn me; nothing would have made me blow my big chance. I met Franco at Broadway and West 110th Street and we spent the whole afternoon and evening together, riding back and forth on subways, talking, holding hands, planning, hoping. We took off, just once, a very small dose, a last time for both of us. The dope was his and so were the works, and I made him promise to come to Synanon, to get his mother to drive him up to Westport and to make sure he'd be there well before one.

It was well after midnight when I kissed him good-bye and took a cab home to my parents.

My mother and father took the occasion seriously; both of

them stayed home from work. They sent Mitchell off to school and then they drove me to Westport.

I thought there must be a mistake. It was a mansion, a huge estate with lawns and shrubs and trees. It made even Grasslands look like a jail. This was too beautiful and too opulent for anything as crummy as addicts. We pulled up in the driveway, the gravel scrunching under our tires, and the moment we stopped by the main door Franco's mother drove in with him and parked right behind our car. We all sat in the reception room, talking in hushed voices. I was nervous and scared. My hopes were unlimited, but my reason told me not to be a fool. Things don't happen like this. They don't provide luxury like this for addicts when they can just as easily shove a few hundred of them into a place like Manhattan General and put them through the meat grinder. There had to be a catch somewhere, but I couldn't figure it out, it was too elaborate, too involved.

Then they called me into an office together with my parents. Three men and a woman introduced themselves by their first names. Then they started firing at me.

"What are you here for?"

"To clean up."

They sneered. "Hah! To clean up. Like Manhattan General! You come here and clean up and then you walk out and start all over again."

"Well, no."

"Listen, this isn't Lexington, Kentucky, either. You're not here to clean up."

"I want to stop using drugs."

"Drugs isn't your problem."

What right did they have to talk to me like that? What did they know about me anyway. "Drugs does happen to be my problem. It's the only problem I have."

"Yeah, that's what you think. We know what your problem is. Shall we tell you? Your problem is that you're a baby. That's what you are. You haven't grown up."

"I'm grown-up enough. I've fended for myself, I've been through more of life and through more hard times than most people you could mention."

"Shut up!" I was shocked by their aggressive way of talking. "You can't put one over on us. We know where you've been. You're not dealing with a bunch of hacks or social workers now. We're all ex-addicts. *We know.*"

I'd gone into Synanon with a load of arrogance. I'd felt important. I was going to participate in something big, something that had already been turned into a movie. And I'd make them sit up and notice when they found out where I'd been and what I'd done and how tough I was. I thought I could shock them and get them to admire me. But here they were, putting me down, trying to make me feel like an insignificant worm.

"You think you know where it's at, dingbat, but you don't know *anything.*"

That name, dingbat, sounded insulting. I wouldn't have minded if they'd called me a motherfucker, that at least would indicate anger, I could respond to that. But what do you say to someone who calls you a dingbat and treats you like a baby?

"What's your name?"

"Cookie Quinn."

"Cookie? Is that the name on your birth certificate?"

"Well, no."

"What is it, then?"

"Barbara."

"Okay, so you're Barbara Quinn."

"But no one has ever called me Barbara."

"That's your name, Barbara."

"But I won't answer to it."

"Yes you will."

Every time I opened my mouth they shot me down. I sank lower and lower into my chair, feeling more and more powerless, more and more childish and foolish.

"You don't come in here for a twenty-one day medical and step right out, dingbat. If you want to become part of Synanon you'll have to stay with us for two and a half years."

I didn't believe them. "Two and a half years! I know I don't need that much."

"You don't know a thing. It's what you think you know that brought you to our front door. We know where it's at. We're all ex-addicts here. We have fifty years of addiction between us."

I didn't believe there really was such a thing as an ex-addict. Once a junkie, always a junkie. They were trying to pull one on me. I kept looking at their arms to see if they had track marks. They did, but I still wouldn't believe it. They couldn't have been addicts, ever. Those marks were put there to fool me.

They sent me out of the room and talked to my father and mother, then they called me back.

"Okay, Barbara, we'll take you in as part of our family. We'll help you to grow up some day. Welcome home." They all hugged me. My head spun. I felt I wanted to cry. They'd treated me so roughly at first and now they were so gentle and loving. I didn't know where I stood with them.

"Well, Barbara. This is it. Kiss Mommy and Daddy good-bye. You're going to cut Mommy loose, you're not going to be able to depend on her anymore. Give her a break. You've clung to her long enough; let her lead her own life now."

I kissed them good-bye and promised to write at least once a week.

"You can't do that, Barbara. You'll have to cut yourself loose from everyone, including your parents. You're not allowed to write to anyone your first three months at Synanon."

"But what about money for the commissary and so on?"

"We'll take care of you here. You'll be part of the Synanon family. If your mommy wants to send anything, let her send a gift to Synanon and we'll make use of it."

They took me upstairs to my room and left me to unpack. I sat by the window and then I saw Franco and his mother drive off. I couldn't wave to them and I wondered why they didn't stay. It seemed so odd; I'd wanted to be with Franco when I cleaned up, finally and for good, and now Franco wasn't sticking by me.

The Synanon people explained it later: "We told him to come back in three months, after you've been passed on to California. We can't help couples that come in together; sooner or later they drag each other down and then we lose both. When you're by yourself the group gives you the strength to hold out."

To say that Synanon was a new experience would be the height of understatement. I was faced, for the first time in my life, with a solid wall of honest reality against which all my attempts at manipulation and pretense were powerless. All my life—at home, in school, on the street, in jails, and in hospitals—I'd been surrounded by people who saw me as an object to be controlled, or an object to be used, and I'd spent my energies in trying to control or use them for my own ends. Here it didn't work. They had my number. They wouldn't let me be an object. They wouldn't let me play roles and they wouldn't let me manipulate them. Helpless baby, seductive sex kitten, world-weary woman, none of those roles worked for me.

I'd brought in lots and lots of makeup. "You don't need that shit on your face, Barbara. That's just a lot of paint you're using as a cover-up. You're trying to create an image. You think it's a defense, but really it's a disguise. We *know* you have a face under it, you might as well let us see the real you. Be yourself." They sent out for some dark dye and had me turn my hair back to its original dark brown. It hadn't been that shade for five years. I kept catching myself in the mirror, seeing myself and yet not seeing myself, a new and strange face and yet familiar, a new Barbara who was trying to be herself. They took me to a dentist to have my cavities filled. "One day, Barbara, Synanon will have your missing teeth fixed. But you'll have to wait a year. You have to earn it first."

Earn it, earn it. That was another refrain. You don't just get things in the real world, you earn them. You earn your stay in Synanon by being part of it and making it work. You earn your way up by proving yourself, by being honest and open and real. You can't play tricks, you can't finagle: You've got to earn what you want.

After dinner on Monday evening, they told me to come downstairs to the basement. "We're going to start the games now."

"Games!" They had games in all the hospitals and jails I'd been to, billiards for the men, ping-pong for the girls. Something to do. Something to fill in the time between the television, and mopping the floors, and rapping, and going back to your ward or your cell. A game.

But not the Synanon Game. No ping-pong table here, only a circle of chairs. Everyone sits down: the people who'd interviewed me, the directors, the new people, myself. And the games start. You call this a game? They're firing at everyone. "Motherfucker!" "Dingbat!" "What do you think you're trying to prove with that fucking shit?"

I remembered it now, I'd seen it in the movie. Everyone gets roasted over his mistakes. The group is merciless, no one escapes. The director is pulled to pieces. Motherfucker! The staff is pulled to pieces. Shitface! The newcomers are pulled to pieces. Dingbat! No one is immune, age doesn't help, length of stay doesn't help, position doesn't help. We're all in the same boat. We're all held responsible for our acts. They're all like me and I'm like them. From bewilderment I change to surprise and from surprise to hope. I'm everyone's equal. I'm as good as everyone—as long as I'm myself and don't pretend to be something special. They all started like me and one day I might be as capable as the others. I have a chance here. I can work my way up. I can earn my position. It's all in my hands. It's all up to me.

I'd kicked on Dolophines under Dr. Tollman, so I wasn't sick. My only problem with drugs was that I couldn't sleep nights. "Yes, Barbara, I know." There was always someone around who understood me, someone who'd been through the same thing. "You'll have to fight that battle here without pills—but you'll have friends to help you." They sat up with me nights when I couldn't sleep, they encouraged me and kept away the terrors, they let me know they understood even when they couldn't do anything direct to help me.

I put on weight and outgrew my clothes. They got me new clothes, but I held on to the old clothes I'd brought with me, just in case. "You don't need those, Barbara. You have as many clothes as you can use. Put your old ones back in the pot where someone else can have them." The pot. For everyone. Everyone shared, no one was favored.

I had a job, helping out in the kitchen, and I pulled my little child act: "I don't know how to do this." "I've never done that." "I don't understand."

"Sure, Barbara, you have to learn. We all have to learn."

"But I might spoil something. I'm sure I'll break the dishes or burn the food."

"Let it burn, let it spill. Next time you'll know better." What could I answer? They'd taken away my excuses. They accepted me with all my mistakes; mistakes at Synanon didn't mean failure.

"You're acting like a sex kitten, Barbara. Stop wiggling your ass. It won't get you anywhere; no one here is interested in children."

"You're acting like a helpless baby, Barbara. We're not authorities here. We don't do your thinking for you. You're responsible for yourself."

"They! They! Them! Don't use those words, Barbara. We're not *They*. It's not you against *Them*. We're all *We*. You too. It's *We*."

Every time I tried to play one of my roles I was pulled up, either by the people I was trying to work on or at the next games. The games were played every Monday, Wednesday, and Friday evening, with everyone there and everyone under attack for his actions and attitudes. They called me a baby and said I was childish and manipulative; that hit me right in the gut. I wished I had drugs when they had me under attack. With drugs I could have been high and if I'd been high I wouldn't have minded what they called me.

They caught on to that: "You've been getting high to escape the truth about yourself, Barbara. That's tough shit to handle, eh baby? A woman of twenty-three and you're still a baby and want people to respond to you as a baby. Tough! Yeah, baby, the truth is hard to handle."

Sometimes it hurt, hurt real bad. I felt crushed by the charges and the frankness. "You have to learn to hurt and accept being hurt, Barbara. You can't feel good all the time. You have to learn how to feel, feel your hurts and your hopes and your love. Dope made you stop having to feel; now you can learn to feel again. You have to learn to be aware of yourself, become aware of your needs, your childishness, your inadequacies, and your insecurity."

Synanon kept my mind busy. I had to grapple with a whirl of new concepts. I was in turn shocked, surprised, intrigued and happy. They wouldn't let me escape responsibility for myself.

They insisted I face up to myself, to what I really was and what I really could do. I'd never before been among people like these: I could hardly put them down as being square, they were all once part of the world from which I'd just come, nor could I put them up on a pedestal as authorities, they were just as likely as me to be pulled to pieces in the next games. I wasn't worse and I wasn't better and I wasn't different; I was simply myself, uniquely myself, and what I would make of myself was up to me. I was kept so busy trying to absorb these new concepts that I didn't even have the time to think about drugs—except during the games. I could have walked out anytime I wanted to and gone to Manhattan to cop. "The door swings both ways," they'd told me when I first arrived. "You can leave as easily as you came. We won't hold you against your will. You have the key to Synanon." I was free to go and that made me free enough to stay.

In my fourth week at Synanon I started getting restless. It didn't seem possible that I could be so long off drugs. How long could I keep it up? Any day I might walk out of there and go down to the city to cop. Did they know that? Did they believe I might do it? How would they feel if I told them? Would they be disappointed in me? Would they try to keep me by force or would they tell me, "You have the key. The door swings both ways," and let me go down to Manhattan to start fucking myself up with drugs again?

I told them. I was too scared not to.

"Sure, Barbara, we know. We all have those feelings. We all had the urge to get drugs. The thing is that if you can talk about it, you can discover those feelings and handle them. Don't ignore your feelings, don't hold things down. Face yourself, talk about yourself."

The next day they told me to pack my clothes. "It's time for you to go to California. You've been here long enough."

They were right. New York was too near. I couldn't handle this sort of freedom and this sort of easy temptation—yet. If I stayed on at Westport I might split, back to my folks, back to Franco, and back to drugs.

They drove me to Kennedy Airport and put me on a plane. "The stewardess is going to come round and offer you a drink,

Barbara. Don't take any liquor. You know liquor is against the rules at Synanon."

I knew. I strapped myself into my seat and waïted for the takeoff. All around me people were sitting; which of them was from Synanon? Which of them was a spy? I'd never been much of a drinker, I didn't really care for alcohol, I didn't like the taste and I didn't like what it did for me. But right now I wanted a drink. Right now I had to drink. It was really their fault. If they hadn't warned me against it I wouldn't have been bothered by it.

My hands were clammy, my throat was dry. The stewardess came to my seat and said to me in her saccharine voice, "Would you like to order your drink now, please."

"Yes," I said. "I'll have a Coke."

☼ CHAPTER TWENTY-THREE ☼

A welcoming committee of two girls and a man came to meet me at the plane in San Francisco. They weren't inmates and they weren't officials. We chatted about Westport and the people they knew there and then we stopped off at a taco stand for some Mexican food. I felt I was in, part of a little group that accepted me without reservations, that let me be their friend and listened to me and joked with me. It was as intimate a group as any I'd ever known at school or in the lesbian bars or on the block.

We went to Sea Wall, the main Synanon facility in San Francisco, a converted warehouse on Lombard Street right by the bay. Gerry Brod, the facility agent who was in charge of Sea Wall, interviewed me on my first evening there. Casually, while we were talking, he asked to see my purse. He opened it and took out my little address book.

"Aha!" he said, looking over my list of johns. "Hey! You've got the same numbers my old lady used to have. She used to work on Broadway, too." I wanted to ask him more about his wife, where she'd turned tricks, whether they'd been married when she was working or if they'd got married later in Synanon.

Gerry took hold of the book between his powerful hands and tore it right across. "Well, you won't be needing *this* anymore."

I was aghast. This was my insurance, the one thing that would keep me in money if I ever needed it. Sure, I was going to go straight, I was never going to go back on the street again, but something might happen, I might need some money, perhaps Synanon wouldn't work.

Gerry threw the two torn halves into the wastebasket. I marked the spot where they fell. I had an urge to jump in after my book. You don't just throw away a book like that: That book was a lifetime of experience, that book was valuable; with a clientele like mine I could have gotten two thousand dollars easily for it from any working girl or her pimp.

My first job at Synanon was as a countergirl. I had to keep the coffee pot filled with water and coffee, clean it between fillings, wipe down the counter, keep cups out and cookies available.

I goofed off every now and again, playing sick. I menstruated rather heavily—junkies more or less stop menstruating when they're on dope and then come on heavily when they're clean—and stayed in bed. Jeannie, a blue-eyed blonde of about thirty who worked in the medical section, came to see me.

"What's the matter?"

"I'm hemorrhaging."

"Nonsense, it's your period."

"But it's very heavy."

"Lying in bed won't help. Keep moving and working. Lying in bed will just give you an opportunity to start tripping out to what you left. Too much brooding by yourself and you'll start getting into your old longings and craziness."

She knew how I ticked. She'd been an addict herself, for only a year, not too strung out, but she was wise to me. She'd been at Synanon a long time.

I was at one of the games, dressed in dungarees and sweat shirt, a cigarette dangling from my lips, cussing and swearing and shooting my mouth off.

Jeannie walked in, Jeannie from the medical section. "Who's this longshoreman?" she asked. Everyone laughed. At me. She'd made a fool out of me. I still wanted to impress them all with my toughness but, instead, they laughed.

"Where did you get a filthy mouth like that?" she asked. She'd shot me down. She had my number; I had to admire her.

When I found out that Jeannie was married to Oscar Camaño, it all made perfect sense. Oscar was a lovely person, tall and lanky, very handsome, the "wizard" of Sea Wall. He was an artist from El Paso, Texas, and his pictures decorated all the walls. He'd been in Synanon for seven years and now he was Gerry Brod's co-worker. Gerry was the authority at Sea Wall, Oscar was the soul; Gerry would lay down a ruling and Oscar would spell it out and explain it and make it acceptable. Oscar had warmth. I tried to use my feminine wiles on him, but he wouldn't respond and I respected him all the more for it; he wouldn't tell me what I wanted to hear but only what was right and true.

Oscar and Jeannie saw that I was a lost child, more lost than most people who came to Sea Wall, and took me under their wing. They gave me the responsibility for making my own decisions. They wouldn't accept my bullshit. They set my boundaries. They were everything I had wanted my parents to be, everything I had wanted from teachers and doctors, from probation officers and psychiatrists. I tried to work for their approval. I watched them at whatever they were doing and modeled myself after them. They lived in a private facility on Clay Street, a three-story house for couples and older residents in one of the best sections of San Francisco, five minutes away by car. I hated it every evening when they left Sea Wall to go home.

Newcomers weren't allowed to go out without a chaperon. About a month after I'd got to Sea Wall I went for a walk with Carol, who'd been in Synanon for a few months. We walked down Lombard Street. Off in the bay the fog horns were sounding. A salty tang was in the air, an atmosphere of mystery and adventure around. I had an urge, a sudden urge, for a pizza. A red hot sizzling pizza with sausages *and* mushrooms *and* anchovies. I hadn't had a pizza since I'd started in Synanon, and I didn't have any money: you don't get walk-around money at Synanon until you've been there for six months and then you start with a dollar a week. Carol had no money, either.

A man accosted us on Lombard Street. He didn't look bad, sort of Italian with curly dark hair and blue eyes. I could turn a quick trick and we'd have money for pizza. I walked away from Carol to talk to him.

"Ten dollars," I said.

"Okay."

I went back to Carol to tell her I wouldn't be gone long. "Then we'll go and have a pizza."

For a moment, Carol agreed, then suddenly she got scared. "You'd better not go. I'll have to tell about it, I'm responsible for you."

"Oh, just once. Nobody has to find out. It's not as if it did any harm to anyone, it's not as if I was going to shoot up or something."

"No, Barbara. I'm responsible for you. I'll have to tell."

"You're chicken."

"Perhaps I am, but I can't let you go. I can't lie about you."

Synanon conditions you to guilt. Carol already had it. She was conditioned to telling the truth. I wasn't conditioned to it yet, but I had a feeling of what it meant. Turning a trick and having my pizza could have been a thrill. Not giving in to it and knowing I could go back to Synanon and let them know I hadn't failed, was also a thrill—a different kind of thrill but just as good. I apologized to the man and we continued our walk along the bay.

After a few weeks as countergirl I was promoted to third cook, responsible for preparing lunch. Then Oscar and Jeannie had me move to Clay Street to take care of the house, do the laundry, and answer the telephone. Jeannie let me play her records—people are discouraged from listening to records in their first few months at Synanon because the tunes often bring back old associations and the associations stir up old longings and desire—and I took special care over their room, spit-shining everything and ironing their laundry with special attention.

"How's Mommy and Daddy?" people would ask me at the games. They were indicting me for being around them so much, for being so dependent on them.

"Don't be ridiculous," I always defended myself. "There's nothing special between us." But I hoped there was, I was glad to have others confirm that Oscar and Jeannie were something special to me.

If it hadn't been for Oscar and Jeannie, I think I might have despaired more than once in my first months at Sea Wall. They gave me strength and a sense of belonging when I felt lost and lonely. Jeannie had a son, Jeffrey, about Mitchell's age, who was living with her parents; that gave us a common interest—and created an added bond.

I moved back to live at Sea Wall after about four months at Clay Street. There were too many complaints from residents that I was becoming detached from the world of Synanon, that I was missing seminars and morning meetings although, of course, I was coming to the games regularly like all residents. I continued working at Clay Street during the day for another couple of months, but now I slept in the girls' dormitory in the Club.

Gradually, as I became able to accept responsibilities, I was put in charge of the girls' dorms. I saw to it that the necessary work was done, assuming responsibility for the actions of others. I became a role model for newcomers, helping them with their problems, listening to them, sharing my own feelings and fears and hopes with them, showing them where they were deluding themselves. I helped new people while they were going through the pain and agony of kicking and sat with them when they couldn't sleep. I talked with them when their urges became too strong and they wanted someone to help them withstand the temptations. I knew where they were at; I could help them be strong.

But I wasn't strong. At heart I was still very much the child. For all my worldliness and all my experience, I was still a child. When I goofed, when I acted irresponsible, when I tried to manipulate others, I got shot down. They tackled me at the games and at meetings, indicting me for my poses, calling me all the names under the sun, making me realize how foolish and immature I was. I was only a child—but I was among friends and my friends would guide me. They understood, they were fighting for me, they were with me all the way.

When I'd been at Sea Wall for about six months I was sent out on speaking engagements, like everyone at Synanon. I spoke to church groups and parents' organizations and civic groups, telling them about my own past as an addict, about the drug problem, about the work of Synanon. It was an important part of the Synanon training: It gave me self-confidence, it brought Synanon to the public, it made people aware of the real dimensions of the drug problem. And it made me become more fully aware of myself. In accepting the past, I was able to face what I had been and what I was striving to become. I learned to be frank and open about my past.

There were two points I always stressed, two incidents that had particularly impressed themselves on me when I came to Synanon. One was the brusqueness of that order, "If you're not here by one, forget it." It had taught me the importance of discipline and the futility of excuses. I knew what I had to do and I had better buckle down and do it. The other lesson, continually impressed on me at meetings and at the games, was that my problem wasn't really drugs; my problem was that I was a baby. I had to be willing to forgo immediate gratification. I had to accept responsibility for my actions—as a grown-up.

Oscar and Jeannie gave me strength. At first I was terribly possessive about them and I became jealous when new people came to Sea Wall and made a claim on Oscar's or Jeannie's attention. Later, as I matured, I came to enjoy sharing them with others. It gave me a special joy to be able to say to a newcomer, "Talk it out with Oscar and Jeannie. They understand, they can help you."

One of those in whom Oscar and Jeannie took a special interest was Joe, a handsome Greek boy from New Jersey. Joe and I were alike in many respects, we were the "little gangsters" of Sea Wall, two rebellious spirits: Joe was James Cagney, I was his gun moll. Jeannie and Oscar became parents to both of us.

Gradually I fell in love with Joe. It seemed inevitable. The group sensed it—and stopped it. "You didn't come to Synanon to have a boy friend, Barbara. You came here to grow up—that's all you're going to get here." When I held Joe's hand they pulled us apart, when I sat next to him they made me move away.

I had to ask Gerry for permission to date Joe. He talked to Joe, then he put it before a meeting. From then on we were allowed to become closer friends but not to flaunt our attraction in public: no kissing, no necking. We were allowed to go out together, even to go to a movie—but always in a group or with a senior member for an escort.

After we'd been dating for a few months, we were allowed to apply for a guest room appointment. The guest room was where couples could go to be alone together. Gerry approved. I went to the girl who kept the register and we were allotted two hours. We had to carry our sheets through the building to the guest room. Everyone saw us. I felt shy and embarrassed, a virgin on her first date, a bride on her wedding night.

Joe was as scared as I was. We sat for a long time just talking softly, just holding hands, just kissing gently. It was the first time I was together with a man as an adult woman.

I came to Joe shy and inadequate, totally inexperienced: all my past sex life, all my experiences from the age of eleven, all my experimentation with me and with women, all my johns and my tricks and my lovers—all was irrelevant. I was starting right from the beginning, learning the meaning of love and life and friendship; learning what men and women are supposed to mean to each other.

For the first time in my life, I was learning the meaning of the word no. It wasn't easy: I couldn't easily take no from others; I couldn't easily say no myself. It took me two and a half years of Synanon to learn to cope with that word. And even then it wasn't easy.

I started reading at Sea Wall. I hadn't read a book since I was fifteen and a student. My first choice was *Siddhartha* by Hermann Hesse. I used the library a lot after that and found that books could give me enjoyment; I relaxed, I became involved with the characters and identified with them. I discovered that what I'd once thought was the real and exciting world was only make-believe. There was wealth and richness in the real world, the world I'd always put down as square. Books opened new doors for me; I read hungrily, trying to experience what others could teach me, trying to make up for the years I'd lived in illusion.

I worked my way up. Synanon paid to have my teeth fixed. I assumed more responsibility. I was put on the sales crew, selling advertising promotions manufactured for Synanon. Sometimes I went out with a team, sometimes I went out by myself, sometimes I went on extended trips with a group and stayed away for a few days. I was a talented saleswoman; I discovered a legitimate outlet for my gift of persuasion. I was somebody. I lived away from Sea Wall now, sharing a brownstone with five other girls.

Joe and I were becoming closer. We asked for permission to marry. Oscar and Jeannie were happy, Synanon gave its blessing and suggested that I should work toward a position at the San Diego facility where I'd be close to Mexico and could get myself a divorce from Eddie. It might take a few weeks until I could get to San Diego, then another few months to arrange the formalities, and then Joe would come to San Diego and we could get married.

Suddenly I became terrified. The responsibilities of marriage frightened me. Did I really love Joe? Could I really make a go of it? Would I start manipulating him? Would I become dependent on him? Would I feel trapped by Joe as I always felt trapped by people who were making too many demands on me? Could I really go through with the marriage? Could I face Jeannie and Oscar if I broke it off?

I was away on an overnight trip with three guys and another girl, Myra. Myra and I shared a motel room. Myra had been sent to Sea Wall from another facility after Synanon found out that she'd had an affair there with Irene, a girl I'd known years earlier from Barbo's in Greenwich Village. Once Irene had turned me on, now Myra turned me on—and I knew she was available.

That night, Myra and I fucked in our motel room.

I hadn't been with another woman since I'd broken with Harriet, over four years earlier. (Partying for pay didn't count—that was always faked.) I'd been eighteen months in Synanon. I felt closed in. I felt the weight of responsibility. I didn't have the guts to marry Joe—and I didn't have the guts to break it off. I wanted someone else to take responsibility for deciding my future with Joe. I wanted to create a situation that would force my decision for me.

Myra and I met regularly on sales trips after that. We felt we could put one over on Synanon. When we stayed away overnight we made out in our motel. When we were on day trips we did only a little selling, then went off to a park or the movies to be together. We necked secretly in our dorm, we necked in the bathroom at Synanon. And still Synanon didn't find out.

I arranged a pajama party at my house with a lot of girls from

Sea Wall coming to sleep over. Someone discovered Myra and me in a compromising position on the floor.

The next day they questioned us as we came back from a sales trip. They brought us up before a general meeting of the whole facility. Joe was there, too, his face ashen.

Both Myra and I admitted it. Joe broke down and cried. I cried too.

"How can you be such an idiot?" Jeannie asked me. "If you wanted attention or something was becoming too much for you, why didn't you tell us and talk it over with people?" They put Myra and me on a ban, forbidden to talk to each other. I lost all my privileges. I had to start again at the bottom. I was relieved: I hadn't been ready for so much responsibility.

A few days later I spoke to Myra in the bathroom. "This place is too much. Let's split."

We spoke to two guys, newcomers, and we decided to walk out together. We passed a church and I suggested that we go in. We sat in the pews for a while, walked around, then came out. I don't know what I had hoped to find in the church, but it seemed the right place to go to after leaving Synanon. We walked off down the road. I felt empty. I didn't know what I wanted. I certainly didn't want drugs. I wanted to be free, but without Synanon I was a prisoner. I needed the love and care that Synanon could give me.

A car was coming down the road. "Hey, quick!" I said to Myra. "Synanon! They're after us. Let's go!" We started running down the street. They stopped the car in the middle of the street and came after us. The two guys made off as fast as they could. Myra and I kept running and then I found myself slowing, slowing, like in a dream, slower and slower. My feet were lead. Gerry Brod grabbed Myra. I let Oscar catch me. The two guys disappeared.

Oscar held me tight. I hugged him. I snuggled into his arms and cried with relief and joy. Oscar and Gerry had come after us; Synanon had showed that it cared.

I was ready now to accept the consequences. "Dingbat!" "Motherfucker!" "Stupid baby!" It was true, I was everything the others called me. I was childish and immature, unprepared to accept responsibility.

Oscar arranged for me to be sent to another facility at Tamales Bay. "You'll have to stand on your own two feet there," he told me. "Without Joe, or Jeannie, or me."

It wasn't quite as Oscar had predicted. Candy, the facility agent at Tamales, and Pat, his girl friend, took an interest in me and helped me get my head together again after my dismal failure at Sea Wall. I'd known Pat from way back in Westport when she'd been in the group that interviewed me and took me into Synanon. She was the only woman among the senior residents at Westport and to have her on my side in Tamales gave me confidence in the future. I was started at Tamales in the dishpan, on the lowest rung of the ladder. Gradually I worked my way up. I put Pat and Candy in the roles that Jeannie and Oscar had played for me at Sea Wall, but they were determined not to let me lean on them and forced me to become more independent. After four months at Tamales Bay I became a trainee teacher under Al Baumann, a former professor who was setting up a revolutionary educational system for Synanon's children. The school leaned heavily on Synanon ideas and the children were involved in what might be described as a continuous encounter highlighted by a special version of the Synanon Game.

From Tamales Bay I was rotated to Santa Monica to teach at the Synanon school there. Oscar and Jeannie had preceded me, and I was glad to be with them again, but our relationship now was on a quite different footing. Jeannie had a new baby that gave her a legitimate outlet for her need to play the mother; she still mothered me, almost instinctively it seemed, patting my head and brushing the hair out of my eyes and fussing over me in numerous other little ways, but what had changed was the fact that I no longer needed her mothering. I could take care of myself.

Candy and Pat also came to Santa Monica. I was Pat's equal now, not her protégée. We shared a room, we confided in each other, we were on equal terms. I had learned to establish a true two-way relationship.

I could have gotten my divorce from Eddie while I was at Santa Monica but everything with Joe had come to an end. There was no urgency. I had no interest in getting involved in another experiment at courtship or another attempt at marriage.

After a while they put me back on the sales crew. I was a good teacher, but I was an even better saleswoman, and I was more valuable to Synanon selling pens inscribed with names of insurance brokers and used car dealers.

In Santa Monica I started going to night school to earn my high school equivalency diploma. I wrote long letters to my mother telling her what Synanon was all about. I was hep to the Synanon Game and to psychological jargon and I started giving her advice, telling her where she had gone wrong and what was wrong with her thinking. I told her with pride that I was reading books and what they'd done for me; in a way, that was a dig at my mother—we didn't have a single book in our house.

I'd been in Synanon for two and a half years. At Westport, when I'd first been allowed to join Synanon, they'd told me that everyone had to stay for at least two and a half years. At Sea Wall a new policy came into force: Synanon wouldn't graduate anyone who hadn't been there five years. While I was at Santa Monica, Chuck Dederich changed the rules again: You were never done with Synanon. Synanon wasn't just a place for addicts; it was a way of life, a place and a concept that would help change the world. You stayed at Synanon and made it your life's work.

I saw that Synanon could become a crutch for some people, as much an addiction as drugs or alcohol. It could become a crutch for me, too. I could become dependent on it and never know again what it was to be myself and take full responsibility for myself. Synanon had taught me to grow up, to cherish my independence, to make my own decisions, and not look to others to run my life or satisfy my needs. Synanon had done a lot for me—perhaps too much. I was comfortable and respected. I had my own garden apartment that I shared with another girl—it even had a swimming pool! I had acquired a beautiful wardrobe of clothes that I'd selected from the donations that flowed into Synanon. I was a successful saleswoman, one of the best. Selling pens. Pens!

I knew there must be something else.

Pat was another one who felt there must be something else. She and Candy had left Synanon and gone back to New York City to work with Mitchell Rosenthal in setting up Phoenix House, a center for drug addicts based on Synanon principles. Pat hadn't wanted to be responsible for making decisions for me, but she had told me that if things worked out well at Phoenix House and if I felt I was ready to leave Synanon, I might find a vocation there working with addicts. It made more sense to me than selling pens.

Then I had a letter from her. She was director of a Phoenix House facility for girls on West Eighty-fifth Street just off Broadway. Things were going well. The program was functioning. Pat was earning a salary. There was room for other experienced people. Pat stopped short of actually offering me a job; that was to be my own decision.

I agonized over it for a few days. Synanon was my home. Synanon would take care of me. Synanon would help me whenever things became too tough for me to handle by myself. Could I give it all up? Could I go back to New York with all its temptations and find a job and support myself and not have Synanon to call on whenever I got into trouble? I felt the answer was yes. Synanon insisted that no one was really ready to leave but I knew better; I knew I was ready, I knew I could make a go of it.

I walked out of Synanon and placed a call to my mother from a store. "I'm calling you collect for the last time, Mother; I didn't want to do it, but I couldn't call you on Synanon's account. I want to come home. There's a job waiting for me. I know I'm ready. I want you to send me the money for my fare home. For the last time. I can't repay you for everything you've done for me in the past and for all the money you've spent on me, but from now on, after this, I'm going to pay my own way. I'm ready to come home now, Mother."

"You know best if you're ready, Cookie."

"Barbara, Mother, not Cookie. Yes, I'm ready. Believe me, I know. I won't ever shoot dope again, I know. You can really trust me, this time."

I went back to my garden apartment and waited until my

roommate had gone over to the Club for the evening. I couldn't tell her. She would have made me face the whole group and they'd have brought it up in a game or at a general meeting. I was strong enough to leave Synanon, strong enough to make my own decisions, but I wasn't strong enough to withstand the pressure from the group.

I left most of my clothes behind and most of the trinkets and possessions I'd acquired. I packed only one small bag that I could carry on the plane. I left a few notes saying good-bye to all my friends, explaining my decision, and thanking Synanon for everything it had done for me. Then I sneaked out and took a cab to Western Union to pick up my money and from there to the Los Angeles airport for the first flight out to New York.

☼ CHAPTER TWENTY-FOUR ☼

I was on my own now. No one was telling me what to do. There were no spies to check on me. The responsibility was mine. When the stewardess offered me a drink I asked for a soda. In January, 1968, a few days shy of my twenty-sixth birthday, I arrived back in New York City. It was snowing heavily; I was wearing the clothes I'd had in Southern California and couldn't help shivering. And I was scared, not of drugs—I knew that I'd never, never go back on drugs—but of the change, the temptations, the responsibilities.

I called my mother from the airport, then took a cab home to Yonkers. I was dying to see Mitchell whom I hadn't seen in nearly three years. I wanted to see how he'd changed—and I wanted him to see that his mother had changed. It was late morning when I arrived. Everyone was up waiting for me. We had breakfast, the first time the whole family had sat down to breakfast together.

"How's Leslie?" I asked Mom.

"She's fine. I see her mother every now and again, and her brother Bruce does my hair every two weeks. She's been in jail since the time you went to Synanon—for forging checks, I think—but she's been home about a week now."

"Make sure you tell her mother about me. Tell her about Synanon. Tell her to get Leslie into it."

I felt I wanted to help every addict. I had a message for them. I had hope. I could show them where help lay.

I called Franco. My call went through to a funeral parlor.

"This must be a mistake," I told them, repeating his number.

"That's our number," they told me.

"I'm sorry, they must have changed it. I'm trying to trace an old friend, he must have moved. Do you know anything about the people who had the number before?"

No one knew anything. Information couldn't help me. Franco's family had moved away. There had been a choice at Westport between Franco and me. I had got there a minute ahead of him and I had been chosen for a new life. I never heard of Franco again.

The next morning I called Pat at Phoenix House and she invited me down to West Eighty-fifth Street. It was strange being back in the old neighborhood. I walked down Broadway, seeing all the old familiar places, the hotels where I'd lived, the corners where I'd hustled, the storefronts I'd leaned against while talking to my tricks, the rooms where I'd taken care of my johns—a dim memory now, their names thrown out in a Synanon trash basket. I walked down Broadway with a sense of power and accomplishment; no one could recognize me, no one knew my secret, no one knew what I'd had to work through to get where I was now.

Phoenix House was based on a system similar to Synanon's, but since it was an agency founded by the city, I had to pass the city's special certification board; my years and experiences at Synanon were considered enough to wipe out my criminal record and to qualify me for a position ordinarily open only to college graduates.

For a few weeks I lived at home, in my old room. Nothing much had changed there except that Mitchell was older and I could really relate to him for the first time in my life. A few days after I'd come back—I was still putting away my clothes—someone rang at the doorbell. My mother answered and called out, "Cookie!" It took me a moment to realize she was calling me. I came to the front door.

"Leslie!"

"Cookie!"

We ran into each other's arms and embraced. So many years had passed between us; little Leslie whom I'd helped across the street, little Leslie with whom I used to play while her brother Bruce was waiting for me in the other room, Leslie who took me to Barbo's, Leslie who got me my first dope.

"Leslie, I want to help you. If you only had the strength . . . if you could do what I did. . . ."

"I'm all right, Cookie."

"It's Barbara now."

"Aw, cut that shit. You're still Cookie. Listen, things *have* changed for me. I haven't spent two and a half years in a jail in Jersey for nothing. I know where it's at now. I've settled down. I'm going steady. I met my old lady in jail; now I'm waiting for her to come out and things will be all right for me."

"Leslie, honest, nothing's changed for you. That's not where it's at, it's not with women. There's a lot more than either you or me knew about in the old days."

"Yeah, I know. But I've changed too. I've gotten away from the old environment; things will be different."

"No, Leslie, nothing's changed. You may have moved away from the old environment physically, but nothing's really changed inside you. You'll get back on drugs unless you *do* something. You've got to get involved with some program. You can't do it by yourself, no one can."

I made her promise to come down to Phoenix House so that I could get her on the program. "Keep in touch, anyway. Think of it as an investment."

I commuted from Yonkers to my new job on West Eighty-fifth Street, but I couldn't live at home more than a few weeks. My mother still saw me as a child, she was forever doing things for me, trying to prove she was indispensable, as if the excellent care she was taking of Mitchell wasn't proof enough. It wasn't what I needed; I needed to be an adult, away from my mother's pressures. I moved into Phoenix House as a resident staff member.

Leslie phoned me once when I was at Phoenix House and told me she'd be coming in soon to join the program. I told her how much I was looking forward to seeing her. My work was with people like her, dope fiends who were wising up, people who felt they'd had enough and wanted to find out what they could do. We had a storefront at Eighty-fifth Street and I sat there, rapping with junkies off the streets, trying to talk sense into them, trying to help them make that final decision to come in and clean up.

I could talk to them in their idiom and tell them where they were at. "You think you have a problem with drugs. Well, let me tell you something, baby, your problem isn't drugs. Your problem is that you're a baby, you haven't grown up." I told them how stupid they were, how much they had to learn to become adults. It hit their guts when I told them about their immaturity.

Many wouldn't believe I'd been an addict myself. "Do you want to see the track marks on my arms?" I asked them. And I'd let them know I was wise to them, I knew all their tricks and all their excuses. They couldn't put anything past me. "I know where it's at, baby, and it's not drugs."

After a few weeks at the storefront, I was made assistant director of a residence facility on West Eighty-eighth Street near Broadway. There I ran encounters and seminars with the addicts, and also what were known as girls' probes—encounters at which we tried to make the girls understand and accept their roles as women. They all had a distorted view of sex; almost without exception, they had all been prostitutes at some point in their lives. I played big sister and Momma to the girls—and to the boys. I spent about three months there, then I was considered ready to take on the task of assistant director at a large new facility at Coney Island.

I was leaving the Eighty-fifth Street office one evening late in May after having spent the afternoon at a staff conference, when I ran into Leslie at the corner of Broadway. She was waiting for tricks.

"*Why,* Leslie?" I asked. "You don't have to do this. Don't you know what's up the block? Do you know what's going on in that house? Did you ever try walking in there?"

"Yes, Cookie, I know. But I'm not ready. I want to fool around a little while longer. I'll be ready for it soon."

"Soon might be too late." I felt sad. Sad for her, sadder still at my own impotence. I had the answer, I could help anyone, help was just up the block. It was so close but I couldn't help my own friend. I couldn't reach her.

She got angry at me: "Where's the old you, Cookie? How come we don't speak the same language anymore? Why do you speak down at me like that, Cookie?"

"It's not Cookie, it's Barbara."

"That's what I mean. You've got to show off all your changes and everything. You've sold out. You're not speaking on my level any more. You're not my friend, Cookie."

I worked for Phoenix House for well over a year. I worked hard with the addicts and had many successes. Leslie didn't call me again and she never showed up at Eighty-fifth Street, but the people at Phoenix House let me know they needed me. They also let me know I needed Phoenix House: "Without the support of Phoenix House we'd all be shooting up again. We need it. We're ex-addicts and we have to help each other. We need to work with addicts, we can't walk away from our pasts."

I didn't want that sort of dependence. I was tired of walking around with a label. I wasn't an addict and I wasn't an ex-addict; I was a person. I had to go out into the world as myself, just Barbara, just *me.* I had to go out on my own, to lead a life of my own, as far away as I could from junkies and ex-junkies. In April of 1969 I resigned.

Through an ad in the *Post* I found a job as salesgirl in an elegant boutique just being opened, Chifforobe on West Fifty-seventh Street, two blocks south of Central Park, one block south of the Plaza, my old stomping ground during my days as a fifty-dollar a tumble whore. I started at eighty-five dollars a week, a big reduction even on what I'd earned at Phoenix.

I had a good taste in clothes. I knew what was fashionable. I knew how to sell. Gene, the proprietor, knew I'd been an addict and I saved him a lot of money: I could spot an addict a mile off, I knew all the tricks of shoplifters. I don't know how many hundreds of dollars' worth of clothes I pulled from girls' pocketbooks as they were leaving the store. Within two weeks Gene had raised my salary to a hundred and fifteen a week. I had it made. It wouldn't take me long to rise to be manager. It was good being responsible to no program and to no obligations, only to myself and my work. I lived my own life. Not an addict, not an ex-addict. Barbara Quinn.

My mother told me how proud she was of my new job. She was telling all her friends they ought to shop at Chifforobe where her daughter worked. One day in October of 1969, Bruce walked into the store.

"Bruce!" Eleven years since he'd been best man at my wedding, fourteen years since we'd been lovers. I recognized him immediately. We hugged tightly.

"Goodness! How've you been?"

"Great, Cookie, great!" He looked around the store and nodded. "Hey, things are looking good for you."

I smiled. "Yes, they've changed. Say, Bruce, how's Leslie?"

He dropped his arms from my shoulder and took half a step back and looked at me silently for a moment, all expression gone from his face. "Don't you know?"

"No, Bruce. What's. . . ."

He put one hand on my shoulder, and said, very slowly, "Don't you know, Cookie? Leslie's dead."

☼ CHAPTER TWENTY-FIVE ☼

Leslie's death drew me back into the drug world. I couldn't keep away from it. This was where I belonged, this was where my duty lay.

Within two weeks I had given up my job at Chifforobe and had taken up a post with New York City's Addiction Service Agency (ASA), working not with die-hard junkies—I could no longer stomach their lying, their cheating and their sorry self-deception—but with those who could still be helped before they had been caught up too deeply. My field was prevention: I spoke to teachers, parents, and civic groups, alerting them to the signs of incipient drug addiction, the danger signals sent out by the child whose mind is a mess and whose world is despair. I showed them how to respond in a way that makes the youngster know that someone is really trying to understand him, that someone really cares and is willing to help him solve his problems—not just to diagnose, lecture, and condemn.

Now I no longer miss the artificial excitement of the drug scene; my new life is rich enough and rewarding enough in itself. One of my happiest experiences in recent years was the three months I spent as director of the Webster Avenue Rehabilitation Center in the Bronx, working with young people in the early stages of addiction, preparing them for entry into full-time therapeutic communities such as Phoenix House and Synanon. They came to me with their problems: I listened to them, felt for them, advised them, chided them, forced them to look through the fog of their illusions, tried to steer them away from drugs and the way of life that fosters addiction. It wasn't a residential program; I couldn't do anything for the young people once they drifted out of the center in the evening and headed for the street, and when they came in in the late morning high on dope I always felt a pang of disappointment in the pit of my stomach. But at least they were in touch with help; sooner or later room would be found for them in a residential program. They had something that I lacked when I got started on drugs, somewhere to turn to, someone who understood. They had hope.

Today, with the rank of Senior Addiction Specialist, I am a special assistant to the Assistant Commissioner of the Addiction Services Agency, a trouble shooter and administrator. I attend City Hall conferences in behalf of ASA, I negotiate with State and Federal agencies, I help create new programs and encourage the setting up of new facilities. I supervise those who go out into the field to make teachers and civic groups aware of the problems—and of the available cures.

In the course of my work I have been called in as consultant by various agencies. My evenings and weekends are busy with engagements. Working in my spare time for the New Jersey Institute of Training, I have advised groups as far afield as Camden, New Jersey, Lawrenceville, Indiana, and Ithaca, New York. In Portland, Maine I directed a workshop on drugs and drug-related problems for camp directors and counselors throughout New England. In Long Island City I taught a ten-week in-service course for teachers on behalf of the New York City Board of Education. I was called in as consultant by a civic group in Ossining, New York and advised them in the setting up of rehabilitation and prevention programs in their community. I have appeared on radio, and currently conduct my own weekly television program, "Drug Line," on Sterling-Manhattan Cable TV where I can bring my message directly to parents and educators with the help of guest speakers—professionals in the field of prevention and rehabilitation, former addicts like myself, and junkies still in the throes of their agony.

I was powerless to help Leslie but I can help other young people before they, too, are beyond help.

☼ EPILOGUE ☼

This is the story of my life.

I have told it all, just as it happened, without softening the language and without pulling any punches. I make no apologies about the past; I have no regrets. What matters to me today is the present, and what I am today is in large part the product of my past experiences, the good with the bad. My strength today is the result of the struggles of my past; without them I would not be the same.

This is also the story of an addict's life, a story familiar to too many thousands of young people—all too little known to the majority of solid Americans, even to the parents, the teachers, and the social workers who should be most directly concerned with the problem. What sets my story apart from the majority is that I am white, that I come from a middle-class background—and that I, eventually, made good.

My story is directed at those who still believe—or would like to believe—that drug addiction is something that happens elsewhere and to others, in the ghettos, in the slums, in the overcrowded cities, to strangers, to hippies, to misfits and outcasts, to the underprivileged and the overprivileged. My story is for the parents of young people who are seeking a sense of glamor or excitement in the drug world, who seek a sense of belonging that their own world cannot provide; who have set out on the path of degradation and self-destruction as a means of drawing attention to their problems, who are calling out in the perverse way of the addict or troubled adolescent for help and understanding.

Perhaps my story will also be read by addicts or by those likely to become addicts. If it is, I hope that it will give them encouragement to seek help where it is available, that they may learn to recognize the illusory nature of the world they live in.

My story is for my parents, good people, well-meaning people who loved me perhaps too much for my own good, who loved me to the point where they denied the evidence of their own eyes, unwilling to see the worst, willing to believe all my lies and fabrications. Nothing I do will ever make up for the pain and anguish I caused them for so many years—and nothing can equal the joy they experienced when they finally knew I was well. I cannot repay them for all they have done for me, but I can express my gratitude for their love and fortitude; not many parents under similar circumstances would have stood by their children as my parents did. If in my story I seem to dwell on their weaknesses, it is not in order to upbraid them but to show others in similar positions how easily they may allow their children to manipulate them and use them to their own destructive ends.

Writing this book has been far from easy. I have had to open myself to the past—a past which had been largely obscured from me by a drug-induced haze. I have had to relive many of the terrors and fears of those days, the agonies and fears, the joys and emotions of my childhood, of my years as an addict, and of the period of my rehabilitation. These were no ordinary writing sessions; each became an emotion-charged encounter that often verged on the psycho-therapeutic. They were painful and exhilarating, and, ultimately, liberating. There were times when I broke down and times when I laughed joyfully.

I must express my thanks also to all those who have helped me in so many ways: to Chuck Dederich, Oscar and Jeannie Camaño, Pat Ryckman, and Candy Latson and all those others at Synanon who threw me a lifeline so many times; to John Sanfratello for his friendship and encouragement; to Geri Wood; to Michael Bernet for helping me to put the pieces together; to Sam Post.

I have done my best to check the chronology and events of this book; if there are minor errors in my recollection, I assume full responsibility.

Barbara Quinn
New York, New York
March, 1971